W. Warner Burke
Columbia University

Organization Change

Theory and Practice

Foundations for
Organizational
Science
A Sage Publications Series

SAGE Publications
International Educational and Professional Publisher
Thousand Oaks ▪ London ▪ New Delhi

For information:

Sage Publications, Inc.
2455 Teller Road
Thousand Oaks, California 91320
E-mail: order@sagepub.com

Sage Publications Ltd.
6 Bonhill Street
London EC2A 4PU
United Kingdom

Sage Publications India Pvt. Ltd.
M-32 Market
Greater Kailash I
New Delhi 110 048 India

Printed in the United States of America

Library of Congress Cataloging-in-Publication Data

Burke, W. Warner (Wyatt Warner), 1935-
  Organization change: Theory and practice / W. Warner Burke.
    p. cm. — (Foundations for organizational science)
  Includes bibliographical references and index.
  ISBN 0-7619-1482-X — ISBN 0-7619-1483-8
  1. Organizational change. 2. Leadership. I. Title. II. Series.
  HD58.8 .B876 2002
  658.4´06—dc21   2002003624

This book is printed on acid-free paper.

        05 10 9 8 7 6

Acquisitions Editor:	Marquita Flemming
Editorial Assistant:	MaryAnn Vail
Copy Editor:	Carla Freeman
Production Editor:	Diane S. Foster
Typesetter:	Siva Math Setters, Chennai, India
Indexer:	Molly Hall
Cover Designer:	Michelle Lee

Organization Change

FOUNDATIONS FOR ORGANIZATIONAL SCIENCE

A Sage Publications Series

Series Editor

David Whetten, *Brigham Young University*

Editors

Anne S. Huff, *University of Colorado and Cranfield University* (UK)

Benjamin Schneider, *University of Maryland*

M. Susan Taylor, *University of Maryland*

The FOUNDATIONS FOR ORGANIZATIONAL SCIENCE series supports the development of students, faculty, and prospective organizational science professionals through the publication of texts authored by leading organizational scientists. Each volume provides a highly personal, hands-on introduction to a core topic or theory and challenges the reader to explore promising avenues for future theory development and empirical application.

Books in This Series

Contents

To the next generation . . .
Brian and Emily, Courtney and Darrin, Donovan and Erin
And to the next generation after that . . .
William and Thomas

Introduction to the Series

The title of this series, Foundations for Organizational Science (FOS), denotes a distinctive focus. FOS books are educational aids for mastering the core theories, essential tools, and emerging perspectives that constitute the field of organizational science (broadly conceived to include organizational behavior, organizational theory, human resource management, and business strategy). Our ambitious goal is to assemble the "essential library" for members of our professional community.

The vision for the series emerged from conversations with several colleagues, including Peter Frost, Anne Huff, Rick Mowday, Ben Schneider, Susan Taylor, and Andy Van de Ven. A number of common interests emerged from these sympathetic encounters, including the following: enhancing the quality of doctoral education by providing broader access to the master teachers in our field, "bottling" the experience and insights of some of the founding scholars in our field before they retire, and providing professional development opportunities for colleagues seeking to broaden their understanding of the rapidly expanding subfields within organizational science.

Our unique learning objectives are reflected in an unusual set of instructions to FOS authors. They are encouraged to (a) "write the way they teach," framing their books as extensions of their teaching notes rather than as the expansion of a handbook chapter, (b) pass on their "craft knowledge" to the next generation of scholars—making them wiser, not just smarter, (c) share with their "virtual students and colleagues" the insider tips and best bets for research, which are normally reserved for one-on-one mentoring sessions, and (d) make the complexity of their subject matter comprehensible to nonexperts so that readers can share their puzzlement, fascination, and intrigue.

We are proud of the group of highly qualified authors who have embraced the unique educational perspective of our "Foundations" series. We encourage your suggestions as to how these books can better satisfy your learning needs: as a newcomer to the field preparing for prelims or developing a dissertation proposal, or as an established scholar seeking to broaden your knowledge and proficiency.

—DAVID A. WHETTEN
Series Editor

Preface

Organizations change all the time, each and every day. The change that occurs in organizations is, for the most part, unplanned and gradual. Planned organization change, especially on a large scale, affecting the entire system, is unusual: not exactly an everyday occurrence. Revolutionary change—a major overhaul of the organization resulting in a modified or entirely new mission, a change in strategy, leadership, and culture—is rare indeed. Most organization change is evolutionary. These two distinctions, planned versus unplanned and revolutionary versus evolutionary, represent core themes of this book. To be unequivocal here at the outset, the emphasis is more on planned and revolutionary change.

The reason for this emphasis is based on the clear and present need for a greater depth of understanding regarding organization change. This need is based on current and future trends that emanate from the external environment in which organizations function. Unlike the situation a few decades ago, the external environment now changes much more rapidly than organizations do. Organizations today are playing catch-up, and certainly this will be true even more so in the future. Capital markets, for example (see Chapter 1), are definitely changing more rapidly than the business organizations that depend on them. Moreover, business organizations in particular do not last as long as they have in the past. Thus, we need to know much more than ever before about how to understand, lead, manage, and in particular, change organizations. And thus, the purpose of this book.

In attempting to understand organizations in greater depth, another distinction is important. Organizations are created and developed on an assumption of continuity, to continue surviving, and to last. The external environment, while continuously "out there," is *not* continuous in the same sense that organizations are. Factors and forces in an organization's external environment are discontinuous, do not fit neatly together in a pattern, are not interdependent, homeostatic, linear, or highly predictable. Forces in the external environment can cause destruction but can cause creativity as well. This continuous-discontinuous theme also runs throughout the book and is analogous to the organizational theory literature; this body of books and articles addresses mainly continuity and stabilization, not discontinuity and change. Sources for help in writing this book had to come from nontraditional sources.

First, as noted, the organizational theory literature is about continuity and stabilization. So one must search diligently for theory about organization change. Such literature exists, and much of it is cited and relied on in this book. In addition to using theoretical references, I have also relied on models of organizations that come from the organization change literature. Models are important because they help to link theory with practice. In fact, models are covered in 4 of the 12 chapters in this book.

A second potential source for knowledge and assistance is the trade literature, professional books written by credible, experienced practitioners such as Peters and Waterman (1982) with their best-seller, *In Search of Excellence,* and more recently, *Built to Last,* by Collins and Porras (1994). These writings typically focus on organization exemplars: This is what to learn from, to model, and to follow. The authors draw conclusions from these model organizations and sometimes even derive principles about how they should be led and managed. Peters and Waterman had eight such principles: for example, "stick to your knitting." Collins and Porras stressed the power of culture as facilitating continuity and stabilization over time. The problem here is that by using popular, actual organization cases as the base from which to derive principles, sooner or later—and today it is much sooner rather than later—the organizations studied and showcased no longer illustrate the principles because things have changed. The model organizations have perhaps fallen on bad times, have become acquired—or worse, have filed for Chapter 11. Thus, the principles become passé, are no longer (if they ever were) relevant, and are soon forgotten. Sticking to one's knitting in this day and age is probably the opposite of what to do in business. In fact, in a recent article, Peters (2001) "confesses" that a number of the conclusions in the 1982 book were guesses and opinions rather than rigorously based on data.

A third potential source is "story" books that have a clear and usually simple maxim to teach. The book tells a story, perhaps based on a metaphor or in allegorical form. A recent best-seller is *Who Moved My Cheese?* (Johnson, 1998). Such books are easy and often fun to read. The author wants us to remember the maxim, and a story is a fine way to do it. These books often sell well. Unfortunately, they tend to *over*simplify the theme(s) they are addressing. Regardless of how charming it might be, organization change is far too complex for a simple story to teach us what we ultimately need to know.

The sources for this book have therefore generally come from the type of organization literature that one would assume—organizational psychology, organization and management theory, and organizational behavior—but not exclusively. The life sciences have much to teach us about change, and in fact have become a recent trend in the organization literature. Even the nontrendy *Harvard Business Review* recently published an article by Bonabeau and Meyer (2001) on "swarm intelligence." The behavior of ants, with their flexibility, robustness, and self-organization (as the authors summarize it) can be applied to certain aspects of running a business and result in significant increases in efficiency. The primary source for this book in this domain is *The Web of Life,* by Capra (1996).

Other sources include literature from chaos theory, from nonlinear complex systems theory, and from as far afield (although highly relevant) as Gladwell's (2000) book, *The Tipping Point.* For an annotated bibliography of these and other primary sources, see the Appendix.

One final point about the nature of this book: The attempt was made to combine and to some degree integrate theory and research with application. After setting the stage in Chapter 1 and providing some background and history in Chapter 2, Chapters 3 to 7 are more about theory and research, and Chapters 8 through 12 deal more with application and practice.

Acknowledgments

I have many people to thank, and I am very pleased to have this opportunity to do so. First and foremost is Ben Schneider, who insisted that I write this book. Throughout, he was incredibly supportive, patient, and persistent that I stay the course. Then there were my three official reviewers for Sage, beyond Ben, two of whom had reviewed my previous work before (Burke, 1982). Len Goodstein was his true self and a true friend in holding my feet to the fire, that is, calling my attention to the need for (a) more examples, (b) better linkage between theory and practice, and (c) better logic as I went from A to C and assumed too much by skipping B. Craig Lundberg gave me feedback in two categories: the "big stuff" and the "little stuff," as he called it. I paid attention to all, but particularly to the big stuff. All of the "stuff" was on target and very helpful. The third Sage reviewer was David Whetten, the overall consulting editor of this Sage series of books. As with the others, it was clear that he had given the manuscript a careful reading. First, he pointed out a major inconsistency in my coverage of theory, which I quickly corrected to alleviate my embarrassment. David and I share a strong interest in and reliance on models. His suggestions along these lines were most helpful. Also, his urging me, as Ben did, to talk about future research needs in the final chapter caused me to take action.

And then there were my friends and colleagues at Teachers College, all of whom amazed me by actually reading the entire first draft. I am immensely grateful. First, Roger Myers, now emeritus, the consummate psychologist who knows how to write and is a stickler about making nouns into verbs, helped to considerably improve my writing of this book. Caryn Block reminded me time and again to remind the reader about points made earlier and how they linked to what I was presently stating. She also urged me to use examples. I did. Arthur Levine, president of Teachers College and a change leader in the world of education, brought his experience and knowledge to my manuscript. His critique and questions were invaluable. Debra Noumair was my idea person. For example, she suggested that I declare myself in the opening chapter. My "points of view" section was the result of that suggestion. She also helped me to think through the ordering of things. Her creativity was much appreciated. Victoria Marsick shares with me the excitement of ideas from chaos theory and the life sciences. I followed many of her suggestions for applying these ideas. Lee Knefelkamp, a scholar of the first order, is superb at helping one to see how seemingly disparate concepts actually intertwine. Her support in my attempt to "bring things together" was most beneficial.

Tony Petrella, a friend and colleague of many years who also read the manuscript, is a true organization change practitioner. What is unique about Tony is that as a consultant/practitioner, he understands and deeply appreciates theory. His comment about my ability to "push practice through the lens of theory" was very meaningful to me.

Finally, and most important, was my assistant Mary Zippo's steadfast support in helping me to get this manuscript onto paper and in readable form. I was fortunate to have her help in word processing skills and the added benefit of her having been an English major. She caught many errors of wording and spelling.

It is appropriate for me to end these acknowledgments with the requisite caveat. Even with all the help that I received, I do in the end acknowledge that the final product is solely my responsibility.

1 Rethinking

Organization Change

M ost efforts by executives, managers, and administrators to significantly change the organizations they lead do not work. By "change significantly," I mean to turn the organization in another direction, to fundamentally modify the "way we do things," to overhaul the structure—the design of the organization for decision making and accountability—and to provide organizational members with a whole new vision for the future. And in the ever increasing world of mergers and acquisitions, 75% fail at this (Burke & Biggart, 1997; "How Mergers Go Wrong," 2000). To survive, especially for the long term, organizations must change and adapt to their respective environments, but typical changes consist of fine-tuning: installing a new system for sales management; initiating a program to improve the quality of products and/or services; or changing the structure to improve decision making without first changing organizational strategy, which is, after all, the basis for decision making.

Examples of significant and successful organization change will be presented in this book. These examples, however, are exceptional. Most organization change is not significant or successful. Organizational improvements do occur, even frequently, and do work, but large-scale, fundamental organization change that works is rare. Why is this the case?

There are many reasons. First and foremost, deep organization change, especially attempting to change the culture of an organization, is very difficult. Second, it is often hard to make a case for change, particularly when the organization appears to be doing well. Nothing is broken, so what's to fix? A paradox of organization change is that the peak of success is the time to worry and to plan for and bring about significant change. Third, our knowledge for how to plan and implement organization change is limited. The primary purpose of this book is an attempt to rectify this limitation, at least to some extent. Let's begin with a fundamental issue.

Accepted knowledge regarding organization change is that we plan the change according to steps or phases. Step 1 is, perhaps, to inform organizational members about the need for change. Step 2 might be to implement an initial project that gradually expands to a larger program of change, and so on. But the actual change itself does not occur according to steps. It's another paradox.

The Paradox of Planned Organization Change

In an Associated Press release on June 1, 2001, Federal Communications Commission head, Michael Powell, referring to the shift to new digital technology, was quoted as saying: "It will be messy and it will be confusing, and we will get a lot of it wrong and we'll have to start over. But that's the creative process, that's the evolutionary process" (*Naples Daily News*, 2001, p. 6A). *Revolutionary* process might have been more accurate; in any case, Mr. Powell described the change process very realistically.

As stated above, when planning organization change, the process is usually linear, that is, Step 1 or Phase 1, then Step 2, 3, and so on. And although an attempt is made in the implementation of change to follow these steps or phases, what actually occurs is anything but linear. The implementation process is messy: Things don't proceed exactly as planned; people do things their own way, not always according to the plan; some people resist or even sabotage the process; and some people who would be predicted to support or resist the plan actually behave in just the opposite way. In short, unanticipated consequences occur. Leaders of change often say something like, "For every step forward we take, we seem to fall back two steps; something always needs fixing to get us back on track."

Provided the change goals are clear and change leaders are willing to stay the course, over time, the process may end up being somewhat linear, or at least a pattern may emerge. But linearity is not what anyone experiences during the implementation process itself, in the thick of things, which may feel chaotic with people in the organization constantly asking the question "Who's in charge here?" Figure 1.1 is a simple way of trying to depict this nonlinear process yet show at the same

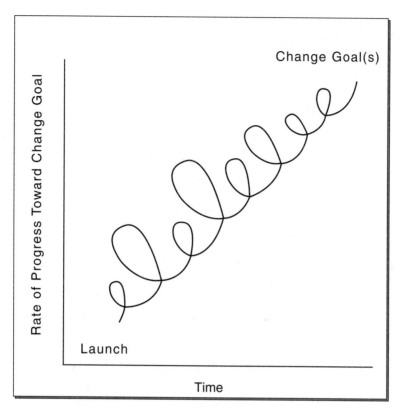

Figure 1.1. Depiction of the nonlinear nature of organization change

time the possibility of an emergent pattern. The loops are of different sizes because no unanticipated consequences are the same. It should be noted that unless there is a change goal in the first place and unless there is some degree of understanding and ownership of the goal, this depiction of organization change is *not* valid.

How organization change occurs, with particular emphasis on *planned* organization change, is the primary theme of this book. The assumption that organizations need to change is embedded in what has been stated so far. I will now expound on this assumption by making the case for organization change. Next, I will declare myself by explaining my points of view about organization change. These points of view provide an overview of the book, or "coming attractions." More than what is to come, these points of view also reveal my biases about what is important, if not critical, regarding organization change. So, here at the outset of our journey, I am declaring myself. Even with these biases on display, I hope you will continue the journey with me.

Making the Case for Organization Change

Changing Corporations

My primary source for this section is the recent volume by two McKinsey consultants, Foster and Kaplan, *Creative Destruction* (2001). In contrast to popular business books such as *In Search of Excellence* (Peters & Waterman, 1982) and *Built to Last* (Collins & Porras, 1994), Foster and Kaplan, with their data from more than 1,000 corporations in 15 industries over a 36-year period, argue that we now are clearly in the "age of discontinuity," as Drucker (1969) earlier predicted.

Consider the following points made by Foster and Kaplan (2001). The first *Forbes* top 100 companies list was formed in 1917. *Forbes* published its original list again in 1987. In 1987, 61 of the original 100 no longer existed. And of the remaining 39 companies, only 18 remained in the top 100, companies such as DuPont, General Electric (GE), Kodak, General Motors, Ford, and Procter & Gamble. These companies survived but, according to Foster and Kaplan, did not perform. Long-term earnings returns by these companies for their investors from 1917 to 1987 were not exactly outstanding: 20% less than for the overall market. Today, only GE performs above the average.

Next, Foster and Kaplan (2001) refer to the Standard & Poor's (S&P) 500. Comparing the 500 in 1957 with those in 1998, only 74 remained, with a mere 12 of those 74 outperforming the S&P index itself. Moreover, "If today's S&P 500 were made up of only those companies that were on the list when it was formed in 1957, the overall performance of the S&P 500 would have been about 20% less *per year* than it actually has been" (Foster & Kaplan, 2001, p. 8). As the authors then ask, how can it be that so many companies do not survive and those that do survive, with few exceptions, perform below average?

Part of the answer rests with the pace-of-change phenomenon that Foster and Kaplan (2001) use as their opening lines. In 1917, the pace of change was indeed much slower than it is today. During that time and continuing on into the 1920s and 1930s, even with the climatic changes of the Great Depression, the turnover rate of companies in the

S&P rankings averaged 1.5% a year. A new company making the list then could expect to remain for about 65 years. As Drucker (1969) pointed out, in those days, change was not a major concern. Continuity was the goal and the way of operating. Vertical integration was the name of the game—that is, owning as much of the production chain as possible, from raw materials to distribution to the customer. But in 1998, "The turnover rate in the S&P 500 was close to 10%, implying an average lifetime on the list of ten years, not sixty-five!" (Foster & Kaplan, 2001, p. 11). Times have changed, and we are living in the age of discontinuity for corporations, not continuity.

The larger answer to Foster and Kaplan's question about corporate survival and performance can be found in a corporation's external environment. Although any organization's external environment consists of myriad factors—customers, the general economy, the changing demographics, and changing government regulations, to name a few—one of the most powerful factors or forces for business, especially those that are publicly owned, is called the *capital market*. Capital markets are "informal aggregations," not highly organized and structured as are corporations. Capital markets consist of buyers, sellers, and others who interact for the purpose of economic exchange. These business people are loan officers in banks, investment bankers, stockbrokers, stock analysts, venture capitalists (those who often help to start companies), and anyone else who has money to invest. Although not acting in concert, these people decide whether your business, your company, and your vision for the future of your organization is worthy of investment. Is your company worth the risk of loaning you $1 million, of buying 1,000 shares of your stock, or investing money to help you with your desire to acquire another business? So, it is this informal aggregation of buyers and sellers that form a powerful force in the organization's environment, determining in part the long-term survival and success of a company. This world is largely a business-to-business arena, and a business can live or die on the basis of the vagaries of the marketplace. The point Foster and Kaplan (2001) make is that capital markets change far more rapidly than do corporations, are based on an assumption of discontinuity, not continuity, weed out poor performers, reward creativity and innovation, and encourage new business entries into the marketplace.

Before going too far with the concept of the power of capital markets determining the fate of corporations, we should pause for a moment and make the most critical point of all, lest we overlook a fundamental. In the end, it is the *consumer*, the customer out there in the organization's external environment, who determines the fate of any business. Will anyone, after all, actually buy our products and services?

By the time my son, Brian, was about 11 years old, he had amassed a huge collection of baseball cards. When I asked him why he had so many, he quickly told me that his collection was an investment. These cards, he informed me, would be worth far more money in a few years than what he'd paid for them. Ah, I thought, here is a teachable moment! So, I patiently explained that his investment would pay off if and only if someone in a few years were willing to buy these cards from him. Brian's reaction to my explanation was something like, "Dad, I don't think you really understand." Obviously, he had a huge psychological investment in those cards.

So, it is the consumer to whom the capital markets folks pay attention. Will anyone out there buy this stuff, pay for these services, and keep on doing so for the foreseeable future?

The primary point made by Foster and Kaplan (2001), then, is that capital markets outpace corporations, the rate of change is considerably different, and the basic assumptions for long-term survival are opposites: discontinuity for the capital markets and continuity for corporations. For corporate survival and success, Foster and Kaplan argue that companies must abandon the assumption of continuity; corporations must understand and mitigate, as they call it,

> "Cultural lock-in," the inability to change the corporate culture even in the face of clear market threats—[this] explains why corporations find it difficult to respond to the messages of the marketplace. Cultural lock-in results from the gradual stiffening of the invisible architecture of the corporation and the ossification of its decision-making abilities, control systems, and mental models. It dampens a company's ability to innovate or to shed operations with a less-exciting future. Moreover, it signals the corporation's inexorable decline into inferior performance. (p. 16)

Changing Government Agencies

Government agencies are also having to deal with changes in their external environments. Take, for example, the National Aeronautics and Space Administration (NASA). The external environment for NASA is just as complex as a corporation's, if not more so. On a daily basis, NASA deals with the public at large, the U.S. Congress, the president and his administration, contractors, vendors and consultants, the scientific community, and various "watchdog" organizations that constantly monitor how taxpayer dollars are spent. Daniel Goldin, the administrator of NASA for about a decade, has significantly affected the organization as a change leader. His mantra of "faster, better, cheaper" has permeated the agency. Goldin is quite clear about who he and NASA serve: the American public through its elected representatives, such as the president and Congress. His response to this critical part of NASA's external environment, under the banner of faster, better, cheaper, has driven and continues to drive the changes at this federal agency.

At the state level, a good example of significant change took place in Ohio, driven by the governor and a desire to be more efficient and customer focused for the people of the state; several separate agencies merged into a much larger one of about 4,000 state employees. The recent merged organization, the Ohio Department of Job and Family Services, has the responsibilities of providing for (a) families in need, especially those on welfare and with children who require special care and for (b) contributing to the Ohio workforce via unemployment support, training, and development. With more federal tax dollars being "delegated" to the states for administration and services, these government organizations have had to deal with significant change.

Changing Higher Education Institutions and Nonprofit Organizations

Institutions of higher education no longer exist exclusively in the non-profit sector. The University of Phoenix, for one, is a profit-making company and by all accounts is doing quite well. Even though they have a fairly sizable campus with classrooms in Phoenix, their forte is distance learning. They are more expensive than many of their competitors, but they focus on customer convenience and service. This relatively recent entrant into the world of higher education has caused a stir and has begun to call into question the long-term survival of many colleges, especially if they drag their feet regarding technology. Moreover, with tuition increasing every year, many colleges and universities may be gradually pricing themselves out of the market. So, even in the domain of higher education, which includes some of the oldest, most traditional types of organizations in the world, the external environment is changing. Unless colleges and universities adapt, their traditions may not last, as least not for centuries as has been true in the past.

With respect to the changing world for nonprofit organizations, consider the case of the A.K. Rice Institute (AKRI). This institute was founded in Washington, D.C., by a group of psychologists, psychiatrists, and related professionals who were keenly interested in the form of human relations and group dynamics training and education that had been developed by the Tavistock Institute in the United Kingdom. In the United States, the founding took the name of A. Kenneth Rice because he was instrumental in bringing to this side of the Atlantic the methods and theory of this form of education. From 1965 until recently, AKRI has steadily grown and found roots all across America via regional organizations affiliated with the national group. AKRI has been both a membership organization (with dues) and an educational institute that holds national and regional conferences (learning laboratory groups) throughout the year. Qualified members of AKRI serve as staff for these educational conferences.

The primary point to be made with this case example of another organization vis-à-vis its external environment is the distinct possibility that AKRI has not been sufficiently *in touch* with its external world. This insularity has been due in part to (a) the desire of members to work and, of course, earn money as staff for the conferences and (b) broader issues of membership per se; that is, what do we get in return for our dues, and who gets selected and why? These issues have been all-consuming. Members not selected or not selected often enough to staff conferences became angry and resentful. Blame was directed at the national organization, which was perceived to be overly restrictive and limited in its decision-making process. Interestingly, the exciting group process of the conferences—learning experientially about issues of authority, leadership, individual/group interactions, and the power of the group as a whole—became the mode members and committees used to attempt to deal with AKRI itself. In other words, the real work before the institute was often left undone because the "sexier" way of working was the conference learning process, as opposed to tackling tasks and accomplishing objectives on behalf of AKRI itself. Confronting AKRI, *the authority*, was more fun than dull and time-consuming committee work.

The problem, therefore, has been the dual and somewhat conflicting missions of the institute, that is, to be a membership organization and serve its members, while at the same time having an educational mission for the public at large. Membership issues often prevented effective accomplishment of the educational mission. And to be effective at the latter, AKRI's external environment needed to be monitored and responded to more directly, instead of indirectly via its members, who were often conflicted between an individual desire to earn money and a desire to give back to and serve AKRI. AKRI has recently launched a significant organization change effort to modify its bylaws and governance structure in support of one mission, the educational one, and to close down its membership structure. Among a number of other consequences, this change will force AKRI to be significantly more in touch with its external environment. And the likelihood is much greater that AKRI will indeed survive and perhaps be even more successful in the future, at least until the external environment changes again.

Summary

The sections in this chapter so far have been about changing corporations, changing government agencies, and changing higher educational institutions and nonprofit organizations, which have served as examples of the critical nature of organizations: their dependence on the external environment for survival. These examples have also illustrated how organizations of all kinds today are having to deal with environments that are changing more rapidly than the organizations themselves. In fact, the remainder of this book could be filled with such examples alone. The ones covered are illustrative only, not comprehensive.

The primary purpose, therefore, of these opening sections was to make the case for the need for a much greater depth of understanding about organization change across all major sectors of organizations. With the rate of change becoming faster and faster and the demands on organizations to adapt and change themselves becoming greater and greater, our learning curve is steep. This book, then, is an attempt to climb that curve and provide more depth of understanding. Our need is to understand organizations more thoroughly, but the greater need is to learn more about how to change them.

Another purpose in presenting these examples of changing organizations and their interactions with their respective external environments was to introduce, perhaps not so subtly, a particular point of view about organization change: that the process begins (and ends, for that matter) with the external environment.

The objective of the following sections is to be more explicit about points of view, to declare myself here at the outset, and to provide with these personal declarations a preview of coming attractions.

Personal Declarations and Points of View

The purposes of this final section of the opening chapter are (a) to provide personal points of view about organization change, especially *planned* organization change, and (b) to address very briefly an overview of what is covered in each of the following chapters.

The Metaphor of Choice

As Gareth Morgan (1997) has so eloquently explained, we can understand the organization via a variety of metaphors, such as a machine, a brain, a psychic prison, or an organism. Morgan appropriately warns us about metaphors: that although they are a way of seeing, at the same time they are a way of not seeing. Metaphors can help but can also limit our perspective and ultimate understanding.

With this warning clearly in mind, the metaphor of choice for this writing effort is the organism. A major strength of this metaphor is the emphasis on the interactions between an organization and its external environment. An organization, therefore, is *not* a closed system, which encourages the view of an open and flexible entity. A second strength, as Morgan (1977) has pointed out, is the emphasis on survival; that is, certain needs must be satisfied for the organization to survive:

> This contrasts with the classical focus on specific organizational goals. Survival is a process, whereas goals are often targets or end points to be achieved. This reorientation gives management an increased flexibility, for if survival is seen as the primary orientation, specific goals are framed by a more basic and enduring process that helps prevent them from becoming ends in themselves, a common fate in many organizations. (p. 67)

Limitations of this metaphor include the fact that an organism is concrete; it is a fundamental of nature, with material properties that can be seen and touched. An organization, on the other hand, is socially constructed, a product of someone's ideas, vision, and beliefs. And although there may be buildings, land owned or leased, machines, and money, organizations depend on the actions of human beings for survival. It is not an autonomic process.

Also, this view suggests that organizations are totally dependent on their environments for survival, overlooking the fact that organizations *interact* with the external world: yes, being influenced, but influencing outwardly as well.

A second limitation is what Morgan (1977) calls "functional unity." Organisms have highly interdependent parts, and each element supports other elements, as in the human being with a heart, lungs, glands, and so on, operating together to preserve the whole. Organizations rarely operate this way. We might argue that ideally, they should, with interdependence and harmony, all elements working for the good of the whole. Yet we know that creativity often stems from conflict and debate and that these kinds of actions by organization members may contribute more to survival than to harmony.

The final limitation that Morgan (1977) notes is the danger of this metaphor becoming an ideology: that organizations *should* be harmonious, that interdependence is always a *good* thing, or that individuals *should* get their needs met on the job.

Bearing in mind these limitations, the strengths of the organism metaphor support the points of view represented in this writing more than any other metaphor. Thus, the choice. Not becoming trapped by the metaphor is nevertheless a highly important goal to strive for as we proceed.

The Theories of Choice

It should come as no surprise that, with the metaphor of choice being an organism, the primary choice here is open system theory, which, after all, was derived from biology. Moreover, the point of view established in this book is that the life sciences, with their theoretical foundations, are more relevant to understanding organizations and change than are the physical sciences. Fritjof Capra's (1996) work is especially relevant, particularly his emphasis on the concepts of pattern, structure, and process. Chapter 3 is devoted to these theoretical foundations.

Types of Organization Change

Think first about evolution versus revolution, a gradual continuous process of change in contrast to a sudden event. That sudden event might precipitate massive turmoil, resistance, and planned change that could lead to eventual organization change. This contrast is actually a useful way to think about the different forms that organization change can take. The language that scholars and practitioners currently use is exemplified as follows:

Revolutionary   vs. Evolutionary

Discontinuous   vs. Continuous

Episodic   vs. Continuing flow

Transformational vs. Transactional

Strategic   vs. Operational

Total system   vs. Local option

Stating this language in terms of one versus the other is for purposes of clarity and understanding, not to suggest that the conditions they describe are mutually exclusive. Pascale, Millemann, and Gioja (2000), for example, have stated,

> The point is: Over time (and even concurrently) organizations need evolution *and* revolution. When they have been limited exclusively to the restrictive precepts of social engineering [for example], they have been handicapped and largely unsuccessful in unleashing authentic revolutionary change. The principles of living systems offer a powerful new recourse. The trick is to clearly identify the nature of the challenge and then use the right tool for the right task. (p. 38)

Revolutionary change or transformation requires different tools and techniques for bringing about successful organization change than do methods for evolutionary or continuous change. The former requires total system events, such as (a) an initial activity that calls attention to the clear need for a dramatic modification of mission and strategy due to changes that have occurred in technology or (b) new, unforeseen forays by a significant competitor. The latter requires improvement measures in how a product is designed, how a service is delivered, or how quality is measured and upgraded. A transformation requires the immediate attention of all organizational members, whereas a continuous improvement action may require the attention of only a certain segment of the organizational population or a phased involvement of all organizational members over time. Chapter 4 provides further detail and examples of these two different forms of organization change. Chapter 6 also addresses this distinction both from a theoretical and research perspective.

Levels of Organization Change

As in the case of the differences between transformational (revolutionary) and transactional (evolutionary), it is very important to understand the different effects of organization change across the primary levels of any social system. These primary levels are the *individual*, the *group* or work unit, and the *total system*. How organization change affects the individual differs from how work units are affected and how the total system is affected. Furthermore, the major focus for change differs as a function of level. At the individual level, the focus of attention is on activities such as recruitment, replacement, and displacement; training and development; and on coaching and counseling. At the group level, the focus is on, for example, team building and self-directed groups. At the total system level, the emphasis is on the different orders of change (first, second, and third): that is, whether the target of change is a subsystem or beyond the initial focus. In other words, other components of the organization will be affected sooner or later by the initial activity.

Chapter 5 is devoted to an examination of these different levels of organization change, how resistance to change differs by level, and how change leaders need to deal with the resistances according to level. The process is not the same for all organizational levels.

How Organization Change Occurs

Let us assume that an organization needs to change itself significantly. Due to major shifts in its external environment, the organization must change its basic strategy and certain aspects of—if not most of—its mission statement, the organization's raison d'être. Change in mission and strategy means that the organization's culture must be modified if success of the overall change effort is to be realized. Change in the culture is in *support* of the changes in mission and strategy; it is the "people" side, the emotional component of organization change, or what a seasoned organization change consultant calls "The Change Monster"—the human forces that either facilitate or prevent transformation (Duck, 2001). So, culture change is our focus. The point of view that I am presenting here is that "you don't change culture by trying to change culture." Culture is "the way we do things around here" and concerns deeply held beliefs, attitudes, and values. Taking a direct, frontal approach to changing values is fraught with difficulty, resistance, and strong human emotion. We therefore start with behavior instead. We start with the behavior that will lead to the desired change in attitudes and values.

When talking about a desired organization change, leaders and managers often say something like, "We need to change people's mental sets." The implication is that attitude is the focus of change. As is the case with values, attempting to change an attitude, one's "mental set," is difficult. So, we begin with behavior changes that if enacted, will eventually lead to shifts in attitudes and beliefs and will subsequently affect values. Although it is absolutely necessary to be clear at the outset of a change effort about the desired values and about the modified culture that is the goal, we do not concentrate on the culture per se, but on the behaviors that will gradually influence the culture in the desired direction. Further thought about this point of view and the theory and research that support this perspective is covered in Chapter 6.

The Content and Process of Organization Change

The *content* of organization change is one thing, and the *process* another. The distinction is important because the former, the *what*, provides the vision and overall direction for the change; and the process, the *how*, concerns implementation and adoption. Content has to do with purpose, mission, strategy, values, and what the organization is all about—or should be about. Process has to do with how the change is planned, launched, more fully implemented, and once into implementation, sustained. The kinds of behaviors required for content differ from those required for process. Determining the *what* requires leadership in terms of taking a stand, declaring what the new world will look like, and composing the story of change that addresses issues of identity and purpose. Determining the *how* requires leadership that, for example, is participative, involves organizational members in the activities that will bring about the change, and recognizes accomplishments. So, for example, composing the story is the content, and telling the story is the process. This distinction between content and process, although useful for our understanding, is not pure. Composing the story of organization change is, after all, a process. In any case, the various ways of understanding the distinctions and overlaps is the subject matter of Chapter 7.

Organizational Models

In addition to theory about organization change, it is useful to have frameworks that help to simplify and focus: *simplify* in terms of reducing the myriad parts and aspects of any organization into more manageable portions, and *focus* in terms of which portions are the most important ones for our attention. A useful organizational model is one that simplifies and at the same time represents reality, a conceptual framework that "makes sense" to people who work in organizations and helps them to organize their realities in ways that promote understanding and action for change. Many organizational models or frameworks for understanding organizations exist in both the academic and applied worlds. The organizational models covered in Chapter 8 are highly selective. They are the ones most closely associated with organization change. For the most part, these models are steeped in open system theory and convey an organismic perspective. They also help to integrate content and process of change.

The Organizational Model of Choice

In making a choice about a model to apply to an organization change effort, certain questions are important to consider. First, in what kind of theory is the model grounded? Organization theory in general or, say, open system theory in particular? If the latter, then an input-throughput-output sequence, with a feedback loop from output to input and vice versa, is absolutely necessary. Second, does the model consist of the most relevant and key factors or components? For example, is the mission included? Third, is the model merely descriptive, or is it prescriptive? That is, for performance to be optimized or for change to be effective, are there certain components in the model that are more important or carry "heavier weight" than other factors? For example, is culture more important than strategy or structure, or vice versa? And finally, are there any unique features of the model?

Although the questions just posed are appropriate, they are also somewhat leading. The Burke-Litwin model of organizational performance and change, the model of choice for me, represents a positive response to these questions. Born from the world of practice, the model evolved and was defined from a major organization change effort in the 1980s at British Airways (BA). Theoretically, the model is grounded in the open system way of thinking. The components of the model come from original work on organizational climate by George Litwin, in the 1960s, and from experiences at BA. (On "climate," see Litwin and Stringer, 1968; for "BA," see Goodstein and Burke, 1991.) Also from these experiences, the model became both descriptive and prescriptive. The model is more normative than contingent in terms of what actions should proceed what other actions regarding a large-scale transformation of an organization. Furthermore, the model is unique in that transformational or discontinuous change is addressed, as well as transactional or continuous change. A full description of the model is provided in Chapter 9.

A model is only as good as its usefulness; thus, Chapter 10 focuses on application. Two large-scale organization change cases are profiled to illustrate how the Burke-Litwin model was employed.

Organization Change
Should Be Data-Based and Measured

With respect to planned organization change, it is imperative that the effort be based on data as much as possible to help ensure success. It is difficult to know what to do next if one does not know what the current situation is. Measures taken over time—Time 1 compared with Time 2, then with Time 3—help to (a) track progress, (b) establish priorities for next steps, and (c) determine what to celebrate regarding milestones reached. Chapter 10 is also devoted to measurement, with the Burke-Litwin model providing the framework and the content for where to gather data and what to measure.

Planned Organization Change Requires Leadership

Change can emanate from any unit, function, or level within an organization. Regardless of its origin, leadership is required. There can be leaders anywhere in an organization. But if the organization change is large scale and transformational in nature, requiring significant change in mission, strategy, and culture, then leadership must come from the top of the organization, from executives, particularly the chief executive. "Leading Organization Change," Chapter 11, concentrates on executive leadership and specifies the change leader's role for each of four, sequenced activities: the prelaunch phase, the launch of the organization change, the implementation phase, and sustaining the effort. The perspective taken herein is that leadership should take the form of specified roles and behaviors rather than a personality orientation. Is personality important? Yes, because leadership is far more personal than management. But charisma, for example, is not required for successful organization change. Neither should we attempt to emulate great leaders, such as Mohandas Gandhi, Margaret Thatcher, Martin Luther

King Jr., Jack Welch, Ronald Reagan, Eleanor Roosevelt, or George Patton. Although lessons can be learned from the lives of these people, in the end, it is how each of us uses our *self* in its own unique formation that makes the difference. A recent article (Brooker, 2001) about Herb Kelleher, the fabled and former CEO of Southwest Airlines, was titled "I Did It My Way." How else could he have done it? And how else could anyone else do it except his or her own way? That is what leadership is about, doing it one's own way, but for purposes of leading change according to key roles and sequenced activities.

Planned Organization Change Is Complex

Charles de Gaulle, the past president of France, once said, "I have come to the conclusion that politics are too serious to be left to the politicians." Similarly, a statement like this could be made about the complexity of organization change. In other words, organization change is too complex to rely solely on the traditional literature in areas such as organization theory, organizational behavior, organization development, and strategic management. As stated in the preface, sources for this book have not been exclusively the "usual suspects." The life sciences and theories related to chaos and nonlinear systems are more useful for our understanding and application. In the final chapter, yet one other clearly nontraditional source, Malcolm Gladwell's book, *The Tipping Point* (2000), is explored to help us understand organization change in more depth. Gladwell helps us understand why major changes often happen suddenly and unexpectedly. He likens these changes to an epidemic, the spread of an infectious disease. These changes are "social epidemics."

Finally, we have returned to the planned sequence of organization change, used in Chapter 11 to apply Gladwell's principles and perspectives. Because we know that unforeseen consequences will occur even in a carefully planned change effort, it is all the more important for us to look far and wide for sources to help us better comprehend the nature of organization change and how to implement it effectively. Gladwell's book is such a source.

Summary

With these personal declarations and points of view, I have attempted to accomplish two objectives. First, I wanted to declare myself—to state my points of view about organization change with biases clearly presented. With these declarations, I have also shown what I consider to be the most important topics for understanding organization change in more depth. Second, my objective was to summarize in a few pages what the book addresses in the following 11 chapters. Now, as you will see in my closing request, I hope that I did not tip my hand too much.

A Closing Request

When you go to a movie theater, the film you came to see never begins at its designated time. What precedes it is a flood of previews and coming attractions attempting to entice you to return to the theater and see these movies as well. Some critics and pundits have been known to complain that these previews show the best parts of a forthcoming film, so that actually seeing the entire movie is not worth one's time. Whether this complaint is valid or not, the danger of having provided the previews of this book is that you, the reader, will now skip the details. But please read on. The richness of organization change is in the details.

2 A Brief History of
Organization Change

Organization change is as old as organizations themselves. The pharaohs of ancient Egypt probably struggled with a need to change the organizations that built their pyramids. And imagine the degree of organization needed, with continual modifications, to successfully construct the Great Wall of China. What we call reengineering today was probably practiced in some form back then.

The first organization change recorded in the Old Testament (Ex. 18:13-27) dealt with what we call today a *loosely-coupled system.* In fact, it was too loosely coupled, and that was the problem. Moses was the client. Having escaped from the tyranny of the Egyptian pharaoh with thousands of Israelites as his followers, Moses had to deal with myriad "social system" issues. Thousands of his followers had direct access to him. Moses was leader, counselor, judge, and minister to all. His father-in-law, Jethro, no doubt because he was concerned for his son-in-law's mental health, suggested what amounted to a reorganization. He proposed that Moses select a few good men to be rulers of thousands. They would have direct access to him and would bring to him only the problems they could not solve. Each of these rulers, in turn, would have lieutenants who would be rulers of hundreds and would have direct access to the rulers of thousands and would bring to them only the problems they could not handle, and so on, down to the lowest, the rulers of 10 persons. This was the birth of one of the first pyramidal organizations. It is possible, of course, that this idea of organization did not originate with Jethro; before Moses's deliverance, the Hebrews had been enslaved by the Egyptians, who had a highly organized society. In any case, changing organizations is not exactly new. What is comparatively new, however, is the *study* of organization change: what systematically seems to facilitate and enhance effective change (*effective* meaning the accomplishment of *planned* change goals) and what leads to failed attempts at organization change. Note the emphasis on *planned* change. Organization change can be unplanned, of course, and more often is. This distinction will be covered in more detail later.

Jethro, along with his client, Moses, were early organization change agents. Since that earlier time, there have been many others we could cite, such as Machiavelli and his client, the prince. Staying with the promise of being "brief," as stated in the chapter title, however, a leap to the 20th century will now be made. Besides, our primary perspective and purpose is to consider the study of organization change, and it has been only recently that organization change has become an interest of scholars. What follows, then, is a tracing of the important forerunners of the modern-day study of organization change:

- Scientific management
- The Hawthorne studies
- Industrial psychology
- Survey feedback
- Sensitivity training
- Sociotechnical systems
- Organization development (OD)
- The managerial grid and OD
- Coercion and confrontation
- Management consulting

An appropriate starting point is during the first decade of the 20th century and the work of Frederick Winslow Taylor, the father of scientific management.

Scientific Management

To understand and appreciate Frederick Taylor's approach to organization change, we need to consider the historical time and content of his work. The time was the late 1800s and early 1900s—his famous book, *Scientific Management,* was published in 1911. Regarding the broader context, we need to recall that (a) the industrial revolution was in full swing, (b) the predominant type of organization experiencing considerable growth was manufacturing, and (c) the primary disciplines providing a strong foundation for (a) and (b) were economics and engineering. It is not surprising, then, that Taylor's conception of an organization was that of a *machine*. An organization, particularly a manufacturing one, should therefore be studied in scientific terms: What is cause, and what is effect? And in terms of operating principles, the machine may be thought of as being based on the idea of a physical entity with movable and replaceable parts.

Taylor's (1980) "scientific management," as he labeled it, was based on four principles:

1. Data gathering: amassing "traditional" knowledge about the way work has been done in the past, via discussions with workers and observations of their work; recording the knowledge; tabulating it; and reducing it to rules, laws, and, if possible, to mathematical formulas. In addition to talks with the workers themselves, methods used were time and motion studies. These consequent rules, laws, and formulas were then applied to the workplace by management, and if applied properly, greater efficiencies were typically realized.

2. Worker selection and development: paying considerable attention to selecting and placing the worker in a job that was as good a match as possible of human skills and ability with the requirements of the job, in other words, the nature of the work itself. Furthermore, Taylor was a strong advocate of training and helping the worker do the best job he or she (mostly "he" during those times) was capable of performing.

3. Integration of the science and the trained worker: bringing together scientific management and the trained worker to "make" the worker and science come together. What Taylor meant was that one could have the best-trained workers humanly possible, but if they did not use and apply the new methods of work, the entire effort would fail. To "make" this integration, to use Taylor's word, he argued that workers needed to be treated well, taking into consideration their wishes and allowing them "to express their wants freely" (Taylor, 1980, p. 21). Moreover, he was a proponent of incentive pay. He added, however, that if a worker refused to perform the new modes of work, then moving that person out (to another job in the company or severing the worker from the company) was the proper step to take. Scientific management did not mean "mollycoddling" the workers, Taylor pointed out. He also stated that "nine-tenths of our trouble comes with men on the management side in making them do their new duties" (Taylor, 1980, p. 21). Obviously, Taylor believed that changing managers was far more difficult than changing workers. For scientific management to succeed, *management must assume new modes of work*, which is essentially Taylor's fourth principle.

4. Redivision of the work of the business: dividing the work of the company into two large parts. The job of the worker was to perform the work itself (shoveling coal, operating a machine, hauling pig iron, and so on), and the job of management was to plan and monitor the work, *not* to actually *do* the work. Managers were to act like scientists, constantly collecting and analyzing data and then planning the next segment of the company's work accordingly. Managers were also responsible for providing the requisite resources for the workers to do their jobs. Taylor stressed the importance of cooperation between workers and managers for this division of labor to succeed.

Taylor demonstrated on a number of occasions that his approach worked; it reduced costs and improved profits. Yet all was not bliss. Frequently, Taylor's scientific management process did not succeed. Executives who used Taylor's methods were too often desirous of quick gains and either only partially or entirely inappropriately applied the methods. Workers resisted methods that appeared to them to be "speedups," used for no other apparent reason than to make more money faster, at their expense.

Not surprisingly, Taylor became controversial. Some supported him strongly; others vilified him. There were during Taylor's lifetime and still to some extent today, *two* Frederick Taylors (Weisbord, 1987):

> Few men ever were such powerful magnets for both admiration and revulsion. [There were] two Taylors. One a mechanistic engineer, dedicated to counting, rigid control, and the rationalization of work, an unfeeling authoritarian who turned his own neurosis into repressive methods anathema to working people. . . . The other was a humanitarian social reformer, who believed workers could produce more with less stress, achieve greater equity in their output, and cooperate with management for the good of society. This [latter] Taylor has hardly been recognized publicly since 1925. (pp. 25-26)

Taylor was probably the first industrial engineering consultant, and, as an organization change agent, he believed deeply that taking a rational, "scientific" approach would provide the best opportunity for change. He recognized that workers were "feeling animals," to use his words, and that they should be treated humanely. Data collected systematically, analyzed carefully, and applied rigorously, if not rigidly, would in the end be the primary set of methods that would achieve the greatest efficiencies and have the most powerful and lasting effect on the organization.

Taylor's impact on organizational work, especially those enterprises that rely predominantly on technology and engineering, should not be underestimated. Some would argue that he is not only the father of scientific management but also the father of the whole field of industrial engineering. Initiatives that today we call *reengineering* and *business process engineering*, for example, have evolved from Taylor. Other related activities of today include ISO 9000, six sigma, and total quality management. These days, it may not be politically correct to claim to be a devotee of Frederick Taylor, but to be involved in any of the techniques and methods just mentioned is to live in his long shadow.

The Hawthorne Studies

Whereas Taylor's work was steeped in the disciplines of economics and engineering, the Hawthorne studies, as they turned out, were significant contributors to psychology and sociology. "As they turned out" is the operable phrase here, because the studies at the outset were not unlike Taylor's, for example, investigating the effects of lighting changes on worker productivity. In the early stages of their investigation, the research team was dumbfounded by the results. The assumed cause-effect linkage between illumination and productivity did not exist. Something else was clearly going on.

Beginning in 1924 and continuing into 1933, the Western Electric Company sponsored a series of experiments for studying worker productivity and morale at its Hawthorne Works, in Chicago. The researchers, from the Harvard Business School were led by Fritz Roethlisberger, T. N. Whitehead, Elton Mayo, and George Homans, and by W. J. Dickson of Western Electric. Full discussion of these studies is presented in Roethlisberger and Dickson (1939).

The studies can be categorized according to types of experiments, types of workers studied, and time period. The four categories of experiments, listed chronologically, were as follows:

1. The illumination experiments

2. The relay assembly group experiments

3. The interviewing program

4. The bank-wiring group studies

The intent of the investigators was to determine the effect of working conditions on productivity and morale. In the illumination experiments, lighting was changed in a variety of ways for a test group consisting of women. A control group was also studied. As lighting was increased, productivity increased, but, to the surprise of the investigators, productivity continued to increase even when lighting was subsequently decreased to significantly less than it had been originally. Other variations were tried. In some cases, even when the researchers pretended to change the illumination, the women responded positively. Throughout these experiments, regardless of whether the workers were in the test group or the control group, production either increased or did not change significantly. The researchers concluded that if light was a factor with respect to employee output, it was only one among many. They further hypothesized that worker attitude was a significant factor.

The next series of studies, the relay assembly group experiments, were conducted with a small group of six women who assembled part of the standard telephone. The variables studied were shorter working periods, incentive pay, personal health, and supervision. The conditions of the study were that (a) the women worked in a special, separate area, (b) they were continuously observed by a researcher, (c) they were consulted by the researcher-observer prior to any change, and (d) although the observer served as a supervisor of sorts, it was clear to the women workers that he was not a formal part of management. Over a period of 2½ years, in spite of many changes, productivity steadily increased to a level 30% higher than it had been before the experiments, and morale among the six women had improved steadily. Their absentee record was superior to that of the other regular workers, and there was no turnover. Also, regardless of the direction of the change the researchers made, output continued to increase over time. The conclusion was that there is no cause and effect relationship between working conditions and productivity. The women themselves told the researchers that the primary factors contributing to the increase in productivity were as follows:

1. More freedom on the job.

2. No boss.

3. Setting their own work pace.

4. Smaller group. (Their pay was based on their performance as a small group, as opposed to the usually larger one of 30 or more; thus, they had more control over the relationship between their performance and pay.)

5. The way they were treated.

This series of experiments had clearly shown the researchers the importance of worker *attitude* and provided information about factors other than physical working conditions that contribute to positive worker attitude. Managers at Western Electric were impressed with these studies, particularly with what they perceived to be a considerable amount of latent energy and willing cooperation that could be tapped under the right conditions.

In an attempt to investigate attitude more thoroughly, a third set of studies was launched in 1928. This program began as a vast data-collection process using individual interviews. Some 21,000 interviews were conducted by 1930. The interviews tended to become counseling sessions, and the researchers learned a great deal about employee attitudes, particularly those relating to supervision, worker relationships, and the importance of perceived status. A major outcome of these interview studies was learning how to teach supervisors about handling employee complaints: teaching them that an employee's complaint frequently is a symptom of some underlying problem, one that exists either on the job, at home, or in the person's past.

The researchers' desire, however, was to investigate social relations on the job more extensively. Thus, the final set of studies was conducted with a bank-wiring group of 14 men. This group's job was to wire and solder banks of equipment for central connecting services. Again, the group was separated for study, and data were collected by observers. The findings of this study concerned the importance of group norms and standards and the informal organization. For example, a group norm regarding rate of productivity significantly influenced the level of individual performance, and informal authority from influential group members often overrode formal authority from the supervisor.

The Hawthorne studies are significant as a precursor to our understanding of organization change for the following reasons:

1. They demonstrated the important influence of psychological or human factors on worker productivity and morale.

2. They signaled the criticality of certain variables for worker satisfaction: autonomy on the job (workers being able to set their own work pace), the relative lack

of a need for close supervision of people who know their jobs, the importance of receiving feedback on the direct relationship between performance and reward, and having choices and some influence regarding change.

3. They ushered in more humanistic treatment of workers on the job.

4. They provided evidence for later theory, such as Herzberg's motivation-hygiene notion. The hygiene portion of Herzberg's theory is that there is no direct cause-effect relationship between working conditions and productivity (Herzberg, Mausner, & Snyderman, 1959).

5. They provided the stimulus and data for much of what we now know about group dynamics, especially in a work context. The bank-wiring group was analyzed thoroughly by Homans, and this study, plus others in the series, resulted in his theory about work groups, his leading-edge thinking about group norms, and his now classic book, *The Human Group* (Homans, 1950).

A quotation from Roethlisberger (1980) is a fitting conclusion for this discussion:

> What all their experiments had dramatically and conclusively demonstrated was the importance of employee attitudes and sentiments. It was clear that the responses of workers to what was happening about them were dependent on the significance these events had for them. In most work situations the meaning of a change is likely to be as important, if not more so, than the change itself. This was the great *éclaircissement,* the new illumination, that came from the research. It was an illumination quite different from what they had expected from the illumination. (p. 33)

Industrial Psychology

Industrial psychology is now called *industrial and organizational psychology,* and the expanded label reflects changes in the field. In earlier days prior to, during, and immediately following World War II, industrial psychology was largely limited to business, industrial, and military organizations. Its primary thrust was testing, along with studies of morale and efficiency. Questionnaires for selection and screening were created by the hundreds and then tested for reliability and validity. As a result of the war effort, psychological testing came into its own. Industrial psychologists were also involved in training and development, especially supervisory and management training, during and after the war.

A research project conducted at the International Harvester Company by Edwin A. Fleishman (1953) during the late 1940s and early 1950s was typical of this era of industrial psychology. It combined supervisory training and the development of a psychological test. This series of studies, conducted over a period of more than 3 years, was highly significant for another reason, however; it provided useful background for our current understanding of organization change.

Fleishman (1953) was interested in the study of leadership and in the consequences of supervisory training: whether supervisors' attitudes and behavior would change as a result of a 2-week training program on leadership principles and techniques. Using several questionnaires, Fleishman took measures before the training and immediately following the program. Measures were also taken from a control group of supervisors and from the bosses and subordinates of both groups, the trained and untrained supervisors. In addition to measures taken right after the training, the same tests were administered at various intervals, ranging from 2 to 39 months later.

These tests reflected two primary functions of leadership: (a) *initiation of structure*, the provision of task direction and conditions for effective performance, and (b) *consideration*, the leader's sensitivity to and consideration of subordinates' needs and feelings. Prior testing had shown that first-line supervisors at International Harvester were strong in initiation of structure but were rarely considerate of their subordinates as people. The training program focused on increasing the consideration function.

Measures taken immediately following the training showed that the supervisors who had received the training scored significantly higher in consideration in comparison with both their own previous scores and the scores of the control group. Further measures taken over time with the trained group, however, revealed a startling outcome. These supervisors not only gradually reverted to their original behavior (not being very considerate) but in a number of cases, they ended up being *less* considerate than the control group.

On further investigation, Fleishman (1953) found that the bosses of the trained supervisors also scored high on initiation of structure and low on consideration. The few supervisors who had considerate bosses continued to score high over time on consideration. There was a direct relationship between the attitudes and the behavior of the supervisors and those of their bosses. Moreover, this relationship was stronger than the effects of training.

Schein (1972) explains the outcome of Fleishman's research directly and succinctly,

The effects of training were immediately related to the culture, or climate, of the department from which the men came. These climates had as much of an effect on the trainee as did the training. Consequently, the training was effective, in terms of its own goals, only in those departments in which the climate from the outset supported the training goals. (p. 44)

As early as 1953, therefore, the knowledge was available that organization change was not likely to occur as a result of an individual change strategy unless the objective of the training was in the same direction as the desired overall organization change.

One final point for this section: There have been many other contributions to our understanding of organization change from industrial psychologists during World War II and the decades that followed. The Fleishman study was singled out because it illustrated a critical point regarding organization change: the difference between focusing on the individual and focusing on contextual variables (such as group norms and organizational culture) and systemic factors (such as structure). These broader issues of organization change will be addressed in the next and later chapters.

Survey Feedback

As noted in the previous section, psychologists rely rather extensively on questionnaires for data collection and for diagnosis and assessment. Leadership questionnaires typically have been associated with a group of psychologists at Ohio State University in the 1950s. Questionnaires for organizational diagnosis, however, are more likely to be associated with the psychologists of the 1950s and 1960s at the Institute for Social Research of the University of Michigan. Rensis Likert, the first director of the institute, started by founding the Survey Research Center in 1946. Kurt Lewin had founded the Research Center for Group Dynamics at the Massachusetts Institute of Technology (MIT). With his untimely death in 1947, the center was moved to the University of Michigan later that year. These two centers initially constituted Likert's institute. The two main thrusts of these centers, questionnaire surveys for organization diagnosis and for group dynamics, combined to give birth to the *organizational survey feedback method.* As early as 1947, questionnaires were being used to systematically assess employee morale and attitudes in organizations.

One of the first of these studies, initiated and guided by Likert and conducted by Floyd Mann, was done with the Detroit Edison Company. From working on the problem of how best to use the survey data for organization improvement, the method we now know as survey feedback evolved. Mann (1957) was key to the development of this method. He noted that when a manager was given the survey results, any resulting improvement depended on what the manager did with the information. If the manager discussed the survey results with his subordinates, particularly through group discussion, positive change typically occurred. If the manager did not share the survey results with his subordinates, however, and failed to plan certain changes for improvement jointly with them, nothing happened—except, perhaps, an increase in employee frustration over the ambiguity of having answered a questionnaire and never hearing anything further.

First, the survey feedback method involves the *survey*, data collection by questionnaire to determine employees' perceptions of a variety of factors, focusing mainly on the management of the organization. Second is the *feedback*, in which results of the survey are reported back systematically in summary form to all people who answered the questionnaire. *Systematically*, in this case, means that the feedback occurs in phases, starting with the top team of the organization and flowing downward according to the formal hierarchy and within functional units or teams. Mann (1957) referred to this flowing-downward process as the "interlocking chain of conferences." The chief executive officer, the division general manager, or the bureau chief, depending on the organization or subunit surveyed, and his or her immediate group of subordinates receive and discuss feedback from the survey first. Next, the subordinates and their respective groups of immediate subordinates do the same, and so forth, downward, until all members of the organization who have been surveyed (a) hear a summary of the survey and then (b) participate in a discussion of the meaning of the data and the implications. Each functional unit of the organization receives general feedback concerning the overall organization and specific feedback regarding its particular group. Following a discussion of the meaning of the survey results for their particular group, the boss and his or her subordinates then jointly plan action steps for improvement. Usually, a consultant meets with each of the groups to help with data analysis, group discussion, and plans for improvement.

Later, Rensis Likert (1967) took the survey feedback approach a step farther by developing his "Profile of Organizational Characteristics," a questionnaire and model consisting of six sections: leadership, motivation, communication, decisions, goals, and control. These six were surveyed within an overall framework of four organizational categories or systems. Likert labeled System 1 as *autocratic,* System 2 *as benevolent autocracy,* System 3 as *consultative* (employees are consulted about matters, but management, in the end, makes the decisions), and System 4 as *participative and consensus management.* Likert argued that System 4 was the most desirable and that most employees felt the same way. Likert thus was able to *profile* an organization according to the four system types along the six organizational dimensions mentioned above.

Thus, survey feedback, this rather orderly and systematic way of understanding an organization from the standpoint of employee perceptions and processing this understanding back into the organization so that change can occur, is a primary method of leveraging organization change. Unless applied appropriately, survey feedback will work no better than any other change mechanism. Used properly, however, survey feedback can be powerful for the following reasons:

- It is based on data.
- It involves organization members directly.
- It provides information about what to change and in which priority.
- It focuses change toward the larger system, not at individuals per se.

In later chapters, this method will be explored in more depth with reference to certain, more current sources, such as Kraut (1996).

Sensitivity Training

From a historical viewpoint, it would be interesting to know how many events, inventions, or innovations that occurred in 1946 had lasting impact through the subsequent decades. Apparently, once the war was over, people were somehow free to pursue a variety of creative endeavors. One such innovative event occurred in the summer of 1946, in New Britain, Connecticut. Kurt Lewin, at the time a member of the faculty of MIT and director of the Research Center for Group Dynamics, was asked by the director of the Connecticut State Interracial Commission to conduct a training workshop that would help to improve community leadership in general and interracial relationships in particular. Lewin brought together a group of colleagues and students to serve as trainers (Leland Bradford, Ronald Lippitt, and Kenneth Benne) and researchers (Morton Deutsch, Murray Horwitz, Arnold Meier, and Melvin Seeman) for the workshop. The training consisted of lectures, role play, and general group discussion. In the evenings, most researchers and trainers met to evaluate the training to that point by discussing participant behavior as they had observed it during the day. A few of the participants who were far enough from their homes to stay in the dormitory rooms at the college in New Britain asked whether they could observe the evening staff discussions. The trainers and researchers were reluctant, but Lewin saw no reason to keep them away and thought that, as participants, they might learn even more.

The results were impactive and far-reaching. In the course of the staff's discussion of the behavior of one participant, who happened to be present and observing, the participant intervened and said that she disagreed with their interpretation of her behavior. She then described the event from her point of view. Lewin immediately recognized that this intrusion provided a richness to the data collection and analysis that was otherwise unavailable. The next evening, many more participants stayed to observe the staff discussions. Observation alone didn't last, of course, and three-way discussions occurred among the researchers, trainers, and participants. Gradually, the staff and participants discovered that the feedback the participants were receiving about their daytime behavior was teaching them as much or more than the daytime activities were. The participants were becoming more sensitive to their own behavior in terms of how they were being perceived by others and the impact their behavior was having on others. This serendipitous and innovative mode of learning, which had its beginning that summer in Connecticut, has become what Carl Rogers (1968) labeled "perhaps the most significant social invention of the century" (p. 265).

Sensitivity training, T-groups, and *laboratory training* are all labels for the same process, consisting of small group discussions in which the primary, almost exclusive source of information for learning is the behavior of the group members themselves. Participants receive feedback from one another regarding their behavior in the group, and this feedback becomes the learning source for personal insight and development. Participants also have an opportunity to learn more about group behavior and intergroup relationships.

T-groups (T is for training) are educational vehicles for change, in this case, individual change. When this form of education began to be applied in industrial settings for organization change during the late 1950s, the T-group became one of the earliest interventions of what became known as *organization development*. See, for example, the classic article "T-Groups for Organizational Effectiveness," by Chris Argyris (1964).

Sociotechnical Systems

As mentioned above, the period immediately following the Second World War was a productive time for innovation and creativity. While in the United States, the serendipitous birth of the T-group was occurring, across the Atlantic, in the United Kingdom, a parallel and highly significant set of social developments was underway. The United Kingdom work emanated from the Tavistock Institute, based in London. There were two action research projects at the institute in the late 1940s. One concerned group relations (similar to the T-group but different regarding the role of the group trainer, called a *consultant*). The other project concerned the diffusion of innovative work practices and organizational arrangements. The former emphasized individual learning about oneself, group, and intergroup dynamics, and the latter focused on organizational matters, especially organization change. Eric Trist was the leader of this latter project. He and his associates began their work at the time in the British coal industry.

The newly nationalized coal industry, then the major source of power in the United Kingdom, was not doing well. There were problems with productivity, turnover, the union, and adaptation to new technology. One exception existed in the South Yorkshire coalfield. Trist and his colleague, Ken Bamforth, a former miner himself, went to take a look. They found that the work organization consisted of the following (Trist, 1993):

> Relatively autonomous groups interchanging roles and shifts and regulating their affairs with a minimum of supervision. Cooperation between task groups was everywhere in evidence, personal commitment obvious, absenteeism low, accidents infrequent, productivity high. . . . The men told us that in order to adapt with best advantage to the technical conditions in the new seam, they had evolved a form of work organization based on practices common in the unmechanized days when small groups, who took responsibility for the entire cycle, had worked autonomously. These practices had disappeared as the pits became progressively more mechanized in relation to the introduction of "longwall" working. This

method had enlarged the scale of operations and led to aggregates of men of considerable size having their jobs broken down into one-man/one-task roles, while coordination and control were externalized in supervision, which became coercive. Now they had found a way, at a higher level of mechanization, of recovering the group cohesion and self-regulation they had lost and of advancing their power to participate in decisions concerning their work arrangements. . . . It was not true that the only way of designing work organizations must conform to Tayloristic and bureaucratic principles. (pp. 37-38)

What Trist had discovered was a new paradigm of work and, interestingly, the coal miners had designed it themselves. Trist went on to conceptualize and further develop the new paradigm, and it became known as *sociotechnical systems,* a new field of inquiry and approach to organization change. Some of the primary principles of sociotechnical systems are as follows (Trist, 1993):

- Work organizations consist of two *independent* yet *interdependent* systems: the technical system (equipment, machinery, chemical processes, etc.) and the social system (individual workers and groups of workers).
- The *work system* is the basic unit, comprising a set of activities that make up a functioning whole, rather than single jobs and tasks.
- The *work group,* rather than the individual jobholder, is central.
- *Regulation* of the system is performed by the group itself, instead of by supervisors (completely counter to Taylor's scientific management notions).
- An individual worker is *complementary* to the machine, rather than an extension of it.

There is more to the sociotechnical systems field than these principles; however, those presented are designed to provide a flavor of sociotechnical systems thinking.

Considering organization change through a sociotechnical lens means that one would gather data about both the social and technical systems but would then consider and act with the perspective that the two are *interdependent:* a change in one system will directly affect the other, and this effect must be treated as another leverage in the change process. For example, changing a piece of software in an organization's information system (the technical) will directly affect how employees who use the software interact with one another in the future.

A final point: Sociotechnical studies need to be conducted at three broad levels, from micro to macro, according to Trist (1993). All three levels are interrelated. The first is *primary work systems,* identifiable and bounded subsystems of a whole organization, such as a department or a business unit. The second is *whole organization systems,* the entire company or institution; they persist, as Trist points out, by maintaining a reasonably steady state within their environment. And the third is *macrosocial systems,* organizations within communities and industrial sectors, as well as institutions operating at societal level, such as national government.

The sociotechnical approach insists that systems are interdependent. Moreover, this approach "has also developed in terms of open system theory [the subject of the next chapter] since it is concerned with the environment in which an organization must actively maintain a steady state" (Trist, 1993, p. 41). For more on sociotechnical thinking, especially regarding the design of effective organizations, see Pasmore (1988).

Organization Development

Both sensitivity training and sociotechnical systems set the stage for the emergence of organization development (OD). As the T-group method of learning and change began to proliferate in the 1950s, it gradually gravitated to organizational life. Sensitivity training began to be used as an intervention for organization change; in this application, the training was conducted inside a single organization, and members of the small T-groups were either organizational "cousins," from the same overall organization but not within the same vertical chain of the organization's hierarchy, or members of the same organizational team, so-called family groups.

As French and Bell (1995) have reported, one of the first events to improve organization effectiveness by sensitivity training took place with managers at some of the major refineries of Exxon (then known as Esso) in Louisiana and southeast Texas. Herbert Shepard, of the corporate employee relations department, and Harry Kolb, of the refineries division, used interviews followed by 3-day training laboratories for all managers in an attempt to move management in a more participative direction. Outside trainers were used, many of them the major names of the National Training Laboratories at the time, such as Leland Bradford and Robert R. Blake. Paul Buchanan conducted similar activities while he was with the Naval Ordnance Test Station at China Lake, California. He later joined Shepard at Esso.

At about the same time, Douglas McGregor, of the Sloan School of Management at MIT, was conducting similar training sessions at Union

Carbide. These events at Esso and Union Carbide represented the early characteristics of OD, which usually took the form of what we now call *team building* (Burck, 1965; McGregor, 1967).

Also during that period, the late 1950s, McGregor and Richard Beckhard were consulting with General Mills. They were working on what we now call a *sociotechnical systems change effort*. They helped to change some of the work structures at the various plants so that more teamwork and increased decision making took place on the shop floor; more "bottoms-up" management began to occur. They didn't want to call what they were doing "bottoms-up," nor were they satisfied with "sociotechnical systems" or "organization improvement," so they eventually labeled their effort "organization development" (Beckhard, 1997). This label also became, apparently independently, the name for the work Shepard, Kolb, Blake, and others were doing at the Humble refineries of Esso.

The first sustained, long-term OD efforts were conducted with TRW Systems, the aerospace division of TRW, Inc. (Davis, 1967), and with the Harwood-Weldon Manufacturing Corporation (Marrow, Bowers, & Seashore, 1967). During the early 1960s, Herbert Shepard, who had left Esso for the academic world at Case Western Reserve, consulted with TRW Systems and worked particularly with internal employee relations managers, James Dunlap and Sheldon Davis. Team building was the primary intervention used in those early days. Later, as OD practitioners became more sophisticated and diversified, TRW Systems began to use a variety of methods. In fact, the external and internal consultants at TRW during the 1960s helped to invent much of the OD technology we use today, such as the organization mirror, "reflecting" back to members of a work unit about how they see themselves compared with how others see them, and other quick techniques for team diagnosis (Fordyce & Weil, 1979).

The primary method at Harwood-Weldon started with an *action research approach* (Coch & French, 1948), conducting a study for the purpose of application and corrective action to some problem, rather than as research that serves the primary purpose of contributing to a body of literature and scholarship; it then gradually incorporated the method of survey feedback developed at the University of Michigan.

OD, then, is an approach to organization change based on applied behavioral science and reliant on the action research approach. It is steeped in the theoretical tradition of applied social psychology, especially the work of Kurt Lewin. In other words, the methodological model for OD is action research: Data on the nature of certain problems are systematically collected (the research aspect), and then action is taken as a function of what the analyzed data indicate. The specific techniques used within this overall methodological model (few of which are unique to OD) are (a) diagnosis, interviews with both individuals and groups and perhaps the use of a questionnaire and observation, followed by analysis and organization of the data collected; (b) feedback, reporting back to those from whom the data were obtained on the collective sense of the organizational problems; (c) discussion of what these data mean and planning the steps that should be taken as a consequence; and (d) taking those steps. In OD language, taking a step is making an *intervention* into the routine way in which the organization operates. And finally, the field of OD is imbued with a strong humanistic value system, making certain that organization members are involved in the change decisions that will directly affect them and that interventions are frequently focused on change in the organization's culture. For coverage of this field, one may refer to the Addison-Wesley series on OD; the volume in that series that provides an overview is Burke (1994). Also, a more recent book series on OD and organization change is now provided by the publishers Jossey-Bass/Pfeiffer of Wiley.

The Managerial Grid and OD

What might be characterized as a special case of OD, a comparatively highly structured approach to change, both individual and organizational, is Blake and Mouton's managerial grid. First, a brief overview of their model relating to the individual manager will be presented, followed by coverage of their approach to change at the organizational level.

Building on the earlier work of Fleishman and his colleagues at Ohio State University in the 1950s (see earlier Industrial Psychology section), Blake and Mouton (1964) took the two dimensions of leadership and initiation of structure and consideration, relabeled them *production* and *people*, respectively, and specified that the typical leader or manager had different concerns about both, some being more concerned with getting the job done than about the people involved, and vice versa for others. They arranged these two concerns on a graph, using 9-point scales to represent the *degree* of concern (Burke, 1997):

The juxtaposition on a graph resulted in what they called the "managerial grid," a two-dimensional model that describes managerial style (Blake & Mouton, 1964). How these two concerns combine for a given manager determines his or her style of management. The greater the concern for production, the more autocratic the manager's style tends to be; the greater the concern with people, the more permissive the management style. Blake and Mouton argue that a manager who has a simultaneously high concern for both production and people (what they label a "9,9 style") is likely to be the most effective. (p. 5)

A few years later, Blake and Mouton (1968) applied the grid model to organization change, calling their approach "grid organization development." Based on a large, cross-sectional study, Blake and Mouton began with an organizational diagnosis that they claimed generalizes to most organizations. Their study showed that managers consider the most common barriers to organizational effectiveness to be (a) communication problems and (b) a lack of planning. Blake and Mouton contended that these two barriers were at the top of managers' lists, regardless of country, company, or characteristics of the managers reporting. They went on to argue that communication and planning as barriers to effectiveness were *symptoms* and not causes of less than optimal performance. Poor planning or the lack of planning stem from senior management's not having a strategy or having a faulty one. Communication problems come from poor supervision and management.

To address these two causes, Blake and Mouton (1968) developed a six-phase approach that addressed the organization's strategic plan and, of course, the style and approach to supervision and management.

The first phase in the grid OD approach was to train all managers in how to become a 9,9, or participative, manager. This usually required 5 days. Phase 2 was teamwork development, in a sense, applying what had occurred in Phase 1 with "cousin" groups to "family" units. In addition, group norms and working characteristics of the team were identified. Phase 3 was intergroup development, which characterized cooperative behavior, as opposed to competition between groups in the organization. Today, this process is often referred to as *cross-functional group work*. Phase 4 consisted of developing an ideal strategic corporate model. Phase 5 was the implementation of Phase 4, and Phase 6 was a systematic critique of the previous five phases, with a particular focus on specific barriers to change that may still exist and need to be overcome. In summary, Phases 1, 2, and 3 were designed to deal with communication problems, and the remaining phases were to address the planning barriers. In addition (Burke, 1994),

Blake and Mouton never state it, but they apparently assume that, unless an organization learns how to communicate more effectively (practice 9,9 management) and plan more logically and systematically (build an ideal strategic model and begin to implement it), its management will never be able to deal optimally with the specifics of running a business. Phase 6 in the grid OD sequence [is designed to get to] the specifics. (p. 121)

Ten years later, Blake and Mouton (1978) claimed success for their approach, but outside their own reporting, there is scant documentation. This is not to argue that grid OD fails. Following Blake and Mouton's approach can lead to successful organization change. It is more a matter of senior management's tolerance for a lock-step approach that is based on one best way to manage, participative, which goes against the grain of many organizational managers. Regarding this final point, it should be noted that there is considerable evidence, despite the beliefs of many senior managers, that participative management is more likely than most other approaches to lead to higher unit and organization performance. See, for example, Chapter 4 in Druckman, Singer, and Van Cott (1997).

Coercion and Confrontation

Although coercion in the form of both nonviolent and violent strategies and techniques may not at first appear to be related to organization change, these kinds of social interventions have indeed been used. Disputes between labor and management have on occasion contained violent actions as well as nonviolent protests, such as company or plant entries being blocked by union members to prevent nonstriking employees from going to work. During the late 1960s, especially at the height of protests against the Vietnam War, attempts were made by students to change their universities. Their tactics were for the most part nonviolent yet highly intrusive, such as occupying the university president's office for several weeks.

Examining these coercive and confrontational strategies and techniques will not occupy a large space in this book (see Hornstein, Bunker, Burke, Gindes, & Lewicki, 1971, for more comprehensive coverage), but certain relevant points pertinent to our study of organization change should not be ignored. Two examples may help to make the point.

Groups, such as unions, minorities, and the disabled, who feel disenfranchised by the organization that employs them and confront or attempt to coerce management for changes, may be understood to some degree by considering *in-group* and *out-group* theory and research. The pioneering experiments of Muzafer Sherif (Sherif, 1966; Sherif, Harvey, White, Hood, & Sherif, 1961; Sherif & Sherif, 1953; 1969) and the work of other scholars, such as Coser (1967) and Deutsch (1969), have helped not only to clarify and provide useful conceptualization in these kinds of situations but also to generate further ideas for dealing with such conflict. For example, the idea of a superordinate goal and/or common enemy is proposed to focus attention more toward cooperation and less toward competition and confrontation. Practical applications of such ideas for organization change may be found in publications such as Blake, Shepard, and Mouton (1964); Burke (1974); and Burke and Biggart (1997).

In the arena of community organizing and change, arguably the preeminent reflective practitioner was Saul Alinsky. His book, *Reveille for Radicals* (Alinsky, 1946) became a handbook for how to organize and challenge accepted authority. Many of his targets were organizations that he attempted to change via coercion and confrontation. The relevance of his work to the dominant view of organization change presented in this book is that, as Peabody (1971) has pointed out, Alinsky's model for building a community organization contains most of the same phases described by Lippitt, Watson, and Westley (1958) in their book on planned change. In other words, even though the underlying value systems and tactics differ, the overall framework for how to conceptualize the main phases of change is essentially the same. The phases of Alinsky's model were *entry, data collection, goal setting,* and *organizing,* which correspond closely to Lippitt and his colleagues' phases of planned change. To quote Peabody (1971):

> The parallels are no coincidence; the study of power requires the keenest observation of social dynamics. Whether or not he read any of these behavioral scientists, Alinsky made similar observations years ago, and applied them to his own imaginative manner. (p. 524)

It can therefore be useful to understand more about change strategies and techniques that do not normally constitute chapters in books for students in psychology, sociology, organizational behavior, and management. Such learning can help either to undermine coercive techniques or to support, say, a disenfranchised group that one values.

Management Consulting

Jethro, of the Old Testament, may have been one of the earliest, if not the original, management consultants. One of the first management consultants of modern times was Frederick Taylor. From the standpoint of establishing a professional service firm devoted to management consulting, the first, at least in the United States, was James O. McKinsey. (According to Drucker, 1974, the first in the United Kingdom was Lyndall F. Urwick, born in 1891.) Born in 1889, McKinsey was younger than Taylor but knew of his work and was influenced by it, especially Taylor's strong emphasis on data collection and deep analysis. Unlike Taylor, however, McKinsey was not an engineer. He was educated in law and accounting (he was a CPA) and eventually became a professor in the Graduate School of Business at the University of Chicago. McKinsey was impressed with the rigor of Taylor's approach and stressed the importance of engineering principles for helping organizations improve and change. In fact, an early name of his firm, around 1938, was James O. McKinsey and Company, Accountants and Engineers. The company actually started around 1923 in Chicago.

Whereas Taylor stressed a scientific approach, McKinsey emphasized professionalism. McKinsey & Co. was, and remains in emphasis to this day, a firm of professional practice, not a business per se. McKinsey believed that three ingredients were critical to establishing a professional practice (Bower, 1979):

1. Unquestioned respectability: McKinsey spent much of his early life getting himself educated and had a goal of becoming a professor of business.

2. Professional exposure: He wrote books devoted particularly to accounting and budgeting and gave numerous speeches and lectures.

3. Reputation: McKinsey wanted to make certain that he had a strong reputation for special competence in an area of concern to management, in his case, accounting, budget control, and business strategy and policy in general.

To say that McKinsey was successful is an understatement. The firm that bears his name today is considered to be one of the most prestigious of its kind.

The McKinsey way of consulting, as it is for most management consulting firms, is to employ a strict problem-solving process (Rasiel, 1999). First, the consultant gathers as much factual information about the client organization's problem as possible. For example, the client's presenting problem (the "presenting" problem may not be the real problem, as most experienced consultants know) may be a sudden drop in sales. Although this presenting problem is real, it is a symptom of something. Finding that "something" is the task. The consultant uses interviews, particularly with people from the sales force; company records that reflect, for example, sales and marketing strategies and tactics; survey data from customers; and accounting and financial information to collect as many facts as possible. Experienced management consultants believe that "facts are friendly" and that being fact-based is the same as being a credible, competent consultant.

Second, after a thorough analysis of the facts, an initial hypothesis is determined, to be tested with the client. A third facet of this problem-solving process is to be highly structured. This means (a) limiting the recommendations for solving the problem to what can realistically be done considering the client's resources, the consulting firm's resources, and amount of time required, (b) proposing a limited number of recommended actions (McKinsey, for example, often limits their recommendations to three, no more, no less; see Rasiel, 1999), and (c) establishing milestones that can be met with targets that can be achieved, along with the assurance that the client will be satisfied.

The roots of management consulting, as mentioned above, come from Taylor. Thus, applying the scientific method of data gathering, analysis, hypothesis generation, testing the hypothesis, and action, basing remedies for the problem on these facts and the hypothesis, is the modus operandi. McKinsey adopted Taylor's approach and added their own structured way of problem solving. Most management consulting firms conduct their business similarly. For more detail on the "McKinsey way," see the book by Rasiel (1999).

Today, management consulting is a huge industry and continues to grow on a global basis. Moreover, major firms today include as part of their practice what has been referred to as *change management*. Even a major accounting firm such as PriceWaterhouse Coopers has a significant practice in change management, which they call "Organization and Strategic Change Services." Change management, then, is an attempt to integrate some of the standard aspects of management consulting (e.g., changing a client's business strategy, modifying its information technology systems, or changing the organizational design and structure) with organization change methods that are based on applied behavioral science, particularly organizational psychology.

Summary

Although the length of this chapter may not correspond to its title of a "brief" history, the coverage provided is only the tip of the iceberg. A full chapter could easily be devoted to each of the 10 forerunners who were summarized. For the purpose of this book, the coverage provided should suffice. It is important to remember the following 10 points:

1. Scientific management set the stage for a systematic approach to organization change; prior to Taylor such rigor had not existed.

2. The Hawthorne studies demonstrated the importance of the human dimension of organization change and contributed significantly to the future of applied behavioral science.

3. Industrial psychology has, and continues to provide today, with the fuller integration of the individual and the organization, the research and theory required for the growth and development of our understanding of organization change.

4. Survey feedback may not be the most important tool for diagnosing and implementing organization change, but it is certainly in the top tray of our tool kit.

5. Even though controversial to this day and not used as prevalently as was true in the 1960s, sensitivity training has provided an unsurpassed mode for learning about group dynamics, interpersonal behavior, and about oneself.

6. Sociotechnical systems furnished what seems today the obvious and yet overlooked critical nature of the interdependence of people and the organizational tools with which they work.

7. Organization development (OD) has given us a systematic approach to organization change with its emphasis on the total system, clear steps and phases of organization change, and an underlying set of humanistic values to guide the entire process.

8. Although highly structured, grid OD has stressed the importance of priorities in organization change and which primary organizational issues need to be addressed.

9. Although unconventional for what we usually think of when considering organization change, much can nevertheless be learned from coercive and confrontational techniques of trying to change an organization or institution.

10. Greater integration of the standard forms of management with those from the behavioral sciences should strengthen our understanding and effectiveness of organization change methodologies and processes.

3

Theoretical Foundations of Organizations and Organization Change

To understand organization change, we must begin with some basics about organizations. This understanding will be grounded in two somewhat different but overlapping theoretical domains:

- Open system theory, which stems from the discipline of biology, especially cell biology
- A theoretical synthesis of recent thinking regarding shifts from physics to the life sciences as the predominate explanatory discipline

In understanding organizations, there is choice about theory. We could include theory from sociology and political science, for example, but as noted in the preface, the standard literature for organization theory based in part on sociology and related disciplines emphasizes stabilization and not organization change. So, an additional choice is to rely on disciplines aligned with open system theory, which is rooted in the life sciences.

Open System Theory

Any human organization is best understood as an open system. An organization is "open" because of its dependency on and continual interaction with the environment in which it resides. Closed systems exist only in the world of nonliving matter. Even a biological cell is an open system because it depends on its environment for survival, for taking in oxygen, for example.

For survival, an organization takes in energy from its environment. Energy is broadly defined and may include money, raw materials, or the work of people. This energy is then transformed into a product or service and returned to the environment. The output may encompass the same segments of the environment or others that were used as energetic inputs. One critical element of input for a business organization is money, which may take the form of a bank loan or the sale of ownership shares. After transformation into a product that is sold in the marketplace (another aspect of the organization's environment), the income from those sales provides additional input. For a profit-making organization to survive in the long term, sales income must become the primary input. The sales income then reactivates the system. This cyclical process is input-throughput (transformation)-output, a feedback loop that connects output to input. Thus, for example, a bank loan (input) provides money to purchase raw materials (more input) so that a product can be made (transformation) and then sold (output) to consumers, and their payments provide money for further input, reactivating the cycle.

To identify the boundaries of an organization, therefore, it is not necessary to consider its name, location, or purpose (though these may add to the definition), but rather to follow, according to Katz & Kahn (1978),

> The energic and informational transactions as they relate to the cycle of activities of input, throughput, and output. Behavior not tied to these functions lies outside the system. . . . Open systems [therefore] maintain themselves through constant commerce with their environment, that is, a continuous inflow and outflow of energy through permeable boundaries. (pp. 21, 22)

Although their boundaries are permeable and open, organizations are also entities with internal elements or parts that are easy to identify: physical and technological parts, such as buildings, machines, desks, and paper (typically, piles of paper!); task- or work-related elements, such as specific jobs, roles (boss, subordinate), or functions (accounting, manufacturing); and suborganizations or subsystems, such as departments, divisions, or business units. Most important, there are the people: male or female, African American or Irish American, skilled or semiskilled, old or young, and so on. All these parts compose a whole, a total organization that represents an entity different from the simple sum of its elements and dimensions, which is a basic tenet of Gestalt psychology. General Motors is more than the sum of Chevrolet, GMAC, Saturn, and the other subsystems. Similarly, a hospital is something more than the operating room and its staff, the various units, beds, nurses, doctors, patients, and so on, put together.

To consider organization change, it is important to take a total system perspective. Although one rarely tackles the entire system at once, one works diligently to keep the total in mind as one goes about changing parts, because the change of one part will affect other parts, perhaps all parts eventually.

Characteristics of Open Systems

Using as an intellectual source the general systems theory of biologist Von Bertalanffy (1950), Katz and Kahn (1978) delineate 10 characteristics that distinguish open systems.

1. Importation of Energy. No human organization is self-contained or self-sufficient; thus, it must draw energy from outside to ensure survival. Take the case of a consulting firm that specializes in conducting employee opinion surveys for client organizations. The energy that the firm draws from its environment comes from various sources, such as a line of credit from a nearby bank; the purchase of raw materials to produce the firm's product and services, for example, paper, high-speed color duplicating machines and services, three-ring binders, or computer disks for on-line processing; revenues from previous client work; and perhaps some temporary workers to help meet peak demands.

2. Throughput. The employees of the firm take these raw materials and other sources from the environment and use them to develop an employee-opinion survey questionnaire, administer the survey in their client organization, collect and analyze the survey data, and prepare a report for the client.

3. Output. Deliver the report, work with the client organization to take appropriate action according to the survey data, and finally, collect a fee from the client organization for the services rendered.

4. Systems are cycles of events. Providing an excellent survey instrument and high-quality service with the delivery of the product will help to ensure that the consulting firm will stay in business, if not result in increased business and insure that the input-throughput-output cycle will continue. Katz and Kahn (1978) used the term *events* (after Allport, 1962) to explain the nature of an organization's structure and boundaries. An organization does not have a physical boundary as a human being does (skin that encloses bones, muscles, organs, and so on) to identify it as a system. An organization's building does not suffice as the identifying feature of structure and boundary, although the TransAmerica Tower in San Francisco comes to mind as an attempt to erect a structure that at least symbolizes the company. Nevertheless, events for the most part, rather than things, provide identity. Social structures, the chain of events between and among people, establish boundaries. For our consulting organization, the identifying and boundary-setting events were contracting, purchasing, hiring a workforce, preparing the survey and providing the service associated with it, collecting monies from the client to purchase more raw materials and to pay employees, and eventually, contracting again with the client for additional work or moving on to a new client. Such a cycle of events is what establishes and identifies an open system—for our purposes, an organization.

5. Negative Entropy. According to general systems theory (Katz & Kahn, 1978),

> [The] entropic process is a universal law of nature in which all forms of organization move toward disorganization or death . . . [but] by importing more energy from its environment than it expends, the open system can store energy and acquire negative entropy. (p. 25)

When an organization is losing money, the managers do not typically ask, "How can we stop this terrible entropic process?" but they do understand that, unless positive action is taken, they and all their employee colleagues may be out of jobs, for the organization will cease to exist under such a condition. For a profit-making organization, storing energy consists in part of having capital and lines of credit. For a private university, it is having a healthy endowment. For the consulting firm that is in the survey business, it is, for example, having the goodwill of clients, money in the bank, good relations with other members of the firm's profession so that referrals for future business will occur, and a solid reputation for high-quality products and services.

The point is that organizations are not self-sufficient; they are unstable and will not survive or grow unless active and deliberate effort is expended. The process of interpersonal trust serves as an analogy. Trust between people is a very unstable process that must be maintained constantly. When one party to the relationship behaves at all strangely or suspiciously, the trust in the relationship is automatically in jeopardy, and deliberate action must be taken for the trusting quality to be regained and maintained. Similarly, constant effort must be expended not only for the maintenance of an organization, but for its very survival.

6. Information Input, Negative Feedback, and the Coding Process. If an organization obtains feedback on how well its output is being received, it can respond to its customers or clients more effectively in the future. This is especially true when the feedback is negative; then, corrective action can be planned and taken. When customers or clients complain about the service they are receiving, the firm's leaders can take action to change some elements within the input-throughput-output and feedback set of events. It is rare for all information in an organization's environment that could be used as feedback to be tapped. Some kind of coding occurs as organizational members are selective and try to simplify all the possibilities into fundamental categories that seem to be most relevant for a given system. The consulting firm would probably pay more attention to negative feedback from clients (good clients especially) than from professional peers. Although professional peers may influence the firm's reputation by what they say in public forums, the clients, after all, provide the firm's income (i.e., input), which is more directly linked to survival.

7. Steady-State and Dynamic Homeostasis. Organizations that survive are typically considered in steady state, but this does not mean that little activity is occurring. As Katz and Kahn (1978) depict it,

> A steady state is not a motionless or true equilibrium. There is a continuous flow of energy from the external environment and a continuous export of the products of the system, but the character of the system, the ratio of the energy exchanges and the relations between parts, remains the same. (p. 26)

Lewin's (1947) concept of quasi-stationary equilibrium is relevant here. An organization's *apparent* equilibrium is actually up at one moment (during one event in the cycle) and down at another, but the overall averaging of these ups and downs gives the appearance of a stationary or steady-state situation.

To counteract entropy, organizations need to grow and to control more and more of their environment—that is, expand the original system. This counteracting process implies change. In terms of Lewin's (1958) concept of equilibrium, the average of an organization's ups and downs does not always remain at the same level. Even so, the basic character of an organization tends to remain the same. To say that Chase Manhattan or the Bank of America is now a financial intermediary institution, for example, is to reflect the organization's movement into a broader field of services, not necessarily to state that it is getting out of the banking business.

8. Differentiation. As an organization continues to offset the entropic process and therefore grows (not always meaning expansion, but sometimes creating new businesses and eliminating old ones), differentiation and elaboration occur; that is, specialization and division of labor evolve. In our consulting firm example, this could be a division of labor consisting of those who work directly with the clients and others who conduct the data processing and analyses.

9. Integration and Coordination. To maintain stability, too much differentiation can occur. A certain degree of unification and coordination is then necessary. According to Katz and Kahn (1978), integration is accomplished through shared norms and values. Organization structure, roles, and authority are the social-system vehicles that managers use to achieve integration and coordination. The current hue and cry about the "silo effect" in many corporations is an outcome of too much differentiation and inadequate integration and coordination.

10. Equifinality. According to Von Bertalanffy's (1950) principle, an organization can attain the same goal from different starting points and by a variety of paths. To increase sales, a clear and specific goal, our consulting firm in the survey business may, for example, concentrate on referrals from current and past clients rather than, say, advertising via direct mail with follow-up phone calls. Either path might achieve the goal of increased sales.

An organization's success and effectiveness in a systems sense is contingent on two processes—openness and selectivity. The organization's managers must operate according to the foregoing 10 open system characteristics, but they should be selective in their inputs and outputs, especially with respect to the feedback they obtain from the environment.

To summarize, open system theory begins with the cyclical process of input (importation of energy)-throughput-output, that is, transforming input into a usable product and/or service. The output into the external environment (a customer, for example) creates the potential for feedback, which in turn generates another form of input so that the organization can correct its throughput to improve its future output, thus helping to ensure long-term survival. So, systems are composed of cycles of events. Within these cycles, it is critical that organizational managers make sure that they store more energy from the external environment than they produce as output. In theoretical terms, this is referred to as *thwarting the natural process of entropy.* In practical business language, it is ensuring that sales are greater than costs. A primary mode of fighting entropy is to obtain feedback on a regular basis about how well the organization is performing so that corrective action can be taken and the organization can remain adaptive (i.e., have a strong capacity to fight equilibrium and change itself).

As organizations do well in offsetting the entropic processes, they tend to grow and develop, which results in greater differentiation of products and services along with the congruent need for integration and coordination. A final characteristic of organization according to open system theory is the principle of *equifinality,* which essentially means that for any given goal, there are multiple paths that organizational members can take to achieve it. In short, it should be clear that managers of organizations need to be constantly aware that they are managing a system that has permeable boundaries, is dependent on its environment for survival, and will go out of existence unless it is actively attended to (managed).

Organization Change Is Systemic

The objective for change is systemic; that is, some aspect of the system, such as the organization's managerial structure or the reward system, is selected for change. Usually, this selection is made as a result of a previous diagnosis and in collaboration with the relevant people within the organization.

The change objective is systemic for at least three reasons. First, when some aspect of the system is changed, other aspects eventually will be affected, thus making for a total system approach. If the leader or change agent works in one part of the organization and does not consider this impact and plan for the consequences of his or her actions for other parts of the system, eventually, the effort is likely to fail (Burke, 1980).

The second reason for an organization change effort to be systemic is based on our knowledge of how to bring about change in an organization. One of the precursors of organization change research and theory is sensitivity training (see Chapter 2), which is educational and individually focused regarding the objective for change, improvement, and learning. Sensitivity training was a primary intervention for organizational change in the 1960s. As we discovered through experience and research, however, although training may lead to individual change (Bunker & Knowles, 1967; Dunnette, 1969; Rubin, 1967) and in some cases, to small-group change (Hall & Williams, 1966, 1970), there is scant evidence that attempting to change individuals will in turn change the organization (Campbell & Dunnette, 1968). The Fleishman research of the 1950s at International Harvester, mentioned in Chapter 2, is further evidence that individual training alone does not affect the total organization for purposes of change.

The target for change, then, is the system, not the individual (Burke & Schmidt, 1971). This systemic target is often the organization's culture, especially the group and organizational norms to which members conform. This approach is based in part on the original work of Kurt Lewin. His theories and research led him to conclude the following (Lewin, 1958):

> As long as group standards are unchanged, the individual will resist change more strongly the further he is expected to depart from group standards. If the group standard itself is changed, the resistance which is due to the relation between individual and group standards is eliminated. (p. 210)

Others since Lewin also have shown in their research that work performance and satisfaction are greater when workers perceive that they influence the formulation of work group norms (Bachman, Smith, & Slesinger, 1966; Bowers, 1964; Hornstein, Callahan, Fisch, & Benedict, 1968; Likert, 1961; Tannenbaum & Kahn, 1957, 1958). Recall also the Hawthorne studies described in Chapter 2. The classic study by Coch and French (1948), based on Lewinian theory, clearly demonstrated this relationship of commitment, norms, and change. Because individual and group behavior in an organization are largely determined by group norms (fundamental to the organization's culture), the changing of certain of these norms and their accompanying values that are integral to culture needs to be a major focus of an organization change effort.

The third reason an organizational change effort should be systemic relates to the open system characteristics of importation of energy and negative entropy. For an organization to survive, energy must be taken into the organization in a variety of forms and transformed into products or services that add value to the consumer, and the entropic process must be reversed. According to Katz and Kahn (1978), "By importing more energy from its environment than it expends, the open system can store energy and acquire negative entropy" (p. 25). It is therefore highly important to pay particular attention to how human energy is used in the organization. Are employees' efforts thwarted because of excessive bureaucracy? Is energy bottled up because of an overly centralized control and authority structure? Are people's efforts dissipated because power and authority are so diffused in the organization that people work at cross-purposes?

Paying considerable attention to the use of human energy can help the organization's leaders change things (norms, rewards, or authority structure) so that this energy can be focused more appropriately toward accomplishment of the organization's goals. Thus, negative entropy is more effectively established.

Open system theory is highly relevant and even expedient for our understanding of organization change. Although necessary to our understanding of organization change, it is not sufficient.

Toward a Deeper Understanding of Organization Change

Open system theory is but a part of a much larger set of theories that constitute a paradigmatic shift from physics—which Kurt Lewin and many others have relied on as *the* explanatory discipline for understanding reality—to the life sciences, or as Capra (1996) refers to the new paradigm, "deep ecology." To use Capra's words,

> The new paradigm may be called a holistic worldview, seeing the world as an integrated whole rather than a dissociated collection of parts. It may also be called an ecological view [in a broader sense recognizing] the fundamental interdependence of all phenomena and the fact that, as individuals and societies, we are all embedded in—and ultimately dependent on—the cyclical processes of nature. (p. 6)

This section relies on the work of Fritjof Capra, the theoretical physicist who has written extensively and clearly for us nonphysicists. His books *The Tao of Physics* (1975) and *The Turning Point* (1982) are prime examples of his ability to span disciplines, to integrate them, and to help us achieve a deeper understanding of science in particular and life in general. His latest contribution, *The Web of Life* (1996), brings us closer to a comprehensive theory of life that has relevance to organizations and organization change.

To continue with the transition from physics to the life sciences and from open system theory to broader and more comprehensive modes of thinking, it was evident that by the 1930s, as Capra (1996) points out, the basis for systems thinking had been derived by biologists, Gestalt psychologists, and ecologists:

> In all these fields the exploration of living systems—organisms, parts of organisms, and communities of organisms—had led scientists to the same new way of thinking in terms of connectedness, relationships and context. This new thinking was also supported by the revolutionary discoveries in quantum physics in the realm of atoms and subatomic particles. (p. 36)

The primary criteria for systems thinking, such as the following, are now well-known and accepted:

- Living systems are integrated wholes with properties that none of its parts have.
- Living systems nest within other systems.
- A part of a system is actually "a pattern in an inseparable web of relationships" (Capra, 1996, p. 37).
- "None of the properties of any part of this web is fundamental; they all follow from the properties of the other parts, and the overall consistency of their interrelations determines the structure of the entire web" (Capra, 1996, p. 39).

But as it turned out, systems theory was not sufficient to achieve Von Bertalanffy's goal of it becoming a mathematical discipline. Mathematical techniques for dealing with the complexities of living systems were not available until decades later. According to Capra (1996),

> Instead of a formal *systems theory* the decade of the 1980s saw the development of a series of successful *systemic models* that describe various aspects of the phenomenon of life. From those models the outlines of a coherent theory of living systems, together with the proper mathematical language, are now finally emerging. (p. 79)

What follows is a brief summary of these emerging theories and models, with an attempt to relate this more comprehensive way of thinking to organization change.

Capra's Three Criteria for Understanding Life

The three concepts that Capra (1996) uses as criteria for understanding life are *pattern, structure,* and *process,* words that are common to us but quite complicated when it comes to explaining life and living systems. These three criteria are totally interdependent, and therefore together form what Capra calls "a new synthesis": a deeper and more comprehensive theory based on certain commonalities that exist across all living systems, from a cell to a human being. It seems useful to learn more about this way of theorizing in order to determine the feasibility of generalizing this understanding to organizations and organization change.

Pattern

The pattern of organization for a living system is "the configuration of relationships that determine the system's essential characteristics" (Capra, 1996, p. 161). This configuration further determines how a living system will be recognized: a normal cell versus a cancerous one, a rose versus a gardenia, a dog versus a cat, and so on. To understand pattern more thoroughly, Capra relies on the work of Maturana and Varela (1987) and their theory of *autopoiesis,* or self-making. Using cell biology as their foundation, Maturana and Varela point out that the key characteristic of a living system, or living "network," as Capra (1996) often calls it, is that it continually produces itself. The function of each component of a plant or human cell is to participate in the production of other components in the network so that the network continually makes itself. A primary component of any cell is its membrane, which is the cell's boundary and maintains the flow of external matter into the cell and dissipates waste into the cell's external environment: in other words, the input-throughput-output mechanism or process of a living system. Other cell components are its nucleus—the location for DNA and the cell's production center containing RNA molecules—enzymes, proteins, oxygen, and so on.

Even though cells interact with their environments exchanging energy and matter via their membranes, the entire system is closed organizationally. According to Maturana and Varela (1987), the cell (and larger living systems) is self-organizing in that its pattern is not determined by the external environment but is established by the system itself. Thus, living systems are autonomous. They interact with their environments to survive, taking in oxygen, for example, but their internal network or pattern of component relationships is not *determined* by the environment. In other words, the environment does not change the DNA. "Autopoiesis, then, is seen as the pattern underlying the phenomenon of self-organization, or autonomy, that is so characteristic of all living systems.... Moreover, the continual self-making also includes the ability to form new structures and new patterns of behavior" (Capra, 1996, p. 168). It should be noted, however, that an exception regarding the cell's relation to its external environment and autopoiesis is that carcinogens (from the external environment) can cause cancer, an altering of the cell's patterns.

It is not too much of a stretch to point out that business corporations are at least to some extent autopoietic networks. Two business organizations may be manufacturing and selling the same kinds of products to the same set of customers or marketplaces and yet internally, be organized very differently and have highly distinctive cultures—both of which define the unique pattern of relationships for each of the respective organizations. Volvo and Toyota illustrate this point.

In summary, autopoiesis means that living systems continually change their structures, renewing themselves while preserving their *patterns* of organization. Components of the system "continually produce and transform one another with cells breaking down and building up structures, tissues and organs replacing their cells in continuous cycles. In spite of this ongoing change, the organism maintains its overall identity, or pattern of organization" (Capra, 1996, p. 218). A fascinating tidbit of Capra's is that "our skin replaces its cells at the rate of one hundred thousand cells per minute. In fact, most of the dust in our homes consists of dead skin cells" (Capra, 1996, p. 219).

Structure

The structure of a living network is the embodiment of the system's *physical* components, their shapes, chemical compositions, size, and the like. Capra's (1996) major source here is the work of Ilya Prigogine (Prigogine & Stengers, 1984) and his theory of dissipative structures.

Whereas Maturana and Varela (1987) focused on the closed nature of living systems, Prigogine (Prigogine & Stengers, 1984) emphasized the openness of a system's structure to input and output. Capra (1996) then pointed out that living systems are both open and closed—open structurally and closed organizationally. *Open structurally* is what is meant by autopoiesis, and *closed organizationally* means that the system's overall pattern remains the same. This seeming paradox is the simultaneous existence of change and stability, which Prigogine refers to as "dissipative structures."

Structure for us human beings is our physical body and its components: skin, bones, muscles, and organs. How we look to ourselves and to others is the particular pattern of these components. The same pattern, "human being," can, of course, be embodied in myriad structures. This example, though perhaps explanatory, oversimplifies the theory of dissipative structures.

From his research with physical and chemical systems, heat convection, for example, Prigogine (Prigogine & Stengers, 1984) discovered that phenomena "far from equilibrium," which produced noise, nonlinearity, and other apparently chaotic conditions, when observed more carefully, closely, and over time gradually revealed new, unique structures and patterns—that is, a new order out of chaos. This back and forth quality of order to chaos to a new order is what Prigogine meant by dissipative structures. (Note the similarity to Lewin's ideas of change.) The structure of a living system, its physical nature, is therefore open to considerable change, but the form or pattern of its components remains the same. As Capra (1996) notes, dissipative structures are not always living systems, even though he uses the idea to understand living systems more clearly. The example that Capra provides of water flowing through a bathtub drain is an interesting image of dissipative structures: That is, water flowing through the drain forms a stable state with self-balancing feedback loops, despite the fact that the water is constantly changing.

The stimulus for structure change in a living system comes from its external environment and triggers reactions and new events within the system. Given a strong enough stimulus of new matter and energy creating consequent reactions followed by feedback loops, from input to output back to input again—far from equilibrium, turmoil, even chaos, can be caused. For the system, a new order may eventually be reached, a new structure may form, and another phase of evolution, perhaps, but the change occurs dissipatively, resulting in equilibrium again, but a different form of equilibrium. The *way* the system deals with this strong stimulus from the external environment, that is, the system's pattern of components, its process of input-output, and its feedback loops, remains the same.

The two criteria of Capra's (1996) synthesis theory of living systems that have been briefly described, pattern and structure, represent different perspectives or aspects but in reality, are inseparable and interdependent. The way a system deals with input from the external environment depends on its internal component relationships, and the nature of the structure that "houses" this pattern depends on its interaction with both the external and internal environments of the overall system. If a new structure forms, its form will be a function of the network, or web characteristics, of the system.

These ideas of pattern and structure from the life sciences help to explain what Foster and Kaplan (2001; see Chapter 1) mean by *culture lock-in*, or the inability to change the culture (or to do so rapidly enough) even in the face of threats to survival from the marketplace. In other words, the way the organization deals with external threats remains the same and, according to Foster and Kaplan, is ineffective. Their argument is that the organization's culture (pattern of behavior) must change.

Process

Capra defines his third criterion of a living system as "the activity involved in the continual embodiment of the system's pattern of organization" (1996, p. 161). In this brief definition, he incorporates the previous two criteria: structure (i.e., embodiment) and of course, the term itself, pattern. Remember that structure and pattern are interdependent. *Process*, then, serves as the connection or link between pattern and the reinforcer of our support for the independent structure. The next logical question is, what does Capra mean by "activity?" He then introduces the term *cognition* as meaning the process of life. Thus, the activity is cognitive, that is, a way of knowing. We psychologists cannot assume that cognition has exactly the same meaning as the way these physical scientists use the term. With this third criterion, Capra relies on the work of Gregory Bateson (1979), who introduced cognition as a concept for understanding life, and again on the theorizing of Maturana and Varela (1987).

Next, Capra (1996) introduces the term *mind*. (As we proceed, it is helpful to our understanding to consider these terms and others already used as both literal and metaphorical, that is, to go back and forth in our thinking.) And it is key to our understanding to distinguish between mind (cognition) and *brain*. Our brain is a physical thing, but our mind is not: It is a process. For us, as higher levels of living systems, the brain is the structure through which the process of cognition or mental activity operates. "The relationship between mind and brain, therefore, is one between process and structure" (Capra, 1996, p. 175). Electrical and chemical activities in our brain that form connections for thought and emotions are analogous to what is meant by *process*. But what about lower levels of life that have no brains or central nervous systems? According to Maturana and Varela (1987), the brain is not necessary for mind or cognition or mental activity to exist. The simplest organism, a bacterium, can *perceive* its environment, can perceive changes, differences between light and dark, hot and cold, higher or lower levels of some chemical, and so on. This process of knowing is much broader than thinking that involves emotion, action, and perception. With humans, of course, cognition also involves thinking, language, and other aspects of consciousness. The concept of mind, as used by these theorists, is more comprehensive than thinking, incorporating emotion, context, and so on. This way of theorizing is not unlike Goleman's (1995) *emotional intelligence*, incidentally, and challenges the Cartesian notions of a mind-body split. Goleman contends that feelings are not separate from thought and that emotional intelligence is an integral part of overall intelligence.

Cognition, or the process of knowing, can be understood only in terms of the living system's interaction with its environment. The living system does not process information the way a computer does, but instead brings its entire being to the interaction. This interacting is what Maturana and Varela (1987) refer to as "structural coupling." With autopoiesis, or self-making, the system goes through continuous structural changes yet maintains its pattern of organization. These recurrent interactions stimulate structural changes in the living system, but the system, remember, is autonomous. According to Capra (1996),

> The environment only triggers the structural changes, it does not specify or direct them. . . . The structural changes in the system constitute acts of cognition. . . . and by specifying which perturbations from the environment trigger its changes, the system "brings forth a world" as Maturana and Varela put it. (p. 267)

Specifying which perturbation is important means that the living system does not react to everything in its environment, but rather, selects. Thus, each living system is distinct with its own mode of environmental interaction. Moreover, the interaction is not a linear cause and effect. The system *"responds* with structural changes in its nonlinear, organizationally closed, autopoietic network [which] enables the organism to continue its autopoietic organization and thus to continue living in its environment" (Capra, 1996, p. 269).

Building on the works of scientists and theorists such as Prigogine, Maturana and Varela, and Bateson, Capra (1996) presents us with his synthesis by way of the three criteria for defining and understanding life. While it is extremely complicated, and therefore overly simplified with the summary provided above, we can nevertheless speculate about the larger meaning for organizations and organization change.

Let us consider a rough approximation of how these ideas from Capra and others are applicable. Effective organizations and, particularly, successful corporations constantly monitor their external environments, but because these environments are so complex and rapidly changing, organizational leaders have to be selective about what they monitor. These leaders then attempt to adapt their organizations to the changes in the environment (the marketplace, for example). Successful adaptation is a function of how congruent the selection made is with the internal organization change. In part, the success of the merger of SmithKline Pharmaceuticals, of Philadelphia, and Beecham, Ltd., of London, may be attributed to the deliberate decision on the part of the top executives to monitor and focus predominantly on the global marketplace—not at the expense of domestic markets, but a shift of emphasis, nevertheless. Internal organization change at the newly merged SmithKline Beecham, especially regarding business strategy, structure, and corporate culture, was therefore based on this selective external environment focus. For more detail about this successful merger, see Bauman, Jackson, and Lawrence (1997), Burke and Trahant (2000), and Chapter 11 in this volume.

The following and final section of this chapter is a further attempt at applying the ideas of Capra and other scientists he cites.

Implications for Organizations and Organization Change

Capra (1996) provides a sweeping summary and then raises an intriguing question:

All living systems are networks of smaller components and the web of life as a whole is a multilayered structure of living systems nesting within other living systems—networks within networks. Organisms are aggregates of autonomous but closely coupled cells; populations are networks of autonomous organisms belonging to a single species; and ecosystems are webs of organisms, both single celled and multicellular, belonging to many different species. . . . Common to all these living systems is that their smallest living components are always cells. . . . thus autopoietic. (pp. 209-210)

Are larger systems, organizations and human societies, autopoietic (self-making) networks?

Maturana and Varela (1987) state that our current knowledge is not sufficient to give a definitive answer. Moreover, they point out, due to language and abstract thinking, human societies are distinct from "lower levels" of organisms and ecosystems. Interestingly, they further state that ants, for example, communicate with one another via chemical exchange; humans communicate with language.

Components of organisms exist to serve the larger whole, whereas societies exist for their components, that is, individual human beings. Furthermore, the laws of nature are not the same as the laws of a society; the latter can be broken, but the former cannot. Humans can choose to interact or not; molecules cannot choose to interact—they *must.*

Even with these caveats and critically important distinctions, one can still see numerous parallels and analogies. For example, organizations and societies have boundaries (membranes); these boundaries are largely social, of course, but can be defined nevertheless. See the previous open system section of this chapter and the work of Katz and Kahn (1978). It is clear that organization change typically is initiated by some "perturbation" in the external environment, but the organization responds in its own unique manner and, in fact, may not respond at all—often to its peril. And although the organization may respond to the disturbances in its environment with some internal changes, say, to its strategy and structure, the organization's pattern of operations among its components may remain essentially the same (e.g., organizational culture). What rarely, if ever, changes is its *pattern,* or as we will see in the next chapter, its *deep structure.*

Additional examples from Capra and others that parallel or help to explain organizations and organization change are as follows:

- Organizations interact with their external environments in a back and forth manner, influencing and being influenced and "bringing their whole being" to the process in much the same way as Maturana and Varela (1987) describe. Recall how Katz and Kahn (1978) state it, quoted earlier in this chapter,

> Systems . . . maintain themselves through constant commerce with their
> environment, that is, a continuous inflow and outflow of energy through
> permeable boundaries. (p. 22)

- Cells take in energy, matter, and the like and dispose of waste; organizations take in energy and "dispose" of products and services and excess human resources at times.

- While cells are autopoietic, they, like human organizations, are not self-sufficient and depend for survival on the external environment.

- Not all elements or disturbances in a cell's environment are responded to; selectivity occurs. So it is with organizations.

- Cells continuously reproduce themselves; organizations continually deal with entropy and in the process, produce themselves.

- A cell's pattern is not determined by the external environment (except for carcinogens, as noted earlier) but by the system itself. For an organization, this is largely true but not entirely. Organizational members are also members of a larger society and culture and therefore bring these "patterns" into the organization's pattern. This statement is consistent with Capra's (1996) point about networks being nested within networks.

- Cells have differentiated components, yet these components exist to support one another in the interest of the whole. This statement corresponds with the open systems concepts of differentiation and integration defined earlier in the chapter. This weblike quality of cells is totally congruent with open systems thinking and supports the ideas underlying the Burke-Litwin model of organizational performance and change described in Chapter 9. The components of this model are designed to support the organizational whole.

- Capra's (1996) third criterion, process, is the living system's mind, cognition, or mental activity. This means that living systems perceive, sort through, and select for internal use certain but not all elements from the external environment. This implies that some form of information processing occurs. Do human organizations learn? Apparently so, but what is not clear is *how* they learn. Interestingly, at the present time, organizational learning is a growing area of interest for scholars and practitioners.

Other examples could be suggested and parallels drawn. And although Capra's new synthesis and the associated theories are not completely and uniformly applicable to human organizations and organization change, this way of thinking nevertheless provides plenty of thought-provoking ideas to warrant our attention and consideration.

One last point: Capra's synthesis takes us a step beyond open system theory. For example, the latter calls to our attention the interdependent nature of an organization with its external environment—dependent for survival yet influential on that environment in terms of output (organizational performance, products. and services). Capra's synthesis helps us to more broadly understand organizational executive actions such as the selective nature of an organization's response to "perturbations" in the environment; and due to the organization's unique pattern (or culture; recall cultural lock-in from Chapter 1) and the autopoietic (self-making) process, the response to the perturbation may be inadequate for long-term survival.

4

The Nature of
Organization Change

As prime minister of Great Britain, Margaret Thatcher was hardly a shrinking violet. "Change agent" would be a more apt descriptor. She worked hard to move her country away from a socialist economic system to a more capitalistic one. She believed strongly in a free-market system. As part of this overall political and economic change effort, she declared that many government-supported organizations, for example, public sector water and electric utilities, would become private enterprises. Prominent among these changing organizations was British Airways (BA). About 1983, she declared that BA would become a publicly owned company, with shares of the company being traded on both the City of London and New York Stock Exchanges. For all its prior existence, BA had been a government-supported organization, and in essence, Thatcher stated that even though it had been the nation's flagship airline, it would now have to survive on its own in a global, free-market system. The British government would no longer, year in and year out, bail it out financially. BA was therefore faced with a need to change itself rather radically if it wished to remain an organization, in this case, as a commercial enterprise. An example of a successful organization change effort, the BA story will be summarized later in this chapter.

During the late 1980s, the general manager of a chemical division within a large, global pharmaceutical-chemical company was concerned about customer service. Customer orders were often delivered late, and as might be expected, the customers were complaining. Why this problem was occurring was not immediately apparent to the general manager, but he quite naturally assumed that it resided somewhere in the way customer orders were handled inside his division. He hired a consultant to tackle the problem. The consultant started with the end state, that is, with the customers' receptions of their ordered products, and then traced the process back through the chemical division's sales and delivery systems. The consultant recommended some organizational structural changes that would result in a more streamlined process. The general manager made these changes in his organization, and customer service improved, as well as overall customer satisfaction.

The two cases briefly described above both illustrate organization change, but as can readily be understood, they are very different in the scope and depth of the change efforts. The first, BA, represented a *revolutionary* change, and the second, an *evolutionary* one.

It is interesting to note that Darwin's theory of evolution has been characterized for many years as a slow, incremental process of change, but more recently, scholars have challenged this view, stating that changes in living organisms actually occur in spurts, or leaps, as perturbations. In other words, a species may live for many hundreds, if not thousands, of years with no significant change, that is, in a state of equilibrium. But eventually, an entirely new species will emerge, replacing the previous one as if overnight. Natural historian Stephen Jay Gould (1977) has been a primary challenger of change being merely gradual and has proposed a new way of thinking and theorizing called "punctuated equilibrium": a steady state for a period of time, then a sudden (punctuated) change, followed by equilibrium again.

Important for our understanding, then, is that change occurs both incrementally and radically. This is true for individuals, groups, and organizations, as well as for even broader domains, such as fields of science and biological species. First, we will consider revolutionary change, then evolutionary.

Revolutionary Change

When scholars independently derive similar, if not the same, theoretical ideas (even though different words may be used), especially if these scholars represent different disciplines, it is time to sit up and take notice. Connie Gersick (1991) recently took notice of how the punctuated equilibrium idea had emerged in six different domains to explain change as revolutionary. In her study, she found commonality of thinking in the following:

1. Levinson's (1978) theory of individual change: We live our lives through a relatively orderly sequence, but at times, many of us, especially around 40 years of age, dramatically change that sequence.

2. Gersick's (1988) group change: Groups do not develop in a linear set of stages; rather, they proceed with not much happening and then recognize (almost suddenly) a need to move forward rapidly in a new way.

3. Organization change (e.g., Tushman & Romanelli, 1985): Organizations do not evolve but are more likely to change via strategic reorientations that demand significantly different patterns of operations.

4. Scientific fields (Kuhn, 1970): Truth is probably not discovered through the accumulation of individual findings, but more likely via paradigmatic shifts, that is, breaks in the prevailing mode of thinking.

5. Biological species (Gould, 1980): Change occurs after long periods of equilibria and then via "rapid and episodic events of speciation" (p. 184).

6. Grand theory (Prigogine & Stengers, 1984): Systems vacillate between some kind of transition and the status quo, or equilibrium. At times of transition, that is, punctuated equilibria, there is no end state that is a given, because during times of transition, system parts interact unpredictably. The change, therefore, becomes revolutionary.

The commonality of thinking across these six theories is in three domains, according to Gersick (1991).

1. Deep structure. Gersick's (1991) definition is as follows:

> A network of fundamental, interdependent "choices," of the basic configuration into which a system's units are organized, and the activities that maintain both this configuration and the system's resource exchange within the environment. Deep structure in human systems is largely implicit (p. 15).

For individuals, it is the underlying pattern of a person's life at a given time (Levinson, 1986). For groups, it is the structure and process a group chooses to accomplish its task (Gersick, 1988). For organizations, it is the underlying culture—the structure itself, that is, organizational design for decision making, accountability, control and distribution of power, and the *way* the organization monitors, reacts to and, in general, relates to its external environment (Tushman & Romanelli, 1985). For scientific fields, it is the paradigm, that is, the pattern and set of standards for how a discipline develops and is maintained or sustained over time through scientific achievements (Kuhn, 1970). Change in scientific fields occurs via a break from the pattern, a paradigmatic shift. For biological species, it is a network of circular and interdependent interactions with feedback loops; thus, no singular unit or part can interact with the environment independently (Gould, 1977, 1980; Wake,

Roth, & Wake, 1983). This network of interacting parts helps to create resistance to change. A perturbation, then, brings about change; change will not occur as a result of life as usual within the species, that is, will not occur in a linear, evolutionary manner. And, finally, for grand theory, collective modes and parameters determine order for the overall system (Haken, 1981).

2. Equilibrium Periods. Gersick's (1991) analogy is helpful here: "If deep structure may be thought of as the design of the playing field and the rules of the game, then equilibrium periods might be compared loosely to a game in play" (p. 16). Specifics of play vary, but the structure and rules remain fixed. The equilibrium period consists of (a) maintenance of the system and (b) choice making of activities, "calling the plays," but within an overall pattern of rules, standards, mores, and circular processes. Part and parcel of equilibrium periods is inertia. One can begin to understand why it is so difficult for systems to change. O'Toole (1995), for example, lists 33 hypotheses for why organizations are resistant to change, from *homeostasis,* "Continual change is not a natural condition of life; hence resistance ... is a healthy human instinct" (p. 161), to the *rectitude of the powerful,* "The best and the brightest have set us on the current course. Who are we to question the wisdom of our leaders?" (p. 164).

Gersick (1991), after reviewing this literature, narrowed the resistance list to three albeit quite powerful barriers to change: (a) cognition, (b) motivation, and (c) obligation. These three are variations of the same phenomenon: resistance. Cognitive frameworks shape our awareness and thinking, how we interpret reality, and how we consider choices for action. In other words, cognitive frameworks, models of reality, and so forth, are useful for understanding reality; yet at the same time, they limit our awareness of other ways to look at reality.

With respect to motivation, change is accompanied by loss of some kind and by uncertainty. Resistance to loss and uncertainty are easy to understand; that is, one is motivated to reduce the loss and uncertainty. Regarding obligation, Gersick (1991) cites Levinson, Tushman and Romanelli, and Kuhn by pointing out "the inertial constraints of obligations among stakeholders inside and outside a system" (p. 18). Stakeholders hold expectations of and assumptions about how the system is supposed to operate. When this equilibrium is disturbed, they put pressure on the system to "get back into line."

3. *Revolutionary Periods.* As Gersick (1991) clarifies,

Incremental changes in a system's parts [will] not alter the whole. As long as the deep structure is intact, it generates a strong inertia, first to prevent the system from generating alternatives outside its own boundaries, then to pull any deviations that do occur back into line. (p. 19)

So, how do revolutions occur? By (a) internal disruptions that pull subsystems and activities out of alignment with each other and/or the environment, for example, intrusion of a "foreign body" from an acquisition or merger and (b) changes in the system's environment that threaten its ability to obtain resources, for example, creation of new technology or severe consolidation of an industry via huge mergers. It is important to note that these internal changes and/or external ones do not in and of themselves bring about revolution. They simply create the need for change.

Revolutionary change, by definition, can be seen as a jolt (perturbation) to the system. As a result, nothing will ever be the same again. Organizations that change their missions exemplify revolutionary change—as in the BA case of focusing on the marketplace, as opposed to years of insularity and allowing the most negative aspects of bureaucracy to be the focus. Although the overall mission for BA remained transportation, the specifics changed significantly, for example, new goals of customer satisfaction and profitability, neither of which had ever been emphasized before. The change of mission affects all other primary dimensions of an organization: leadership, strategy, structure, culture, and systems. In Gersick's (1991) language, the *deep structure* has been affected significantly.

It should be reiterated that the fundamental mission of an organization is to survive. Most of the time, organizations survive by continuously fixing problems and trying to improve the way things are done. Sometimes, however, survival depends on an entirely new raison d'être with completely different products and/or services. The BA case is such an example and will be described in more detail later in this chapter.

Evolutionary Change

No doubt, more than 95% of organizational changes are evolutionary. As noted above, the resistances to revolutionary change are indeed strong. The second case vignette, at the beginning of this chapter, (improvement in customer service at the pharmaceutical-chemical company), is illustrative of evolutionary change. Most organizational change consists of improvements, incremental steps to fix a problem or change a part of the larger system. Most organizational change in Japan, for example, is referred to as *kaizen,* meaning continuous improvement: changing the way a product is packaged before shipment to the customer, instituting a new form of commission on sales for how salespeople will be compensated, developing a new set of products or services for an emerging market on the basis of demographic shifts, acquiring a smaller company to augment current business lines, and installing a new leadership development program for the top 300 executives in the organization, to name only a few examples. These examples illustrate evolutionary changes. Any one of these examples, however, could be part of a larger change effort that might be revolutionary. But if any one of these partial changes does not affect the whole and the deep structure of the organization is not fundamentally modified, then the change is evolutionary.

In an attempt to further clarify the meaning of evolutionary change in organizations, let us consider the writings of Weick and Quinn (1999) and Orlikowski (1996). Instead of evolutionary, these scholars use "continuous change" as their label. The meaning is the same, nevertheless. For Weick and Quinn, continuous change means "the idea that small continuous adjustments created simultaneously across units, can cumulate and create substantial change. That scenario presumes tightly coupled interdependencies" (p. 375).

The "looser" these interdependencies, the less likely that overall organization change will occur. The change is more likely to remain primarily within subunits of the organizations—although not necessarily exclusively. Ultimate organization change could occur depending on managers' abilities and desires to diffuse innovation from one unit to other units.

Orlikowski (1996), as cited in Weick and Quinn (1999), has also helped with definition and clarification. She had noted the following:

> Each variation of a given form is not an abrupt or discrete event, neither is it, by itself discontinuous. Rather, through a series of ongoing and situated accommodations, adaptations, and alterations (that draw on previous variations and mediate future ones), sufficient modifications may be enacted over time that fundamental changes are achieved. There is no deliberate orchestration of change here, no technological inevitability, no dramatic discontinuity, just recurrent and reciprocal

variations in practice over time. Each shift in practice creates the conditions for further breakdowns, unanticipated outcomes, and innovations, which in turn are met with more variations. Such variations are ongoing; there is no beginning or end point in this change process. (p. 66)

I would question Orlikowski's assumption that "sufficient modifications may be enacted over time that fundamental changes are achieved." Although possible, it is unlikely. Overcoming inertia and equilibrium, as Pascale, Milleman, and Gioja (2000) emphasized, is difficult, if not impossible, without a discontinuous "jolt" to the system. Organization change does occur with continuous attention and effort, but it is unlikely that fundamental change in the deep structure (Gersick, 1991) of the organization would happen.

Another example of continuous change is the relatively new field of organizational learning (Argyris & Schön, 1978). Watkins and Marsick (1993) define organization learning as follows:

Advocates may differ about specific details, but in general, they agree that the learning organization,

1. Is not just a collection of individuals who are learning—instead, learning also occurs simultaneously at various collective levels within business units and sometimes within an entire company.

2. Demonstrates organizational capacity for change.

3. Accelerates individual learning capacity but also redefines organizational structure, culture, job design, and mental models (assumptions about the way things are; see Senge, 1990).

4. Involves widespread participation of employees and often customers in decision making, dialogue, and information sharing.

5. Promotes systemic thinking and building of organizational memory. (p. xii)

Further examples of recent summaries of organization learning include Huber (1991), Miller (1996), Easterby-Smith (1977), Mirvis (1996), and Lundbeg (1989).

In concluding this section, it should be noted, of course, that all organizational changes do not lead to improvement, just as revolutionary change is not always good or doesn't always produce a significantly better organization. The following two cases do represent successful change, the first revolutionary, the second evolutionary.

Revolutionary Change: Case Example

This chapter began with a brief illustration of radical change, albeit over time. British Airways (BA) in the 1980s experienced significant organization change, a fundamental modification of its deep structure.

Described at the beginning of this chapter were the external forces threatening BA's survival—the edict handed down by Prime Minister Thatcher and the growing deregulation of international air traffic; that is, many fares were no longer being set by governments but instead were being determined by the marketplace. We will now pick up the story by summarizing what happened, with emphasis on the organization's internal changes.

In an attempt to become more competitive and cost conscious, an early decision made by the CEO, Colin Marshall, was to reduce the workforce from about 59,000 to 37,000. This act got everyone's attention and, as might be expected, drew lots of criticism. Marshall stayed the course, however, and went on to emphasize a mission of providing superior service and to focus on a strategy that would increase market share and customer satisfaction.

These changes of mission and strategy began to affect the deep structure of BA but were not sufficient to complete the change. Marshall knew that he had to change the BA culture. Historically, BA was formed from the former pilots and staff of the Royal Air Force of World War II and quite naturally, had evolved into a command and control culture that was engineering- rather than market driven. BA had a terrific maintenance and safety record, but passengers seemed to be incidental to the whole process. It was a question of what to change in the culture while keeping those aspects that could continue to support the superb maintenance and safety records.

To be more specific about the culture change aspect, a series of programs and activities were launched to move BA from a bureaucracy laced with military residue to a service business in which passengers were treated as human beings rather than as another form of baggage. The initial programmatic effort was a 2-day orientation to the new culture called "Putting People First." The program challenged the prevailing wisdom about how things were to be done at BA.

The next activities were to focus even more intensely and directly on the culture. Nick Georgiades, the head of human resources at the time, conceptualized this aspect of the change effort in terms of a "three-legged stool." The "seat" was the new, desired culture, to be more customer focused (Burke, 1994):

The three legs were (1) "Managing People First" (MPF) program, a five-day residential experience to help managers learn about how to manage their people in such a way (more participatively, for example) that they would be more service oriented; (2) performance appraisal, where half of a manager's evaluation was based on results and half on how the results were achieved, the how being an incorporation of the behaviors and practices emphasized in the MPF program; and (3) pay for performance, rewarding managers according to how they were rated in (2) above. (p. 137)

Another program was to train all human resources staff within BA on consulting skills so they would be in a better position to help the MPF participants apply what they had learned.

A guiding rationale for conducting the MPF program and spending considerable effort with follow-ups to ensure change in the BA culture was supplied by the research work of Ben Schneider and his colleagues. In a series of studies reported in Schneider (1980, 1990a) and Schneider and Bowen (1985), this is what has been consistently demonstrated (Burke, 1994):

How "front line" people in a service organization [in this case, banks, therefore, tellers, loan officers] are treated by their respective supervisors has a differential effect on customer satisfaction. In bank branches where front-line employees were managed more participatively as opposed to bureaucratically—following procedures strictly, for example—customer satisfaction was significantly higher. (p. 137)

With BA, of course, being a service business, the same principle was applied. Although ticket agents and cabin crew employees needed some technical training in how they served the customer, the primary emphasis was not with them per se, but rather with their managers.

The MPF program was therefore designed and conducted to help managers to manage more participatively, openly, respectfully, enthusiastically, and with greater trust in their subordinates. Managers cannot manage the myriad of hour-by-hour contacts that employees who have direct contact with customers encounter every day, those 50,000 "moments of truth," as Jan Carlzon, another successful airline CEO, described in his popular book (Carlzon, 1987). Managers can, however, work with their subordinates in an involving manner that will in turn have a positive effect on customers. (Burke, 1994, p. 137)

Many other activities were involved in this large-scale change effort, for example, changing the entire financial function from one of government accounting and reporting to one of providing annual financial statements for stockholders and monthly income statements for managers. Also, Marshall essentially created a marketing function in BA where, prior to his arrival, for all practical purposes, none existed.

It is now a matter of record that BA transformed itself (Goodstein & Burke, 1991). By the end of the 1980s, BA was one of the most profitable airlines in the world and had improved its service record from what passengers used to refer to BA as standing for "bloody awful" to what was then considered "bloody awesome" (Power, 1989).

In summary, the revolution at BA began as a result of a "disruption" from the airline's external environment. Internally, the initial disruption was the huge reduction of BA employees by more than 20,000. Then, through a planned series of activities and interventions, the culture (deep structure) was gradually shifted from a militaristic, bureaucratically driven way of doing things to one that was focused significantly more on service to customers and on being competitive in the workplace. The organization in a span of some 6 to 7 years had fundamentally changed, had transformed itself.

Evolutionary Change: Case Example

This case concerns a comparatively small professional services firm that is close to a century old. The firm, a partnership, consists of about 50 partners, with approximately the same number of associates, plus administrative and technical staff. The firm is relatively small, deliberately. They are a specialty house providing highly individualized services to corporations primarily. Their mission is to remain specialized, not to provide a broad array of general services for clients. They serve more than half of the *Fortune 500* corporations, and more than half of their revenue comes from clients they have served consistently for more than 20 years. The firm serves clients in 400 U.S. cities and in 15 foreign countries. Although growth of the firm is a goal, the partners do not favor "rapid growth, mergers, and branch offices." In fact, the firm is located in only one building in a large metropolitan area in the eastern United States.

The structure of this professional services firm is rather simple and straightforward. At the top is the managing partner (the CEO equivalent), and working closely with him is a small executive committee consisting primarily of department heads, or as they prefer to call them, "practice group chairs." Following the managing partner and the executive committee are the senior partners, then the junior partners (recent entrants into the partner status), followed by the associates (most of whom have partner aspirations), and the staff.

The organizational consultants working with this firm were initially asked to meet with the managing partner and some of his executive committee members to explore ways of evaluating the performance of their senior and junior partners and eventually, to cascade the process down to include the associates. The managing partner had heard about something called a "360-degree feedback process" and wondered if this kind of procedure could be used to measure and reward performance. The consultants who were asked to meet with the managing partner and his colleagues had considerable expertise in this type of feedback process, as well as in the broader arena of organization change and development.

Briefly, a *360-degree feedback process* gets its name from a "full circle" procedure of rated behavioral practices. The behaviors rated are usually in the domains of management and leadership. The central person rates himself or herself on a set of behavioral practices concerning leadership and/or management and is also rated by three other categories of raters on the same set of behavioral practices (examples will be provided later in the context of this case). The three other categories of raters are the central person's supervisor, the person's peers, and the person's direct reports or subordinates. The self and three other sets of raters comprise the full circle, or 360 degrees, as it is often called. Incidentally, instead of the overly popularized and metaphorical label, a more accurate description would be *multirater* or *multisource feedback,* because other raters may be included, such as clients or customers.

The feedback process consists of the central person comparing his or her self-ratings with how the others (one or sometimes two supervisors and a minimum of three peers and three direct reports) rate him or her on the same set of behavioral practices. The degree of congruence/divergence in the ratings is, of course, the main focus of attention.

In the exploratory discussion with the managing partner and his colleagues, the consultants quite naturally asked many questions and in due course, offered opinions and suggestions. In addition to finding a way to evaluate partner performance, the managing partner also stressed the need for more leadership especially from among the senior partners, identifying potential leaders among the junior partners, and the need for more teamwork. The consultants explained in detail how a multirater feedback process works and then offered the opinion (actually the expression of a value that the consultants hold) that using this kind of procedure as a measure of performance for certain organizational purposes was not wise. That is, to employ multirater feedback in the service of performance appraisal and then to base organizational rewards (incentive compensation, promotion, etc.) accordingly would create the strong possibility of rater bias. To base evaluations and rewards on the rating procedure would mean that one's ratings become somewhat public, that is, known to those who make decisions about performance evaluation and rewards, certainly to the managing partner and his executive committee. In other words, what would likely drive the process are the rewards to be obtained, not so much one's desire to be a more effective leader or team player. Moreover, when one knows that his or her ratings of someone, especially one's supervisor, will be used for evaluative purposes, as compared with individual and organization development purposes, the ratings are likely to differ. It is not necessarily a matter of using multirater feedback for organizational administrative purposes (for example, performance appraisal) versus using the process solely for individual and organization development. As London (2001) has pointed out in his coverage of the "debate," it does not have to be one or the other:

> [The feedback process] can be used for both development and administrative purposes, but this takes time. The organization may need to start by using MSF (multisource feedback) for development alone to establish a culture of interpersonal trust and attention to development. (p. 383)

With respect to the professional services firm, this multirater feedback process was a first for them. For more coverage concerning the use of this process for purposes of individual and organization development, see Bracken (1996) and Church, Waclawski, and Burke (2001).

The consultants therefore urged the managing partner and his executive committee colleagues to use the multirater process for individual and organization development purposes. Individually, the purposes would be to increase one's self-awareness in particular (studies have shown a positive link between self-awareness and performance, e.g., Church, 1997) and to provide for increased personal and professional development in general. Organizationally, the purposes would be to (a) select behavioral practices that are leader-, manager-, and teamwork-related to fit with the managing partner's objectives and (b) encourage partners via the feedback process, that is, coaching by the external consultant, to work on improving their leadership qualities and to improve these in the context of enhancing teamwork in the firm. Furthermore, the consultants urged the firm's leaders to authorize that the multirater feedback process be confidential, so that only the person being rated and the external consultant directing the overall process and providing the feedback and coaching would have access to and knowledge about the individual's ratings. Finally, the consultants assured the managing partner that when a sufficient number of feedback sessions with partners had been conducted, an overall summary of all the ratings would be provided.

The consultants then recommended that the behavioral practices be as tailored to the firm's change needs, mission, and values as possible. The recommendation was *not* to use off-the-shelf or "general purpose" practices but instead, to go through the process of identifying and selecting behaviors that they, as the firm's leaders, thought made the most sense, that is, in terms of aligning partner behavior more closely with desired values and change directions for the firm.

At the end of the discussion of almost 3 hours, the managing partner and his colleagues told the consultants that they would talk further among themselves about what was being recommended and let the consultants know within a week or two. There was no expectation by the consultants that a decision by the firm's leadership would be made that day. Rarely do potential client organizations make a decision to move forward that quickly. Besides, in this case, the consultants had attempted to persuade the managing partner and his executive committee members to move in a different direction than what had been asked for in the first place, namely, a change from an administrative appraisal to a developmental one.

The firm's leadership did decide to move forward with the consultant's recommendation (otherwise there would be no story to tell!), and the process began.

The Tools for Assessment and Ratings

To start, the consultants asked for certain materials and documents from the firm, such as their mission statement, strategic plan, statement of values, and any other information that addressed their desired future state. Being rather conservative and careful regarding organization change, these materials provided by the firm suggested a course of action that encouraged continuous improvement, as contrasted with a significant and sweeping change of mission—they wished, you will recall, to remain relatively small and specialized. Although they wanted to expand their services to new clients and broaden their base, the range and nature of these services would continue as they were. They considered themselves among the best at what they did, their specialty, and wanted to remain so. They had good reason to believe that they were (and still are) among the best, because their clients list was indeed desirable, and more than half of their clients stayed with them for long periods of time (more than two decades).

Behavioral Practices

On the basis of these documents and some selected interviews, the consultants, from their data bank of hundreds of behavioral practices that had proved to be effective in other organizations, developed a working list of behavioral practices that were as relevant to the firm as possible. These behavioral statements were categorized according to the firm's list of values, for example, promoting a courteous, collegial, and trusting culture. Through a collaborative, back and forth, iterative process with the client firm that required about 3 months, the consultants and the firm's leadership agreed on a final list of 59 behavioral practices. In the end, at least half of these behavioral statements were written "from scratch," that is, expressly for the firm. Much debate about the right phrase and proper word had ensued.

The 59 practices were then arranged into a rating questionnaire using a 5-point Likert scale. Each of the behavioral statements was rated twice—first, according to the extent to which the person being rated practiced that specific behavior, and second, according to how important the behavior was to the part of the firm represented by the partner being rated. Comparing the behavior in terms of how much it is practiced with how important it is viewed to be helps the individual being rated decide how much change in the given behavior may be needed. If the behavior is not seen as very important, little, if any, change may be required. If there is a gap—the behavior is perceived to be highly important, but the person is rated as practicing it very little—then behavior change may be needed. The 59 practices were categorized according to the firm's 12 primary values. An example of a practice for 6 of these values used in this multirater feedback process is shown in Table 4.1.

In addition to the 59 behavioral practices, three other rating instruments were used in this feedback process. These additional three were

Table 4.1 Main Values of Professional Services Firm With Behavioral Practice Example

Value	Behavioral Practice
• Solidifying and maintaining close client relationships	• Solicits and responds to client feedback regarding the quality of service provided.
• Promoting a courteous, collegial, and trusting culture	• Relates in a courteous and professional manner, regardless of the level of the person with whom he/she is dealing.
• Working effectively in teams	• Promotes an atmosphere of teamwork, cooperation, and coordinated effort among people.
• Developing, mentoring, and training others	• Plans and reviews personal development goals jointly with associates.
• Developing the business	• Effectively manages and balances priorities among many different projects, relationships, and clients.
• Leading and managing	• Provides a vision of the future that captures the commitment of people.

related more to one's personality than to specific behaviors. There were two primary reasons for adding these three questionnaires.

First is the matter of context. One's day-to-day behavior is in part a function of the situation and in part due to a person's temperament or personality. In a sense, one's behavior is foreground and the personality underlying the behavior is background. Thus, in providing feedback to a person about behavior, that form of feedback can be understood more thoroughly if one can also see the rated behavior in the context of his or her nature, that is, personality and temperament. An introverted individual behaves differently from one who is extraverted. Linking this dimension of personality to behavior can help one more clearly understand feedback from others.

Second, the firm's leaders wanted to encourage their partners to assume more leadership, and they wanted to understand more about the potential for leadership in the firm, especially from among the junior partners.

It should be noted that providing leadership and management in a professional services firm is not exactly easy. There are clearly exceptions, but professionals—lawyers, accountants, and consultants—do not as a rule join firms to be managers or leaders. They join because they want to *practice* law, *consult* with clients, or *analyze* a company's financial situation. They do not want to lead and certainly do not want to manage other professionals. They definitely do not want to have to be concerned with such mundane matters as budget, hiring other professionals, generating a business plan, providing performance feedback to others, determining compensation, and so on.

So, the managing partner wanted to know whether he could count on more help regarding leadership for the firm—or was his firm like most other professional service enterprises in this regard?

What follows is a brief description of the three other instruments of assessment that were used in this feedback study.

Myers-Briggs Type Indicator

Based on Carl Jung's theoretical notions about individual differences, the Myers-Briggs Type Indicator (MBTI) assesses a person's degree of strength of preference along four continua of personality dimensions (Briggs & Myers, 1943). Briefly defined, these dimensions are as follows:

- Extraversion-introversion: the degree to which individuals differ with respect to sociability and being energized while around others, as compared with introversion, which stresses keeping more to oneself and being energized more while alone than with others.

- Intuition-sensing: the degree to which individuals depend more on intuitiveness and hunches for assimilating information, as compared with a preference for concrete, fact-based information, that is, more a function of what a person sees, touches, hears, smells, and so on.

- Thinking-feeling: the degree to which individuals differ with respect to what they do with information once they take it in, that is, whether one (a) uses primarily thought processes such as logic, analysis, and objectivity or (b) prefers instead to rely more on emotional consideration when making decisions, for example, feeling domains such as interpersonal relationships, values, and certain internal, personal standards.

- Judging-perceiving: the degree to which individuals prefer order, planning, achieving closure, and decisiveness, rather than keeping one's options open and "going with the flow," or spontaneity.

A person's results on the MBTI become eight preference "scores": when compared with norms based on many thousands of others' scores, how strongly one prefers thinking to feeling, judging to perceiving, extraversion to introversion, and intuition to sensing.

Although it would be possible to have others answer the MBTI as a rating of the central person, this other-rating is not typical. The MBTI is lengthy, well over 200 questions, and has strengths of reliability and validity; thus, it serves the feedback process well with self-ratings only.

NEO-Personality Inventory

Also a self-rating instrument only, the NEO-PI provides measures that are linked to the "Big Five" factors of personality (Costa & McCrae, 1985). The NEO-PI is also lengthy, with 240 items, and is based on extensive research and practice. NEO stands for three of the five factors briefly defined below:

- Neuroticism: the higher the score, the more one tends to be anxious, depressed, and angry.
- Extraversion: very similar to the same measure on the MBTI; that is, the higher one's score, the more the individual tends to be gregarious, warm toward others, and outgoing.
- Openness: primarily meaning open to ideas and new learning; the high-scorer's behavior is likely characterized by curiosity, a love of intelligence, and creativity.
- Agreeableness: the higher the score, the more one tends to be cooperative, trust-worthy, kind, and sympathetic toward others.
- Conscientiousness: High scorers on this factor tend to be reliable, well organized, responsible, and disciplined.

There is some overlap with the MBTI, and the feedback to a person needs to highlight convergence where it exists, such as the obvious extraversion dimension and intuition with openness and perhaps judging with conscientiousness. Consistency across instruments helps to convince the person receiving the feedback that his or her responses are credible.

Leadership Assessment Inventory (LAI)

This instrument was included to determine the extent to which partners in the firm preferred leadership as compared with management. It is possible, as noted above, that many of the partners preferred neither. If the latter, a person's scores would be relatively low when compared with a large set of norms. The LAI consists of 18 items that measure an individual's preference for leadership as compared with management. It is based on the thinking of Burns (1978), Zaleznik (1977), and

Burke (1986). See Chapter 9 for more coverage of this kind of thinking. The LAI is a multirater instrument including self-, supervisor-, and sub-ordinate- but not peer ratings. Due to the content of the 18 items, peer ratings are not as relevant or as reliable as those from supervisor and subordinates. In addition to an overall preference score for leader com-pared with manager, individuals receive ratings on five subfactors, namely, determining direction (five items), influencing followers (five items), establishing purpose (three items), inspiring followers (three items), and making things happen (two items). For more information regarding the LAI, see Sashkin and Burke (1990) and Van Eron and Burke (1992).

Data Summary of the Firm's Partners

The 50 partners in the firm were rated the highest on practices cate-gorized as "Solidifying and Maintaining Close Client Relationships" and "Promoting a Courteous, Collegial, and Trusting Culture." Their "Teamwork" ratings were fairly strong, but "Developing the Business" resulted in so-so ratings, and the lowest were "Leading and Managing." In fact, the lowest-rated practice of all was "Provide a Vision of the Future That Captures the Commitment of People." Moreover, the rat-ings on the LAI reflected little desire for service as a leader. Management activities were not exactly popular, either.

The MBTI pattern of the firm did not fit norms for the United States very closely. As compared with 25% for the U.S. population, 56% of the partners scored as *introverts. Intuition* was 68% compared with 25% for U.S. norms; *thinking* was 72% compared with about 50% for U.S. norms; and 62% scored *judging* compared with approximately 50% for U.S. norms. This overall combination, among the 16 possibilities for the MBTI of introversion, intuition, thinking, and judging, is represented in less than 2% of the U.S. population. This firm's partners may not be like most American personalities, but they may not be that different from other professional service firm populations. Although some research has indicated that perceived leaders in organizations are likely to be higher on intuition and a bit higher on perceiving rather than judging (Van Eron & Burke, 1992), the only dimension conducive for leadership in our professional services firm is intuition. So, there may be some potential in the firm for leadership but in the main, not a clear, strong profile for it.

The results on the NEO-PI were well within the normal range for neuroticism—no problems here—and showed consistent scores on extraversion (rather low), with openness and conscientiousness being strong. Agreeableness was in the average range.

Conclusion

The lead consultant in this case made the following points and recommendations to the managing partner and executive committee of the firm:

- This professional services firm is indeed highly *professional:* the strong emphasis on serving clients promptly and effectively; the internal firm norms of courtesy, respect, and collegiality; and their clarity about mission and the identity within the larger professional community, that is, strong specialization.
- Although a reasonable amount of teamwork in the firm seems to exist, there is insufficient attention being paid to mentoring and providing professional development for junior partners and associates.
- The leadership picture is rather bleak. Although there may be leader ability among the partners, there is little motivation.

The latter two points overlap. Mentoring is a form of leadership.

Approximately halfway into this consultant-client relationship of about 3 years, the managing partner hired a senior partner from another firm to help with leading and managing. This seasoned outsider enjoys leadership and appears to be quite good at it. The consultant discussed this decision with the managing partner and suggested these options for the future: This method of providing further leadership for the firm could be followed and/or focus could be made on changing the firm's reward system in such a way that internal leadership could be reinforced more strongly, and in terms of recognition, be placed on an equal footing with effective client work.

Much more could be stated about the interesting culture of and the issues facing this firm. However, the point of providing this case example is this: Organization change for this firm comes slowly; it is clearly evolutionary in nature. Future work is on leadership development, whether internally or externally in terms of new hires, or both. The firm needs to do a much better job of (a) mentoring, (b) considering the firm more as a business and less as a "professional club," and (c) learning how to improve from the kind of process they have spent considerable time and money on, their multirater feedback program.

This professional service firm is not in trouble. There has been no need for a sea change. Evolutionary change is therefore quite appropriate. Continuous improvement is their slogan.

Summary

The primary purpose of this chapter was to make clear that all organization changes are not the same. An important distinction is the difference between revolutionary (later to be referred to as transformational) and evolutionary (later to be referred to as transactional) change. The inclusion of the two case examples was intended to clarify the distinction between the two.

Revolutionary change, perhaps by definition, occurs in leaps, spurts, and disruptions, not in an incremental, linear fashion. Our understanding of revolutionary change has been enhanced and emboldened by similar findings across disciplines and multiple levels of analyses. These similarities are quite remarkable. Deep structure, as explained by Gersick (1991), is perhaps the key concept to understand the nature of revolutionary change more fully.

Evolutionary change is characteristic of most organizational change. This form of change is typically aimed at attempting to improve aspects of the organization that will lead to higher performance. The fundamental nature, or deep structure, of the organization, its culture, for example, remains undisturbed. The primary mission of the organization remains the same, and the primary rationale for its strategy to implement the mission also remains intact. Yet major organizational changes can occur, such as modifications of the structure, installing a new system of information technology, or launching a new line of businesses. These kinds of changes are simply evolutionary when it comes to a comprehensive understanding of organization change.

5

Levels of
Organization Change

INDIVIDUAL, GROUP, AND
LARGER SYSTEM

We now know the importance of considering organization change in systems terms (Chapter 3). An organization is a totality, a whole with interacting parts or components. To change a part may be *organizational* change but not organization change. To change a part of the component does not constitute organization change. To understand organization change as thoroughly as we can, however, it is useful to analyze, to examine the various pieces and parts and how they affect and are affected by each other and by the whole. Also, to understand organization change as thoroughly as we can, particularly in light of the fact that the process is so complex, it is critical to consider multiple perspectives. In the previous chapter, our perspective was to distinguish between revolutionary and evolutionary change. Although overlap exists across the two perspectives, separating them helps us to understand more clearly that organization change occurs quite differently depending on whether the change goal is to improve operations or to turn the organization in an entirely new direction.

The perspective for this chapter is to examine change at three different yet overlapping organizational levels. So, our perspective is to look more to the internal organization. Just as organization change differs according to whether it is evolutionary or revolutionary, the same can be said for change at different levels in the organization.

Our analysis in this chapter examines three levels: the individual, the group, and the total system. There is more to an organization than these three broad levels, of course. The prefix "inter" comes to mind. Individuals in organizations relate with one another, so there is the interpersonal level. Groups in organizations relate with one another, so there is the intergroup level. And organizations relate with other organizations, so there is the interorganizational level. We will touch on these other "inter" levels, but our main focus will be on the three broad ones.

Organizational behavior and change can be at least partially understood according to the three broad levels that comprise this chapter, but we must constantly bear in mind that individuals in organizations always behave in context. The context is at the interfaces, that is, relations with others, or as Capra (1996) would put it, "networks within networks."

With this caveat in mind, let us now proceed with an analysis of organization change at the level of the person, the group within the larger system, and then at the totality: the organizational level.

Change in Organizations at the Individual Level

First, an assumption: An important context for addressing these different levels of change is that an overall direction for organization change has been determined. Changes at the individual level are therefore designed and implemented to facilitate, that is, to help the organization to move in its new direction. This assumption is critical to our understanding. Many, perhaps most, changes at the individual level in organizations are not in the service of moving the total system in a new and different direction. Training programs, for example, are often conducted because another competitor in the industry is doing it, and to remain competitive, "We had better do it, too." This "keeping up with the Joneses" mentality accounts for many changes at an individual level that rarely, if ever, affect the whole.

Now let us consider three primary change examples for individuals that can be in the service of helping to implement organization change.

Recruitment, Selection, Replacement, and Displacement

This category of individual change concerns getting, placing, and keeping the right people in the right roles and jobs to facilitate the larger change effort. For example, almost three decades ago, General Foods, now a part of the Phillip Morris Corporation, decided to try an experiment with a new plant start-up that if successful, would be disseminated throughout the company in the interest of its becoming more competitive in the food industry. As reported by King (1972), the plan was to design this new manufacturing organization, a food-processing plant, according to the criteria of Likert's (1967) System 4. This meant that major tasks would be accomplished by teams and that first-line supervisors would be team leaders rather than operate more traditionally as supervisors, giving close individual supervision. Status differences among all employees were to be minimized. There would be no executive dining room, for example, but one cafeteria for all, and a participative approach to management was to be practiced. The top management group for the plant, the general manager and three operating managers (operations service, manufacturing, and technical) had been selected by corporate headquarters according to the new plant design criteria; that is, these individuals were compatible with and committed to managing their organization according to the participative management premises of System 4. The objective of the selection process, therefore, was to find people who were also compatible with a participative approach. Team leaders would be expected to manage participatively.

The selection process was managed by the top team with the assistance of an organization development consultant. The principles that guided their work were as follows:

1. All selection decisions would be made by the people who were to work with those selected.

2. Decisions would be based on how applicants behaved in collaborative and conflicting group situations.

3. All applicants would receive feedback from the decision makers regarding why they did or did not receive job offers.

4. The selection process would reflect as much as possible the types of tasks and relationships that would be characteristic of work in the plant; that is, status differences were minimized, the process was personalized, there was a growth and development emphasis for all employees, communication was two-way, and considerable activity took place in small groups.

5. Psychological tests would be used but only as secondary information, and the results would not become a part of an individual's employee file.

6. Contact between those who were already members of the organization and those who were strong prospects would gradually become more extensive and open as the selection process progressed.

King has described in detail the 2-day process for the selection of team leaders. The process included a plant visit, a detailed description of the new organization, role-playing exercises, a battery of psychological tests, group decision-making tasks, and simulation exercises of plant work. As King (1972) pointed out,

> The selection decision makers must obtain an accurate indication of whether or not the candidate is likely to function well in a participative organization. At the same time, prospective employees need accurate information to assist them in deciding whether or not it is advisable for them to join such a new system. (p. 201)

King's report was written about 9 months after the start-up of the plant. During that time, only two people had left the organization, absenteeism was less than 1%, and productivity had exceeded original expectations. This early success was sustained (Walton, 1975), but the managerial and change process associated with it did not spread to the overall parent company. Walton (1975) has hypothesized several reasons for this lack of diffusion within General Foods and within six other similar situations of organizations in the United States, Canada, the United Kingdom, and Norway. Some of the reasons included an inadequate pilot project, a poor model for change, confusion over what was to be diffused, and deficient implementation. An eighth organization, Volvo, of Sweden, was an exception. The success of an initial pilot effort there was effectively diffused into other parts of the overall organization (Gyllenhammar, 1977). This more effective diffusion was due to an effective pilot project, a better model for change, less confusion about what to diffuse, and better implementation than the other organizational examples. Also, as work by Levine (1980) has shown, innovative enclaves in organizations that are incompatible with the overall culture and are unprofitable remain isolated and do not diffuse whatever innovation they develop.

The opportunity to select people for a new organization in a planned, systematic way is rare. The advantages of such an opportunity are clear (King, 1972):

> Many difficult problems in overcoming resistance to change are obviated. New norms, different from traditional norms in industry, can be developed. Rather than the problem of changing established roles and role expectations about how supervisors or employees "should" act, roles are established anew. The newness of the physical setting and technology is congruent with the institution of a new approach to organization and interpersonal relationships. (p. 201)

Although still relatively rare today, selecting employees in this deliberate, planned way does occur. The Saturn automobile division of General Motors was started and has continued to operate according to many of these more participative ways of selecting and working with people. Procter & Gamble has used similar practices, and some of the newer hi-tech companies in places like Silicon Valley do the same.

Replacement and displacement in the interest of organization change also occurs. The brief story of revolutionary change at British Airways (BA) related in Chapter 4 began in part with reducing the workforce by more than 20,000 people. This displacement occurred over some period of time, because early retirements and other forms of natural attrition were predominantly used. The main objective, nevertheless, on the part of the CEO at the time, Colin Marshall (today Lord Marshall), was to reduce bureaucracy and move BA toward a more market-oriented, customer service enterprise. In other words, this huge reduction in the workforce was in support of the overall organization direction and change effort.

Finally, a key replacement tactic in many organization changes is to recruit a new leader from inside the organization but more often, from the outside. Marshall, the change leader of BA, was recruited from an outside yet similar industry, Avis Rent-A-Car, a service organization in the broader travel industry. Lou Gerstner was recruited from outside the computer industry to change IBM (and he has). Many other examples could be given.

The point is that frequently, a deliberate tactic for organization change at the individual level is to infuse the system with new leadership, especially at the top.

Training and Development

Again assuming that a training program is designed and conducted to help bring about organization change, most of the time, the effort is directed toward individuals in managerial positions. How this approach to training was implemented was described in Chapter 4 with the brief story of the change at BA. Let us now consider another example also conducted by a service organization, a global bank.

Citicorp, now known as Citigroup, with its recent merger with Travelers Insurance, launched a unique training program, "Managing People," early in 1977. The corporation's top management was concerned that, along with its rapid growth in the late 1960s and 1970s, the increasing strain on managers to continue to produce profits and adapt to rapid change had caused mounting "people problems" in the organization. More and more people were feeling like cogs in a (money) machine. Because it was accepted by top management that people were the organization's most important resource, particular attention had to be paid to managing this resource more effectively. William Spencer, president of the corporation at that time, publicly stated in a filmed introduction to Citicorp's program, "The management of people is probably a greater skill mandated than individual brilliance. Even the most brilliant person, if there is little or no ability to manage people, is a lost cause in our operation" (Burke, 1982, p. 244). He was talking about what Daniel Goleman (1995) today calls *emotional intelligence.*

To begin the process, a study was conducted (a) to identify the best management talent within the organization, (b) to determine the specific set of management practices that seemed to distinguish the best from average managers, and (c) to design a training program based on these superior practices. A criterion group of managers was thus established by asking senior executives to identify subordinate managers within their respective groups who were outstanding and would most likely be taking their places as senior executives within the next decade. They indentified 39 such managers. The researchers then asked these same senior executives to identify 39 additional managers within their groups who were satisfactory managers but not as effective as the first group. The researchers next arranged for 353 subordinates of these 78 managers (39 in the "A" group [outstanding] and 39 in the "B" group [satisfactory]) to rate their bosses on 59 management practices culled from a list of hundreds. The ratings were done with 5-point Likert scales. Some of the practices rated were as follows:

- Your manager communicates high personal standards informally—in conversation, personal appearance, and so forth.
- Your manager tries to make the best use of staff members' skills and abilities when making assignments.
- Your manager works with staff members (subordinates) to reach mutual agreement on their performance appraisals.
- Your manager uses recognition and praise—aside from pay—to reward excellent performance.
- The work group meetings your manager conducts serve to increase trust and mutual respect among the work group members.

The A group was rated significantly higher than the B group on 22 of the 59 practices, regardless of their management situation in the corporation. Another eight practices differentiated between the two groups but only under structured conditions of management, such as in a back-office operation of check processing. The A-group practices were then used as the basis for design of the training program. Because this group had been identified as outstanding managers, and subordinate ratings had further identified some of the specific practices that these managers did exceptionally well, it followed (to Citicorp's top management) that the larger population of managers should be trained to adopt this special set of people-management practices. Prior to participation in the program, managers were rated by their subordinates on the selected practices.

The 5-day program then consisted of training in clusters of these practices, with each training day devoted to one cluster. The five clusters were (a) getting commitment to goals and standards, (b) coaching, (c) appraising performance, (d) compensating and rewarding, and (e) building a team for continuity of performance. Training techniques included case method, role practice, group problem-solving and decision-making exercises, and occasional short lectures. For each day of the program, the managers received a computer printout of their ratings by their subordinates on that day's cluster of practices. This feedback for the manager was the most powerful part of the training program, because managers focused their learning and improvement objectives on the practices that received the lowest ratings. In its first 3 years, about 2,000 Citicorp managers went through the program. It continued to be popular and highly valued among Citicorp managers for at least another 15 years.

This Managing People program of Citicorp's was designed to change the management of the organization from an insensitivity and results-only mentality to a management group that was more people focused, with a better blend of getting results and managing subordinates in a more participatory and caring fashion. Although some qualitative studies were done over the years to determine the degree of success of the Managing People program, its ultimate payoff is not clear. The fact that the program continued for almost two decades supports the belief that it had value for Citicorp. In any case, the value was primarily individual in nature and unclear as to its value for the organization as a whole. Assuming that change did occur, it was certainly evolutionary, not revolutionary.

Coaching and Counseling

Counseling in an organizational work setting, or as we prefer to call it today, *coaching,* is not exactly new. Counseling was recognized as a tool for individual development and organizational improvement at least 70 years ago, when the Hawthorne studies were conducted (Dickson & Roethlisberger, 1966). When counseling/coaching is used for purposes of furthering organizational change, we have the problem of integrating individual needs and organizational goals. This is not an easy problem to solve (Beer, 1980),

> Since the requirements of system-wide change may not be in the interest of the individual, and vice-versa. However, if the counselor [coach] can relate equally to the demands of organization change and to the needs of the individual, he is in a unique position to help the individual and the organization renegotiate a new psychological contract. (p. 190)

The new psychological contract, then, is an attempt to integrate individual improvement objectives with organization change goals.

Most of the time, coaching and counseling occur informally with internal organizational professionals, usually in the human resource function, serving in the helping role. These informal encounters may be carried out during lunch conversations, brief and spontaneous talks with a manager before or after an intense meeting, phone conversations with a manager about scheduling the next time together in which a current problem is discussed incidentally, and so forth. One of the most important times is when the coach/counselor is helping his or her client (usually a manager) deal with feedback that is experienced by the client as negative (Crockett, 1970). Defensive feelings are the most common ones, and the more the coach/counselor can help the client talk about those feelings, the more the client will be able to move on to a problem-solving mode of behavior.

More recently, the term *executive coaching* has become incorporated into our language. Actually, coaching today occurs at all levels of management in an organization, but "executive coaching" has more panache. In any case, this form of coaching currently consists of providing help to a manager or executive in much the same way an athletic coach works. Witherspoon and White (1998) have specified at least four roles that executive coaches play:

1. Coaching for *skills:* The focus is on tasks that a person has to accomplish and the skills and competencies required. An example might be a highly important speech that the executive has to deliver, and the help needed concerns how best to "win over" the audience.

2. Coaching for *performance:* The focus here is broader and encompasses the executive's entire job, and the help needed is how to perform the overall job effectively. An example would be an executive's job change from operations or line responsibility to staff; in the former job, success would be defined more in terms of supervision, whereas with the latter, job success would be defined more in terms of how well one can influence others to accomplish tasks when formal authority is minimal.

3. Coaching for *development:* Here, the focus is on the future; it is more about helping the manager/executive with career choices and about the next job.

4. Coaching for the *executive's agenda:* In this case, the manager/executive decides what is needed. An example would be to help with a forthcoming meeting that the executive must lead; the help provided might be designing the meeting, how the executive could share leadership, how certain difficult subordinates could be managed in the meeting, and so on.

Determining at the outset the need that the executive has for coaching more clearly defines the particular role the coach will play. In other words, distinguishing among these four possibilities helps the coach to respond more directly and precisely to what the executive may require. It is also useful to think about the coaching sequence:

- Gaining *commitment* to the coaching process via an agreement or "contract" between the coach and the executive about the work to be done
- *Assessing* the problem presented by the executive, which determines for the coach which of the four roles to play
- *Action* to be taken by the executive following a given coaching session
- Follow-up on the part of the coach after the executive's action(s) in which the coach helps the executive learn from his or her experience

This synopsis of what comprises executive coaching helps to illustrate how change at an individual level can facilitate organization change. More specifically and also currently, coaching/counseling is frequently conducted as part of a multirater feedback process in which help is provided in understanding the feedback more clearly and in planning change in one's behavior accordingly. If the content of the feedback is congruent with organization change goals, then this individual process helps to leverage the change. We will return to this type of leverage for organization change in Chapter 10 and by implication, in Chapter 11, which is about leading organization change.

Individual Responses to Organization Change

Individuals' reactions to significant change in organizations, change that directly affects them, has been likened to the psychiatrist Elizabeth Kubler-Ross's (1969) description of the five stages that most people go through when they are faced with a terminal illness. The struggle begins with (a) shock and denial, (b) moves to anger, (c) to bargaining, or attempts to postpone the inevitable, on to (d) depression, and finally, to (e) acceptance. Not everyone moves through all these stages; some never move beyond denial. And so it is with organizational behavior. Some organizational members fight the change "to the death," constantly denying that the change is necessary. Others embrace the change readily and move with it. Most people are somewhere in between and move through all stages.

Levinson (1976) has argued that whether change is resisted or embraced, all change is nevertheless a loss experience, particularly a loss of familiar routines. And the more that what one leaves behind is psychologically important, the more likely one's behavior will take the form of resistance. Levinson further argued that all loss needs to be mourned (a bachelor party on the eve of a groom's wedding, most often a joyful change, could be thought of as a mourning ritual) and that people should have an opportunity to discuss and deal with their feelings if they are again going to be able to perform effectively on the job. He went on to state,

> Most organizational change flounders because the experience of loss is not taken into account. When the threats of loss are so severe as to increase people's sense of helplessness, their ability to master themselves and their environments decreases. To undertake successful organizational change, an executive must anticipate and provide means of working through that loss. (p. 83)

Resistance

The phenomenon of resistance to change is not necessarily that of resisting the change per se but is more accurately a resistance to losing something of value to the person—loss of the known and tried in the face of being asked, if not forced, to move into the unknown and untried. Feelings of anxiety associated with such change are quite normal.

Another form of loss that leads to resistance can come from one's experiencing a lack of choice, that is, the imposition of change, or being forced to move to some new state of being and acting. Thus, people are not simply and naturally resistant to change. What comes closer to a universal truth about human behavior is that people resist the imposition of change. Brehm's (1966) research and his theory of *psychological reactance* help to explain this human phenomenon. When one's feeling of freedom is in jeopardy, the immediate reaction is likely to be an attempt to regain this sense of freedom. This reaction is so strong, in fact, that people frequently will not bother to defend their beliefs and may even change them to oppose others' attempts at changing them. In some cases, the issues of advantage and change are in conflict, leading to a situation in which people may prefer to continue on a path that is not in their best interests rather than to give up the feeling of free choice.

Research shows, for example, that when a smoker is *told* to stop smoking, his or her typical reaction is either to continue as usual or increase the rate. Brehm's theory is that when people believe themselves free to behave in a certain way, they will experience psychological reactance (that is, they will resist) if that freedom is threatened or eliminated. The degree of ease and success with which an organization change is introduced is therefore directly proportional to the amount of choice that people feel they have in determining and implementing the change.

It is also important and useful to consider the *kind* of resistance that is being manifested. Hambrick and Cannella's (1989) distinctions are helpful in this regard. In other words, diagnostically, one should determine whether the resistance is blind, political, or ideological:

Blind Resistance. Some people, no doubt a small minority, are simply afraid and intolerant of change—any change. Two kinds of responses may be useful here. One is to provide as much reassurance as possible: Moving into something unknown is always discomforting, at least for a while, but things rarely turn out as dire as we imagine. Second, allow time to pass. Some people in this category merely need time to get used to the idea; it is just their nature to react defensively at first, like a reflex, but not necessarily forever.

Political Resistance. Here, the persons involved believe that they stand to lose something of value if the change is implemented, such as loss of one's power base, status, job, income, and so on. With this kind of resistance, one needs to counter with negotiation, trading something of value with something else of value. Also, one might argue long term versus short term: Yes, for a while we will be losing some things, but over the long haul, we stand to gain much more.

Ideological Resistance. Some people may genuinely believe that the planned change is ill-fated (it simply will not work, and here are reasons why) or in violation of deeply held values (this change is the wrong thing to do, and here are reasons why I feel this way). In other words, the resistance comes from honest, intellectual differences and/or genuine beliefs, feelings, or philosophies that are different. Under these circumstances, it can be useful to counter with strong persuasion based as much as possible on data, facts, and substance. Mere opinion will not be persuasive. Careful prediction from and linkage to this information is absolutely necessary.

It also should be noted that resistance to change is not necessarily a bad thing. Apathy is worse. At least with resistance, there is energy, and the person cares about something. Moreover, resistance is a natural human response and, like one's defense mechanisms, should be respected. There are reasons for defenses to be in place. As the paragraphs above have attempted to explain, there are reasons for resistance. Understanding these reasons is important if the organizational change agent wishes to be successful.

To summarize, change usually involves a shift away from a known situation, with all its familiarity, comfort, and advantages. The people concerned are exchanging the known for the unknown, certainty for uncertainty, existing patterns of behavior and adaptation for the need to evolve new patterns, or tried rewards for untested ones. In addition to the uncertainty of the satisfactions to be gained from the new situation, the people being asked to make the change are required to spend a great deal of effort and psychological energy in getting to know the new situation and in tolerating and coping with frustration until they can evolve new work or living patterns. In psychological terms, newness and the need to cope with it constitute stress. If the long-term rewards to be gained from the change are no greater than those enjoyed formerly, the stress cost outweighs the future advantage. If the new advantages outweigh the old but are not well understood by those making the change, again, the effort involved will not seem worthwhile. Only if the advantages are greater and are desired sufficiently to outweigh the efforts required to make the transition are people likely to embrace change willingly.

Individuals Coping With Change

There are at least three ways to help organizational members deal with change: conceptually, achieving closure, and participation.

Frequently, giving people a way of thinking about what they are experiencing can be useful. The framework developed by William Bridges (1986) is an example. First, he distinguishes between *change* and *transition*. Change, he states, is something that "starts and stops, or when something that used to happen in one way starts happening in another" (Bridges, 1986, p. 25). Transition, on the other hand, is a psychological process extending over a long period of time and cannot be "managed" in a rational way, that is, unlike change. People in transition, Bridges contends, move through three phases:

1. Ending and letting go. People must let go and stop identifying with the old before they can embrace the new (Bridges, 1986):

   > They have to let go of who they were (role, position, title, etc.) and where they have been if they are to make a successful transition. A great deal of what we call resistance to change is really difficulty with the first phase of transition. (p. 25)

2. Going through the "neutral zone." People in this second phase experience ambiguity, confusion, and perhaps despair and a sense of meaninglessness. Bridges (1986) refers to it as "no-man's-land," but it is also a time of reorientation, and gradually, a new "psychological place" can be considered.

3. Making a new beginning. People may begin to learn new skills and competencies, make new relationships, and develop a new vision for the future.

Conceptual frameworks such as this one by Bridges can be useful. Jick's (1990) caution and perspective need to be heeded, however:

> These basically optimistic theories about how people eventually embrace change, while psychologically accurate, are somewhat simplistic. Most people will work through the emotional phases they delineate; some will do so more quickly than others. But others will get stuck, often in the first stages, which encompass the most keen and jagged emotions. . . . People get stuck for two basic and obvious reasons: "Change" is not some monolithic event that has neat and tidy beginnings and ends; and people's subjective experiences of change vary considerably as a result of individual circumstance. [Moreover] frameworks that presume periods of psychological sorting out while the change is being digested are somewhat flimsy in helping us deal with multiple changes. How are we to be in "defensive retreat" with one change, in the "neutral zone" with another, while adapting to a third? If these changes are also rapid-fire, a fairly common situation in these upheaving days in the political and economic arenas, it becomes clearer why some people "resist." (p. 5)

Achieving closure is most relevant to the disengagement phase, letting go of the past. As Jick (1990) implies, this is easier said than done. Although there are individual differences, most, if not all, people have some need to complete "unfinished business," and at some level, energy will be spent in an attempt to "finish the thing." For example, when one has an argument with someone that stops, for one reason or another, short of resolution, one tends to continue the argument mentally, even though the other party is no longer present. People spend mental and emotional energy in an attempt to finish, to resolve, or to complete the argument. So it is with organizational change. When newness is thrust on organization members, replacing, say, formal ways of doing things, with no time to disengage and "finish the business" of the former way, they will spend energy trying to deal with the incompleteness. This energy may take the form of continuing simply to talk about the former ways or, even more resistantly, sabotaging the new ways. What is referred to as "resistance to change" often reflects energy devoted to closure attempts. Providing ways for organization members to disengage from the past, at least to some extent, helps them focus on the change and the future.

An actual case example of achieving a reasonable degree of closure occurred at one of the centers of the National Aeronautics and Space Administration (NASA). Due to the obsolescence of the technology involved, the center director had to terminate a certain rocket program as part of a larger change effort. Several hundred scientists, engineers, and technicians were affected. The center director held a brief ceremony for all these people that symbolized the "death and burial" of the program. He also made a toast to the group commemorating the fine work that had been done on this program in the past. Follow-up interviews indicated that this NASA executive achieved closure for his part of the agency. (For more detail about this closure experience, see Burke, 1994, pp. 147-148.)

Finally, getting people involved, or *participating* in helping to make the change work, can go a long way toward resolving resistance. A principle of behavior that is central to effective management in general and managing change in particular is "Involvement leads to commitment." Stated a bit more elaborately, the degree to which people will be committed to an act is a function of the degree to which they have been involved in determining what the act will be. This is a commonsense principle of human behavior that is corroborated by considerable research. This principle helped to explain why so many elegantly and appropriately designed plans never get implemented. When a single person or small group of people plan a change that will involve a much larger group of other people and fail to involve the others in the planning, the likelihood of successful implementation is diminished. The larger group is likely to perceive the plan as something being imposed on them, and their reactance is aroused. Although they may agree that the plan is intrinsically logical and appropriate, there will be no *psychological commitment* to it if they have not been involved in the planning itself and have had no influence on its content or choice in whether to contribute to it. This lack of psychological commitment does not necessarily cause complete resistance to implementation, but the best that can be expected (unless organizational loyalty is extraordinarily high) is slow, reluctant compliance. Getting people involved, then, can not only mitigate resistance but can also potentially contribute to a more effective overall change process.

Change in Organizations at the Group Level

The primary work group, whether it is a top management team, a packaging unit at plant level, or a district sales team, is the most important subsystem within an organization. The work group serves as the context and locus for (a) the interface between the individual and the organization, (b) the primary social relationships and support of the individual employee, whether or not he or she is a manager, and (c) a determination of the employee's sense of organizational reality. The extent to which members of a group work well together and the extent to which they, as a group, work well with other groups in the organization will determine in part the overall effectiveness of the organization.

Work groups have always been important for organizational effectiveness. We first recognized this systematic importance in the Hawthorne studies (see Chapter 2). This importance is increasing. The single individual who knows many of the functions and specialties within an organization is becoming more and more a rarity. Groups of various specialists attempting to produce something that is greater than the total of their individual specialties are becoming more the rule than the exception. Newer organizational structures, such as the matrix design and networks, require an increase in group activities.

Team Building

Organization change efforts typically rely heavily on the use of work groups. These "family" units within the organization have to make changes in the *way* they conduct their work. Their unit goals may need to be entirely different, their roles within the unit may need to be modified, and so forth. Conducting team-building activities is often an activity in support of the larger organization change. And the more the work unit has at least one goal that is common to all group members and the accomplishment of that goal (or goals) requires cooperative interdependent behavior on the part of all members, the more likely a team-building activity is in order. Dyer (1987) has developed criteria to help determine whether team building is needed, for example, in the case of difficulty between the team leader and members or difficulty among team members; and Beckhard (1972) has provided a set of four purposes for team building:

1. To set goals or priorities

2. To analyze or allocate the way work is performed according to team members' roles and responsibilities

3. To examine the way the group is working—its processes, such as norms, decision making, communications, and so on

4. To examine interpersonal relationships among members

Beckhard (1972) pointed out that all these purposes are likely to be operating in a team-building effort, "But unless *one* purpose is defined as *the* primary purpose, there tends to be considerable misuse of energy. People then operate from their own hierarchy of purposes and, predictably, these are not always the same for all members" (p. 24). Thus, Beckhard's order for the four purposes is important. The reason for this ordering of the purposes is as follows: *Interpersonal* problems could be a consequence of group members' lack of clarity regarding team goals, roles and responsibilities, or procedures and processes; problems with *procedures* and *processes* could be a consequence of group members' lack of clarity regarding team goals or roles and responsibilities; and problems with *roles* and *responsibilities* may be a result of group members' lack of clarity about team goals. To begin a team-building effort with work on interpersonal relationships may be a misuse of time and energy because it is possible that problems in this area are a result of misunderstanding in one of the other three domains. Clarifying goals, roles and responsibilities, or team procedures and processes may eliminate certain interpersonal problems among team members; clarifying roles and responsibilities may in itself eliminate some of the problems with the team's working procedures and processes; and clarifying team goals and their priorities may in itself eliminate certain problems team members have with their roles and responsibilities.

A smoothly operating group of people in a work unit, or in a temporary task force, for that matter, can be highly beneficial to an overall organization change effort, particularly if the group is the top management team of the organization. To have everyone pulling in the same direction is critical to the success of an organization change effort.

A well-honed, highly cohesive, smoothly operating work unit or task force can have adverse consequences for the overall good of the organization, however. Kanter (1982), for example, has addressed the importance of linking teams with their environments. She points out that this linkage has six dilemmas:

1. Suboptimization: Too much team spirit can cause insularity, with members losing sight of their team's role and function in the larger organization.

2. Turnover: A highly cohesive team has a difficult time accepting new members.

3. Problem of fixed decisions: Norms and ground rules can become rigid, and prior decisions may become immutable.

4. Stepping on toes and territories: A highly cohesive team can feel powerful and believe that no one else can understand what they know; their expertise should therefore have great influence in the larger system.

5. NIH: "Not invented here" is the problem of ownership and transfer, a reluctance to share and to be influenced by other individuals and groups.

6. As Kanter (1982) put it, "A time to live and a time to die" (p. 122): Groups have life cycles and after a high of effectiveness, may then dip to ineffectiveness.

Self-Directed Groups

It may be that as part of a larger change effort, management has decided to "flatten" the organization's hierarchy, that is, to eliminate several layers of supervision. Usually with such changes, the span of control for a given manager or supervisor broadens from, say, 1:9 to 1:20 or more. Organizational members need to learn more about how to manage themselves individually and in work units. So-called self-directed or self-managed groups have become much more prevalent in organizations as of late. With many organizations downsizing and delayering to become more nimble and adaptable to rapid changes in their marketplaces, the growth of self-management, particularly in groups, has significantly increased.

Hackman (1992) has (a) delineated the key features of self-directed groups, paying particular attention to the authority and leadership issues, (b) specified the behaviors that distinguish self-directing from the more traditional modes of operating, for example, taking personal responsibility, mentoring and managing one's own performance, actively seeking guidance when needed, and helping others in the group, and (c) suggested conditions that foster and support the kinds of self-direction that will contribute both to personal satisfaction and to group achievements, such as having clear and engaging goals, a supportive structure for the unit, expert coaching and consultation, and adequate material resources. Paying attention to Hackman's criteria and conditions should lead to greater team effectiveness for self-directed groups. In any case, evidence is beginning to emerge that self-directed groups can indeed be successful. In a comprehensive meta-analysis of 70 studies, Goodman, Devadas, and Griffith-Hughson (1988) concluded that self-directed groups had a positive impact on productivity. In another study by Pearson (1992), attitudes on the job were favorably influenced as well.

As one might expect, there are problems to overcome for self-directed groups to be effective:

- Group members must learn to share power and leadership.
- Effectively managing differences and conflicts within the group is critical to success.
- Not all group members are equal with respect to skill and ability, experience, knowledge, and expertise. Managing these differences is key to success, that is, deploying the human resources of the group toward task accomplishment in an efficient and effective manner.

It is likely that for overall organization change to be successful now and in the future, there will need to be more and more reliance on self-directed groups. Why? Because change is ever more with us, organizations need to be as flexible and adaptable as possible for future survival. A part of this greater adaptability is a flatter hierarchy with more rapid decision making and less bureaucracy.

Intergroup

Work units or groups in organizations that are normally dependent on one another—such as marketing people working with operations people, research and development with manufacturing, or headquarters with field as they exchange information, hand off one aspect of the production process to another unit, and so on—will from time to time experience problems and issues with one another. Each group has its own mission, but for that mission to be accomplished, each group occasionally must rely on the other. This mutual dependence, or interdependence, is a natural setting for conflict.

The original research in intergroup conflict, which set the stage for how we deal with it in practice today, was conducted by Sherif and his colleagues in the late 1940s and early 1950s (Sherif, Harvey, White, Hood, & Sherif, 1961). In a series of studies with groups of boys at summer camp, Sherif and his colleagues demonstrated how to develop strong in-group feelings with two separate groups by creating opportunities for success and enhancing pride and then showing how these feelings translated into competitive behavior when the two groups were placed in a win-lose situation. Experiments were also conducted in reducing the conflict and in establishing a cooperative attitude between the two groups by focusing on a superordinate goal, that is, a goal that could only be accomplished via cooperative efforts between the two groups. These experiments were also conducted over a period of years with adults in industrial organizations (Sherif & Sherif, 1953). Blake, Shepard, and Mouton (1964) summarized Sherif's work and demonstrated refinements of the processes in work done with actual groups in conflict, such as staff and line, headquarters and field, sales and operations, and management and union. Alderfer (1977a) has provided an overview and summary of intergroup relations, as has Schein (1980).

It is important to distinguish between real conflict between groups and what Harvey (1977) referred to as "phony conflict." Otherwise, what action to take remains unclear. According to Harvey, the difference is that real conflict involves substantive differences. One party says, "The research project is technologically feasible," and the other says, "Not according to my understanding of the data." Phony conflict, however, consists of negative, even hostile blaming behavior that occurs when *agreement is mismanaged.* One party says, "I told you the project couldn't work. Look at the mess you've got us in," and the other says, "Don't blame me. It would have worked if you had done your job." Harvey argued that such conflict is a symptom, not a generic process. As a symptom, conflict may be reflected as real differences, or it may be symptomatic of agreement that people are not willing to acknowledge: For example, all members of a team believe that a project is doomed to fail, but no member will voice this agreement because they also may believe, perhaps incorrectly, that the team leader is fully behind the project.

Harvey (1977) further argued that when managers and consultants fail "to distinguish between real and phony conflict they collude with maintaining the problem they are attempting to solve" (p. 166). In a phony conflict situation, all members—regardless of group—know what the problem is and what solution is required. They are reluctant to act because of action anxiety, negative fantasies, fear of separation, real risk, and psychological reversal of risk and certainty (Harvey, 1974). Confronting reality, recognizing, and acting on the implicit agreement may require more risk than people in the situation feel like taking. Thus, there is an underlying agreement not to discuss the implicit agreement, but it is not being exposed and managed. According to Harvey, it is highly important to bring this agreement to the surface and help manage it toward action.

Real conflict between groups involves substantive issues, and the two (or more) groups express competitive behavior, not merely blaming one another. Within each group, we are likely to find that members are close and loyal to one another. Their internal differences are submerged; group climate is formal, serious, and task oriented, rather than informal, playful, and oriented toward members' psychological needs; the group leader is more directive and less participative; activities are structured and organized; strong norms exist that demand loyalty to the group from each member; and there is considerable energy to resist the other group.

Once it has been determined that real conflict exists and that there is motivation within both groups to work on the problems, action to resolve the conflict is warranted. As the earlier coverage of experiments about intergroup conflict by Sherif and others suggested, the first action step for resolving conflict among groups is to establish a superordinate goal. For a description of action that is based on the theoretical foundations briefly described above and on the earlier work of Sherif and colleagues, see Burke (1974).

Group Responses to Organization Change

The more that work units in the organization are involved in helping to plan and implement change, the more they are likely to embrace rather than resist the organization change effort. Resistance by organizational groups, on the other hand, can take at least four forms (listed in no particular order).

"Turf" Protection and Competition. "To change our unit is to endanger a central and core competence of the organization" is an expression often heard during times of organization change. The work group, function, department, or business unit is fighting for survival and will muster every rationale, fact, and guilt-inducing behavior to justify its continuation.

Closing Ranks. "Circle the wagons." "One for all and all for one." In a recent structural change at a university, the anthropologists were asked to divide themselves among two or three new academic departments. They refused, declaring that they must remain as a group and join only one department, none of which they liked, incidentally. Their arguments and feelings were that the president was attempting to destroy their identity and function in the university by dividing them.

Changing Allegiances and/or Ownership. To avoid having to deal with the organization change, a group may opt for becoming a separate entity, that is, formally departing from the parent organization. The group can be "spun off" as a separate business and go its merry way. Leveraged buy out (LBO) is one form of separation. The group may join another division within the organization but remain intact. The group may become a "wholly owned" subsidiary and have to survive on its own but remain intact and maintain its autonomy. A spin-off, LBO, or subsidiary may be a carefully planned and deliberate action as part of an overall change effort for the organization. Just as likely, these kinds of actions are ways of avoiding conflict and having to deal with difficult change issues.

The Demand for New Leadership. Analogous to distinguishing between real and phony conflict, there are times and circumstances in which the group leader is simply not capable of dealing with and leading a change effort. Under these conditions, perhaps the leader should be replaced. There are times, on the other hand, when the leader is quite capable, but the followers in the group revolt as a way of resisting the change. In other words, they collude with one another to resist their change leader by suggesting, if not outright averring, that their leader is incompetent. This form of resistance is a deeper psychological process and may reside more in the collective unconscious of the group than in their consciousness. Bion's (1961) theoretical distinction between a work group (conscious of its task and the passing of time) and what he calls a "basic assumption" group (colluding to destroy the leader, that is, assuming that the leader is no longer a leader) is useful for more thoroughly understanding this form of resistance. After all, organization change generates strong emotions for organizational members; feelings may "run high," as the expression goes. People may be aware of their feelings but may not always be conscious of what may be causing them.

Ways of dealing with change for individuals—conceptually, achieving closure, and participation—apply to groups as well. A few additional points regarding group action are worth our consideration.

Achieving closure at a group level, for example, conducting a brief "funeral" for a former program or the past ways of operating and then celebrating the new way or program, may be more beneficial than remaining at an individual level. Sharing feelings, that is, having an opportunity to discuss these feelings with people who are going through the same experience, is often valuable, a worthwhile expenditure of human energy.

Conducting group problem-solving meetings off-site, where members can participate in determining the specific change actions that will directly affect them, may be highly beneficial.

Finally, it may make sense to recompose a group, not changing its function necessarily, but changing its membership. It may be that new skills and technology are needed for a particular work unit to go forward in support of the larger organization change effort. Or it may be that the members are so resistant to the change, for whatever reasons, that they need to be reassigned—as Kanter (1982) noted, a "time to die." In other words, for the overall common good, the local group must be recomposed.

Change in Organizations at the Larger-System Level

An organization change effort rarely, if ever, begins all at once with the total system, especially in a large organization. Beginnings typically involve an individual, a group, a program, such as management training, or an already recognized need to make a significant change, in the organization's structure, for example. The previous sections in this chapter have dealt with much of the groundwork that either leads to large-system change or facilitates it. In this section, we shall consider some of these previously described interventions in the context of an attempt to change a large organization, a system composed of multiple groups, functions, and processes. In examining large-system change, we shall briefly consider the orders or levels of change, the phases of large-system change, the change focus (mission or structure), some examples of change processes at the larger-system level, and finally, change at the interorganizational level.

Orders of Change

Because change at the larger-system level is so complex, it is useful to think strategically about different orders of change. Kimberly and Neilsen (1975) have suggested three orders of change. (*Order* refers to the level of the ultimate target for change.) For *first-order* changes, the initial focus is some subsystem of the organization. The change would occur as a result of an intervention in a particular unit or division (subsystem) within the organization. The unit may be a relatively autonomous business line or the top management team, and the intervention could be team building, with a change objective of developing more collaborative, consensual decision-making behavior. First-order change, then, is within a subsystem; and although change in that unit will have some consequences for the larger system, the likelihood is that, unless other complementary and supplementary changes are also occurring in related parts of the total system, the change within the initial subsystem will be short-lived. For an excellent and classic example of this point, see the Hovey and Beard case (Whyte, 1955).

Second-order change means that the target is a subsystem or process that is beyond the initial focus but that will be affected if the initial effort is successful. The focus is frequently a category or a particular set of subsystems within the organization. An intervention may take place with one group of employees, first-line supervisors, for example, when the ultimate objective for the change effort is to affect all workers below these supervisors in the organizational hierarchy. If we want to decrease absenteeism and turnover among the workers who are accountable to these supervisors, our initial effort may be a training program for the supervisors in which they would have the opportunity to learn more about human motivation, the consequences of certain kinds of rewards and punishment, and effective ways of providing feedback on worker performance. With proper application of this learning, the supervisors would help reduce absenteeism and turnover, our ultimate target for change.

Third-order change eventually influences some organizational process or outcome that is affected by multiple factors. Wherever the interventions or series of interventions are made, the ultimate objective of the change effort is larger, to increase productivity, for example. Staying with this example, because multiple factors affect productivity, no single first-order or even second-order change is likely to be successful. Also, for third-order change, there is likely to be a chain or sequence of factors that eventually leads to higher productivity. We may begin with changing managers' behavior regarding the way they treat their subordinates, for example, by getting them to manage more participatively. This change in turn will affect work climate and subordinate motivation, which then may lead to greater individual and group performance and finally, to increased productivity. Third-order change means the involvement of multiple factors in some causal sequence toward an ultimate goal.

Documenting change at the first order is fairly straightforward, at the second level, it is more difficult, and at the third, very difficult, as we shall see in the next chapter. Nevertheless, we must understand that changing the entire system is a third-order change.

Change Phases

One of the first psychologists to help us understand organization change at the larger-system level was Kurt Lewin. His rather simple three-phase model set the stage for the more elaborate and comprehensive models we embrace today. These more recent models are explained in a later chapter. For now, let us briefly examine what is meant by these three phases.

Although applicable to the larger system, Lewin's (1958) three-phase model for change, interestingly, was explained at the group level. The term *step* is often used in describing Lewin's model, but *phase* is a better word because the steps are not discrete; they overlap.

Lewin (1958) argued that in Phase 1, we must *unfreeze* the system. This unfreezing phase may take a variety of forms: creating a sense of urgency about the need for change, educating managers to behave differently, merging with another organization, and so on; but the underlying notion is that the system must be "shaken up," must be confronted with a compelling need to do business differently, and must be "thawed" from its present way of doing things so that in a new, more malleable, perhaps even vulnerable state or condition, the system is accessible and amenable to change interventions.

The second phase, then, is *movement,* or changing the organization: moving in new directions with different technologies and ways of operating. Lewin's (1958) point was that the system will *not* move or change in any meaningful way unless and until an unfrozen condition has been achieved.

Once change, or movement, is underway, the third phase, *refreeze,* must be initiated (Lewin, 1958). The change that has occurred cannot be allowed to dissipate or drift away. The new, changed condition or state therefore needs to be reinforced, or undergirded, with a process and infrastructure in place to maintain the new system. This means, for example, having a different reward system that reinforces the behaviors that are congruent with the new, changed organization. In other words, organizational members see a clear and direct relationship between what the organization's mission and strategy are and their individual roles and responsibilities. Other examples could be noted, such as organizational structure and information systems. The point is that as the new state is "frozen" in the early stages of change, it is delicate, somewhat vulnerable, and until jelled, is subject to further change that may not be desired. Thus, reinforcing the new state is just as important in the change process as shaking up the old one was in Phase 1. Chapter 11 will provide more about sustaining a change effort.

We examine in more depth this phased way of thinking about, planning, and implementing organization change in Chapter 7.

Change Focus

In a sense, the question here is, where do we start with our change effort, what comes next, and then where do we focus? The answer to "Where do we start?" depends on what is initiating the change in the first place, particularly from the organization's external environment, and how deep the change should be. Are we talking about revolutionary or evolutionary change? If revolutionary, then the focus is on deep issues such as the raison d'être of the organization, its purpose, mission, and related matters, for example, strategy. We will also focus on issues of leadership and organizational culture. If, on the other hand, the changes needed are not as fundamental or transformational in nature— that is, what seems to be required is some fine-tuning, improvements here and there, or changing some important parts of the organization but not the entire system—then we are talking about evolutionary, or transactional, change. The focus, therefore, is on matters such as organizational design and structure, the information system, or perhaps management practices.

Staying with our theme, larger-system change, implying more transformational than transactional change, we start with a focus on the bigger picture—mission, leadership, and culture—followed by a focus on the more transactional dimensions. The focus of change in the latter case is on the support and infrastructural aspects of the organization that will reinforce the transformational changes: organizational structure (*after* the new strategy has been determined), the reward system (to reinforce new behaviors), information technology (to align with and support new operations), new roles and jobs for people, improving the climate of groups and teams, and so on.

Change Processes

In general, *process* here refers to mechanisms that facilitate the overall change effort, such as communication systems (newsletters that tell stories about successful changes that support the overall effort; videos of the CEOs championing the cause, etc.) and training programs that focus on the new skills and behaviors needed to make the change work. More specifically, process refers to certain interventions meant to significantly implement the change effort, such as in the following two examples.

Large-Group Intervention. This kind of activity involves bringing together a large, key group of organizational members (e.g., the top 100 executives or all 500 first-line supervisors) into one room for a day or two to address a significant organization change issue, for example, determining the new mission and set of guiding values for the organization or responding to an organization-wide survey with action plans. This kind of intervention requires a significant amount of design and logistical planning, yet it can be powerful for moving the organization (a huge step) toward the change goals. For more information about this kind of large-scale intervention, see the book by Bunker and Alban (1997) and the article by Burke, Javitch, Waclawski, and Church (1997).

Survey Feedback. The historical development and brief description of what this kind of intervention entails is provided in Chapter 2.

Suffice it to say here that in support of an overall change effort, an organization-wide survey helps to achieve the following:

- Establish data points at a particular time that can serve as milestones or benchmarks for how well the change is progressing; further value is provided when a "Time 1" assessment is compared with a "Time 2" measure, say, a year later.
- Establish priorities about which aspects of the organization to emphasize for change and in what order to address them.
- Send messages, by the content of the questions that are asked, to organizational members about what is important in the change process.
- Keep the change effort data-based.
- Involve large numbers of people in the organization change effort via feedback and action-planning processes.

For more information on this kind of organizational intervention, see Kraut (1996).

Interorganizational

Currently and probably for some time yet to come, larger-system change comes about by way of mergers and acquisitions, strategic alliances, joint ventures, and the like. There are a number of reasons for these joinings, two in particular: (a) the opportunity to share resources that neither organization by itself has and (b) the opportunity to improve cost-effectiveness by reducing redundancies. By their very nature, these decisions and occurrences force organization change. This is particularly true of a merger in which two organizations of relatively equal size and scope come together as one. But most of these joinings fail, especially mergers and acquisitions. Using the criteria of what is promised by the leaders of merged and acquiring companies and the objectives of the decision to join ("achieving synergies" is a phrase often bandied about), there are many more failures than successes. Burke and Biggart (1997) conducted a study of interorganizational relations and found that this majority of failures could be attributed to the following primary reasons or conditions:

- Insufficient clarity about goals and how to measure progress toward the goals
- Imbalance of power and control between the two organizations when they merged or, say, established a strategic alliance or joint venture
- Imbalance of expertise, status, and/or prestige between the two parties

- Overconfident and unrealistic notions about future success of the relationship, that is, holding a belief of having sufficient control over key variables
- Lack of a contingency plan (as we address in Chapter 1, organization change including these joinings never unfolds as foreseen)
- Lack of perceived equity, for example, distributions of key jobs and roles

Conditions for success regarding organizations' coming together are the opposite of those on the failure list. To clarify, here are a few examples:

- Having a superordinate goal, that is, a goal or goals that can be accomplished *only* through the cooperative efforts of the two parties. See the section on "Coercion and Confrontations" in Chapter 2 for the original research in this domain, the work of Sherif (Sherif & Sherif, 1969) and Blake, Shepard, and Mouton (1964).
- Having a balance of power, expertise, and status.
- Creating mutual gain.
- Having a committed leader.
- Alignment of rewards—in the early stages of a merger or acquisition, it is important to consolidate various compensation systems into one.
- Having respect for differences.
- Achieving equity.
- Having realistic assumptions about what can be accomplished and in what time frame.
- Having good luck!

In an informal discussion with senior executives who had recently been through an acquisition (some the acquirers and some the acquired) and were about to go through yet another one, I asked them what they had learned from their previous experiences. The following is a quick summary of what these executives said:

1. They emphasized the importance of having a vision for the future (sound familiar?).

2. They noted that having a rationale behind the joining and explaining this carefully to all those affected is critical.

3. They stressed the importance of being open and honest about the change.

4. They pointed out how important it is in the early stages to have informal relations between the two parties, such as going to a ballgame together, having meals together, and so on.

5. These executives argued that rapid decision making was imperative even if some of the decisions would have to be changed later. They pointed out that people cry for structure and order and this need should be addressed.

6. The seven executives emphasized the importance of what they referred to as "walking the talk," meaning matching words with actions, or the absence of hypocrisy (Chapter 11 elaborates on this aspect of leading change).

7. They stated that in midst of this kind of organization change, typically, the customer is forgotten. With so much time and energy being focused inwardly, conducting the business and serving customers suffers.

Although these executives made some interesting and unique points, as can be seen, there is considerable overlap with the findings from the study by Burke and Biggart (1997).

To see how a successful merger changed two organizations, SmithKline Beckman of Philadelphia and Beecham of London, into a new, single organization that required the coming together of two companies as well as two nationalities, see Bauman, Jackson, and Lawrence (1997) and Burke and Jackson (1991). And to see how a strategic alliance that cut across three companies and three nationalities (United Kingdom, France, and Germany) affected the internal organization change effort of British Aerospace, see Evans and Price (1999). Finally, as already cited, for an overview and analysis of interorganizational relations in general, see Burke and Biggart (1997).

System Responses to Organization Change

Again, with strong efforts at following a planned process to bring about large-scale organization change, including heavy use of involvement and participatory activities as well as clarity of direction with strong leadership, successful organization change can occur. The change at BA and successful merger of SmithKline Beecham are good cases in point. Yet even with successful changes, resistance occurs along the way, and when success is not achieved, the resistance dominates and lingers. We will touch on five examples of resistance to larger-scale change.

Revolution Becomes, at Best, Evolution. When a transformational change is attempted, in the end, only some components of the organization are changed or perhaps just some fine-tuning occurs. The old culture is simply too powerful, the bureaucracy too pervasive. Even though the perturbation(s) from the external environment may have been strong, say, a significant technological change in the industry (such as going from analog to digital in the communications industry), the organization's response to this external shift is insufficient, and the deep structure (pattern) does not change.

Insufficient Sense of Urgency. In this instance, which happens often, the case for change is simply not compelling. The question is obvious: "Why change?" Many people in the organization lack the motivation to tackle an organization change process and program because they harbor disbelief about the need, serious skepticism, a lackadaisical attitude, or a combination of these responses. For whatever reasons, not enough organizational members are convinced that change is required, and there is not a critical mass to move the organization in another direction.

"This Too Shall Pass." This response is typically a function of history. Time and again, management has tried this and tried that, taking on the latest fad for improving the organization, or the "flavor of the month," as this process is sometimes called. And people believe the cliché, "The more things change, the more they stay the same." So, organizational members' response is to "Wait 'em out." The response shows more apathy than it does active resistance.

Diversionary Tactics. This category of response is indeed resistance and reflects a strong desire on the part of organizational members to sabotage the effort in one way or another. One way is to create a crisis that must be addressed before any change can get underway. Sales may drop all of a sudden, a technological glitch may pop up, or some waste products may be declared as toxic. There are many possibilities. Another more common form is to argue that the *timing* for such a change is wrong. There are far too many other things "on the plate," as the expression goes. "We have residual problems from last year that still need fixing"; "People are stretched to the limits, too much stress, we simply cannot afford to pile yet another organizational initiative onto their agenda." "This kind of effort will divert us from the *real* work, manufacturing and selling our products, or attending to customer needs." The point is that people will grab at anything to avoid, if not sidetrack, the change.

Lack of Followership. "Well, the platform may be burning, but if you think I'm going to follow this CEO into the flames, you're out of your mind!" This response is, of course, similar to if not the same as the one mentioned earlier in the group-level section. Followers, or more accurately, potential followers, collude or even conspire with one another to find fault with the leader. And if there is no followership, by definition, there is no leadership. Without leadership, *intended* change will not occur.

Coping With Responses to Change at the Larger-System Level. Many of the coping mechanisms at the individual and group level are applicable at the larger-system level: achieving closure regarding the previous way of doing things, providing conceptual frameworks to help people understand more clearly what is happening to them, and involving organizational members in the process of planning and implementing the change.

In addition, we can easily point to the list of responses and resistances and then suggest antidotes. First and foremost is the issue of making a compelling case for the need to change. A clear example is the change at British Aerospace. The top 100 executives were complying with the CEO's desire to bring about change, but a deep commitment on their part was lacking. A senior and highly respected executive in the company was given the assignment of "making the case for change." He conducted an "environmental scan" and showed trends regarding the past, present, and "If things continue as they are," what the future would look like. These trends were in the categories of sales, technological shifts, what and how their competitors were doing, and likely scenarios for the future with respect to the aerospace industry, which currently can be described as a shrinking marketplace. British Aerospace is, of course, loaded with engineers. The senior executive's presentation to the company therefore was, quite appropriately, in the form of many bar charts, line graphs, and myriad statistics. An engineer himself, he argued that if they remained as they were at the time, within a decade or less, they would be out of business. Critical to this senior executive's success in getting the message across was his knowledge of the audience. Although he was a senior executive, he was nevertheless one of them, an engineer, and therefore knew how to talk to them, using appropriate language, supporting documentation, and the proper medium (charts with data). From that time to the present, there has been a significantly stronger commitment to the overall organization change effort (Burke & Trahant, 2000; Evans & Price, 1999).

To combat apathy and responses such as "This too shall pass," the change leaders must demonstrate as clearly and strongly as possible that (a) this time, the change initiative is different (due to a compelling and pervasive need) and (b) we are in this for the "long haul," that is, showing at the outset that persistence will prevail. The British Airways story of change had both these qualities.

With respect to diversionary tactics, it is incumbent on the part of change leaders to be as clear and committed as possible to the organization change goals and objectives and to establish a set of priorities— to address strategy first and then to tackle structure, and so on. And although it may not be desired, for the change to be successful may mean that certain saboteurs must be dealt with by job changes, early retirements, or outright severance from the organization.

Finally, two points: (a) Described briefly above are examples of the kind of leadership that will attract followers, and (b) if revolutionary change is called for, the deep structure of the organization must be changed. This means changing the culture particularly, perhaps new leadership with a different mission and strategy, followed by addressing the more transactional aspects of the organization, such as structure, with respect to decision making and accountability, teamwork, and so on.

Summary

We have considered organization change in this chapter from the perspective of levels: individual (including interpersonal), group (including intergroup), and the larger system (including interorganizational). The point of the parentheses following each of the three is to emphasize that taking this perspective is somewhat limited. Organizations are far more complex than merely three levels. In fact, the interactions across these levels are very important. As we proceed with additional chapters, these interactions will become more salient.

Considering organization change according to these three levels, although limited, is useful nevertheless. As noted, organization change must start somewhere, and understanding how it can start at each of these levels helps us to more clearly understand how to plan and how to lead and manage the overall change. This chapter was intended to deepen this understanding by addressing the nature of change at each

(Text continues on page 119)

Table 5.1 Summary of Levels of Organization Change According to Primary Change Example and Whether Evolutionary or Revolutionary Change

Organizational Level	Primary Organization Change Example	Evolutionary Change	Revolutionary Change
Individual	• Recruitment, selection, replacement, and displacement	Operational: Place people in positions as a consequence of changes that are underway.	Strategic: Place people in positions that are key to the overall change effort (King, 1972).
	• Training and development	Facilitate targeted change (e.g., people management skills, as in the Citicorp example).	Facilitate large-scale culture change, as in the British Airways example.
	• Coaching and counseling	Conduct at all levels in the organization for purposes of general improvement.	Conduct primarily with change leaders to enhance overall change effort.
Group	• Team building	Conduct team-building activities throughout the organization to improve teamwork and cooperative behavior.	Conduct team building with top executive group initially to model behavior desired for overall change effort.
	• Self-directed groups	Promote the adoption of self-directed groups due to structure change (i.e., eliminating some layers of management in the hierarchy).	Promote the adoption of self-directed groups to enhance culture change in the direction of values that encourage participation, involvement, autonomy, and greater teamwork.

(Continued)

115

Table 5.1 (Continued)

Organizational Level	Primary Organization Change Example	Evolutionary Change	Revolutionary Change
	• Intergroup	Use conflict resolution techniques to reduce inappropriate intergroup competition.	Use conflict resolution techniques to promote cross-functional and interunit cooperation to reduce "silo effects" that in turn serve to change organization culture.
Organization	• Orders of change	First order	Second and third order
	• Change phases	Lewin's three phases	Lewin's three phases
	• Change focus	Issues such as structure, systems, work unit climate, motivation, and performance management	Deep issues such as purpose, mission, strategy, culture, and leadership
	• Change processes	Those that promote problem solving and continuous improvement	Those that facilitate large-scale change, such as large-group interventions and survey feedback
	• Interorganizational	Acquisitions, strategic alliance, consortia	Mergers, large-scale acquisitions, strategic alliances, partnerships

Table 5.2 Summary of Responses to Organization Change According to Organizational Level

Organizational Level	Resistance	Coping With Change
Individual	• Has to do with losing something of value to the person	• Transitioning: ending and letting go, going through the neutral zone, making a new beginning
	• Forms: blind, political, and ideological (Hambrick & Cannella, 1989)	• Achieving closure: dealing with unfinished business
	• Apathy is worse; with resistance, there is energy, and the person cares about something	• Participation: helping to make the change work
Group	• "Turf" protection and competition	• The sense for individuals as listed above
	• Closing ranks: "circle the wagons"	• Conducting a closure ceremony (e.g., "funeral")
	• Changing allegiances and/or ownership	• Conducting group problem-solving sessions, preferably off-site
	• Demand for new leadership	• Recompose the membership of groups

(Continued)

Table 5.2 (*Continued*)

Organizational Level	Resistance	Coping With Change
Organization	• Revolution becomes, at best, evolution	• The above for individual and group are applicable for the organization level as well
	• Insufficient sense of urgency	• Ensuring that a compelling case for the change has been made
	• "This too shall pass"	• This time, the change initiative is different—we mean it, and we are in it for the long haul
	• Diversionary tactics: sabotage, timing is all wrong, too many initiatives and other things on our plate as it is, and the change is a way of avoiding our real work	• Strong, effective leadership

level, the likely responses in general and resistances in particular that occur at each level, and some examples of coping mechanisms at each level. Moreover, these three levels of understanding are not discrete. Individuals reside within groups and groups within the larger organization. And although our analysis, taking the organization apart by level, is helpful, we must remain highly cognizant of the fact that we are dealing with totalities, wholes, and systems.

This chapter covered a lot of ground. Tables 5.1 and 5.2 are therefore attempts at further summary. Also, in Table 5.1, the intent is to provide linkage with Chapter 4, that is, by including examples at the three organizational levels that show both evolutionary change and revolutionary change.

In Chapter 6, we take a closer look at research regarding organizational change and at further theory, in this case, theory that is more closely related to the research.

Organization Change

RESEARCH AND THEORY

The objective of this chapter is to provide a guide through the mazes of both organization change research and organization change theory. Although we will review the compilations and summaries of research studies from the appropriate sources, for example, the *Annual Review of Psychology*, when it comes to theory, we will not rely on the "usual suspects," such as textbooks on organization theory, but will explore the less typical literature instead. Organization change theory barely exists, and we must therefore seek other theories that may begin to inform us in such a way that in a decade or so, a clearer and more definitive theory about organization change per se will emerge. For our theory bases, then, we will explore domains such as nonlinear complex systems theory, stemming from chaos and related theories, and some of the more fundamental psychological theories such as the one developed by William James and C. G. Lange, more than a century ago, known today as the James-Lange theory (James, 1890; Lange, 1885/1922). But first, let us see what research tells us about organization change by examining the literature of the past 25 years or so.

Reviews of Organization Change Research

One of the early reviews of organization change research was the *Annual Review of Psychology* chapter by Friedlander and Brown (1974). Writing under the banner of organization development (OD), these authors framed their review of research in the field in terms of "target of interventions" that led to outcomes. The two broad categories of interventions were people and technology, with the former emphasizing organizational processes, such as communication, decision making, and problem solving, and the latter emphasizing organizational structures, such as task

Figure 6.1. Approaches to organization development
SOURCE: F. Friedlander and L. D. Brown, Organization Development, 1974, *Annual Review of Psychology*, 25, pp. 313-341. With permission, from the *Annual Review of Psychology*, Volume 25 © 1974 by Annual Reviews www.annualreviews.org.

methods, job design, and organizational design. These two categories of interventions could lead to two outcomes: human fulfillment and task accomplishment (see Figure 6.1). "These components interact in the techno-structural and human-processual [their term, not in the dictionary] systems on behalf of the objectives of human fulfillment and task accomplishment—and the environment obviously interacts with all these components in terms of input to and output from the organization" (Friedlander & Brown, 1974, p. 315). Their framework is reflective of an open system approach to conceptualizing organizations.

Friedlander and Brown's (1974) main conclusions from their review of the research literature at the time were as follows:

- Research showing change in the techno-structural category was clearer and more definitive than studies investigating the human-processual (their language) approach. They attributed this difference to types of measurement tools, that is, techno-structural change is easier to measure than the more abstract and less objective human processes domain.

- "OD today is a long way from being the general theory and technology of planned social system we would like to see it become" (Friedlander & Brown, 1974, p. 335).

Although there was some evidence at the time that OD interventions had an effect on organizational performance, remembering the differences noted above, the pervasiveness of the impact was not clear, and there was no overall guiding theory.

Three years later, Alderfer (1977b) provided a review of the research up to that time and concluded that "the overall quality of research . . . is showing increasing signs of both rigor and vigor as more careful studies . . . are being conducted and reported" (p. 197). Alderfer, unlike his two predecessors, did not use an overall framework or model to discuss his review of the literature.

In a subsequent summary of theory and research in organization change, three Europeans wrote a wide-ranging, cross-cultural review of the field (Faucheux, Amado, & Laurent, 1982). Their review differed somewhat from Alderfer's conclusions 5 years earlier. Citing the work of Porras (and his colleagues), one of our foremost researchers in OD and planned change, Faucheux et al. (1982) reported that there remained a "paucity of good research and particularly fundamental research" (p. 350). For example, there was even evidence to counter "that changed process caused changed outcome" (p. 350). In other words, part of Friedlander and Brown's model dealing with the outcomes of human processes (see Figure 6.1) was not substantiated. Faucheux and his colleagues called for a stronger linkage between the social and the technical approaches. This sociotechnical linkage (see Chapter 2) and the need to account for the broader context of organization change, such as understanding the relationship between a given organization and the society within which it resides, are critical. They contended that bringing about true organization change that is measurable and endurable requires such a linkage. This way of thinking is quite compatible with Capra's (1996) notion of networks (systems) embedded within networks (systems).

With the passage of another 5 years, the lament was similar: "Despite more sophisticated research methods, OD research results are still inconclusive. One can find support for many different conclusions, among the results reported in the studies" (Beer & Walton, 1987, p. 343). Hence, these reviewers raised an all-important question: "Why should this be so?" They stated that organization change research "suffers from problems," which are described as follows:

1. This kind of research attempts to determine causation. Most researchers rely on traditional scientific methods, working hard to identify the effects of some change intervention, such as team building, structure change, survey feedback, training, a shift in business strategy,

installing a new information system or compensation plan, and so forth. What is overlooked is the larger system, the interconnectedness of the various parts (sound familiar?), and the context, changes that are occurring in the industry, for example. As Beer and Walton (1987) pointed out, "Exogenous variables and intervening events will always prevent any powerful conclusions. . . . Even worse, normal science methodology can damage the experiment itself" (p. 343). The authors then presented a very interesting example, a study by Blumberg and Pringle (1983). These researchers described an intervention that included job redesign and worker participation in managing a mine. Blumberg and Pringle had a control group and an experimental group, as normal science would dictate. In this case, however, the control group discovered what was going on with the experimental group and resented the latter's advantage. Moreover, the control group of miners then voted to stop the whole process, and no further changes occurred.

2. Most research on organization change is a "snapshot," not a longitudinal view. Thus, it is difficult to determine how permanent a change may be.

3. Beer and Walton (1987) used the word *flat* to signal the third problem. What they meant is that much research methodology and instrumentation is quite precise, but the meaning and interpretation of the data are anything but precise. History is often ignored, as is environmental context. The authors also pointed out that quantitative methods are not very useful for understanding an outcome that has multiple causes.

4. The research often does not fit the needs of the user. "Good science can be antithetical to good action" (Beer & Walton, 1987, p. 344). The use of highly technical, if not esoteric, statistical procedures can make research outcomes so complicated that managers and executives in organizations (users) end up with glassy eyes wondering what all of this may mean. Also, researchers often equivocate about results and use phrases such as "On the other hand" and "This outcome can only be expected under these conditions." The researchers, certainly from their point of view, are using proper language for normal science. The users expect something quite different, such as simple declarative sentences.

Beer and Walton (1987) went on to state that organization research may be at a turning point—continuing as is will lead only to studying isolated and episodic events. Going in another direction, namely "action science," as Argyris, Putnam, and Smith (1985) call it, may be the better choice. This means moving away from typical positivistic assumptions regarding research in organizations and toward a process that (a) involves the users in the study, (b) relies on self-corrective learning, say, trying certain assessment methods and then modifying them along the way as trial and error yields knowledge, and (c) occurs over time, not episodically. As Beer and Walton noted, the literature about this kind of choice regarding organization change research has begun to grow. See, for example, Carnall (1982), Morgan (1983), and Legge (1984).

In addition to the four problems covered by Beer and Walton, at least two more can be identified, the researchers themselves and determining *what*, if anything, changed:

1. Numerous studies have shown that the research can affect the outcome (Rosenthal, 1976). The degree to which the researcher is directly involved makes a difference: collecting data from organizational members, as a more distant observer, or not directly intervening in the organization at all and relying exclusively on archival information. Clarity must be sought, therefore, about the objective of the organization change research. Is it for evaluative purposes, and are the organization's members the primary users? If so, then from the outset, these organizational members need to be involved, as Argyris (1970) has argued, in decisions about what data to collect and how to collect them. This increases the likelihood that appropriate data will be collected and analyzed with valid inferences being made. It further ensures that the data will be used. If, on the other hand, the primary user is the scientific community, then more objectivity with the process is necessary, with a greater reliance on data that are more likely to be objective: as archival information, financial outcomes (although these need to be chosen carefully because "creative accounting," for example, is not dead), and independent assessments of the organization's effectiveness, such as Dun and Bradstreet ratings.

2. With respect to a more complete understanding of what, if anything, changed, the work of Golembiewski, Billingsley, and Yeager (1976) is enlightening. They drew distinctions among three types of change, which they labeled alpha, beta, and gamma. *Alpha* change concerns a difference that occurs along some relatively stable dimension of

reality. The change is typically a comparative measure before and after an intervention. If comparative measures of trust among team members showed an increase, after a team-building intervention, for example, then we might conclude that our organizational intervention had made a difference. Golembiewski et al. (1976) assert that most evaluation research designs consist of such "before" and "after" self-reports.

Suppose, however, that as a result of our team-building intervention, a *decrease* in trust occurred—or no change at all. One study has shown that, although no decrease in trust occurred, neither did a measurable increase occur as a consequence of team-building intervention (Friedlander, 1970). Change may have occurred, however. The difference may be what Golembiewski et al. (1976) call a *beta* change, a recalibration of the intervals along some constant dimension of reality. As a result of a team-building intervention, team members may view trust very differently. Their basis for judging the nature of trust changed, rather than their perception of a simple increase or decrease in trust along some stable continuum. In other words, their *standard* for judging what trust is may have changed.

A *gamma* change "involves a redefinition or reconceptualization of some domain, a major change in the perspective or frame of reference within which phenomena are perceived and classified, in what is taken to be relevant in some slice of reality" (Golembiewski et al., 1976, p. 135). This involves change from one state to another. Staying with the example, after the intervention, team members might conclude that trust was not a relevant variable in their team-building experience. They might believe that the gain in their clarity about roles and responsibilities was the relevant factor and that their improvement as a team had nothing to do with trust.

Thus, selecting the appropriate dependent variable—determining specifically what might change—is not as simple as it might appear. This is especially important when self-report data are used.

In summary, we have learned over the past three decades that measuring organization changes is not simple. Following traditional methods of normal science may be straightforward, but the results may not be. Determining cause and effect in organizations is difficult because so many variables are involved and most can be controlled. In our attempts to measure organization change, we must also be clear as to who the research is for. If the users are other researchers, then following normal science may be important. If the users are the members of the organization being studied, then they need to be involved and normal science is not necessarily appropriate. The emerging field of action science may need to be followed.

More Recent Approaches to Research and Theory

The Shift From "Normal" Science

So-called normal science methods originated with the physical sciences and were adopted by the social and behavioral sciences. But the physical sciences have not stayed exclusively with "normal" methods. Chaos theory, nonlinear systems theory, and related concepts and theories, such as fractals, have precipitated changes in research methods. As Svyantek (1997) and his colleagues have pointed out (e.g., Svyantek & Brown, 2000; Svyantek & DeShon, 1993), organizational researchers need to move in similar directions. Svyantek (Svyantek & Brown, 2000) refers to this kind of direction as a "complex-systems approach" to the study of organizations, meaning that organizational behavior can rarely be explained by analysis, that is, breaking down the system into its component parts:

> Explaining the behavior of a complex system requires understanding (a) the variables determining the system's behavior, (b) the patterns of interconnections among these variables, and (c) the fact that these patterns, and the strengths associated with each interconnection, may vary depending on the time scale relevant for the behaviors being studied. (p. 69)

With respect to their third point (c), Svyantek and Brown cite an example by Koch and Laurent (1999) regarding the measurement of reaction time. With respect to light, sound, a machine, or the human nervous system, reaction time changes may occur in milliseconds, whereas for change in "corporate performance, the time scale might be in months or years" (Svyantek & Brown, 2000, p. 69).

Svyantek and Brown (2000) went on to point out some fundamental differences between traditional (normal science) approaches to the study of organizations, that is, the use of linear methods such as regression, and complex systems approaches that rely on nonlinear methods; with respect to the latter,

> [The] data gathered consist of multiple measurements of both independent and dependent variables, and these data are then graphed. The predictions made are more molar and qualitative than the predictions in traditional approaches. The

value of these predictions is based on the degree to which a consistent pattern of behavior is found in the system across the repeated measurements. The results of such an experiment are used to make predictions that are context-specific. (p. 69)

Relying on the work of Liebovitch (1998) and Richter (1986), Svyantek and Brown (2000) proposed two nonlinear concepts "that have explanatory value for understanding social systems . . . *phase space* and *attractor*" (p. 70).

Phase space consists of a depiction of multiple behavioral measurements over time (the phase aspect). The depiction can be a three-dimensional graph (the space aspect) that shows how a particular behavior can be affected by, say, three different variables over time. Richter (1986) has provided examples of this phase space method: how an individual's responses in a particular situation may be affected by his or her level of aggressiveness, fear, and guilt, all at the same time and over time. Patterns of behavior can then be traced.

Attractors are these patterns of behavior. They have two primary characteristics: sensitivity to initial conditions and stability.

Sensitivity to initial conditions means that an organization's history is highly important. (A number of years ago, a colleague of mine, also an organization change consultant, and I were working together. He kept saying to the client, "Spare me the history!" I thought it was a mistake then, and I am even more convinced today.) By way of positive feedback, early behaviors in an organization's developmental stages get reinforced and stabilized. Two organizations in the same domain (e.g., business) that originated at the same time under similar, if not identical, conditions can become very different from one another over time. Small differences at the beginning can lead to large differences years later, due to highly specific, even undetectable, behaviors being consistently reinforced in the first year.

A personal consulting experience recently illustrated this attractor characteristic dramatically. After almost 150 years of independent existence, two banks in a large metropolitan area decided to merge. These two businesses were remarkably similar. Both were founded at about the same time, in the mid-19th century, in the same community of the larger metropolitan area; and ten decades later, they were almost equal in size in terms of number of employees, number of directors on the respective boards, annual revenues, and number of branches. Moreover, the announcement of the deal was touted as a "merger of equals." At the outset, the consulting project seemed easy. Such similarities would no doubt make the integration of the two banks quick and smooth. In reality, the merger was anything but quick and smooth. The corporate cultures of the two banks, despite all those similarities, were entirely different. The culture of Bank A was loose, risk taking, rather spendthrift, and led rather than managed, whereas Bank B could be characterized as tight, risk averse, highly cost conscious, and managed, not led. The descriptors of the two cultures are examples of multiple behaviors that represent the phase space concept. A century earlier, small, undetectable but different behaviors in each of the two banks were positively reinforced (and became attractors), and decades later, these differences loomed large. It took more than 2 years for the merger to even be accepted, much less integrated. And these were not huge organizations in the first place, about 1,700 employees in each. This example is explained later in considerable detail in Chapter 10.

The second characteristic, *stability*, can best be understood analogously, as an organization's culture. Interestingly, Schein (1985) has stressed the importance of a founder's behavior in shaping an organization's culture, especially in terms of what he or she emphasizes and values.

In a sense, then, this nonlinear approach helps us with a new way of thinking about the research process, phase spaces, and with a more focused content regarding what to study: attractors.

In summary, the primary point is that measuring organization change is extremely complex and therefore requires extremely complex approaches and methods. Although still useful, "normal" and traditional approaches to research nevertheless are limited indeed.

The Organizational Change Research Theory of Porras and Colleagues

Although by no means exclusively, in the early 1990s, theory and research most closely associated with OD were reflected largely in the work of Jerry Porras and his colleagues. They have reviewed and to some extent consolidated the literature on organization change research and theory (Porras & Robertson, 1992; Porras & Silvers, 1991). To begin with, Porras and Robertson (1992) have provided some useful distinctions to help us understand organization change more thoroughly: planned versus unplanned change and first-order versus second-order change.

Planned Change. This is a deliberate, conscious decision to improve the organization in some manner or perhaps to change the system in a deeper, more fundamental way.

Unplanned Change. In this case, the organization has to respond to some unanticipated external change, for example, creation of a whole new technology that affects the very core of the business, as was true for Swiss watchmakers when the digital version came on the scene. In unplanned change, the response is adaptive and often spontaneous.

First-Order Change. This form involves what we today refer to as "continuous improvement" (the Japanese call it *kaizen*); that is, the change consists of alterations or modifications in existing system characteristics, such as eliminating a layer of management or administration in the organizational hierarchy, rather than a shift in some fundamental way, such as change of organizational mission. In Chapter 4, we referred to this first-order level of change as *evolutionary.*

Second-Order Change. This form is radical, more fundamental change. We earlier referred to this form as *revolutionary,* a change of the organization's deep structure (see Chapter 4). The change is paradigmatic.

Quite naturally, Porras and Robertson (1992) then placed these concepts into a 2 x 2 arrangement (see Table 6.1). Although this arrangement is rather neat and easy to grasp, it oversimplifies, unfortunately. Revolutionary change can be planned after all (see, for example, Goodstein & Burke, 1991), and so can evolutionary change (see Chapter 4).

In a related paper, Porras and Silvers (1991) distinguished between first-order (they classified organization development, OD, as first-order; again, see Table 6.1) and second-order, or what they referred to as "organization transformation." With respect to the former classification, OD, they concluded,

> Much of this research is fragmented and does not build on work done by other authors laboring in a similar arena. More effort should be directed at the development of a paradigm for OD, and thus researchers must build more consciously on each other's work. (pp. 69-70)

And concerning the latter, organization transformation (OT), Porras & Silvers (1991) stated,

Table 6.1 Types of Organizational Change

Order of Change	Change Category	
	Planned	*Unplanned*
First	Developmental	Evolutionary
Second	Transformational	Revolutionary

SOURCE: From Organizational Development: Theory, Practice, and Research, by J. I. Porras and P. J. Robertson, 1992, in M. D. Dunnette and L. M. Hough (Eds.), *Handbook of Industrial and Organizational Psychology* (Vol. 3, 2nd ed., p. 722.), Palo Alto, CA: Consulting Psychologists Press, Inc. Used by permission.

> Although the broad outlines of the field may be sketched (e.g., a focus on vision, conscious change, etc.), there is still considerable diversity in this area and consequently many different directions for future development. It is therefore difficult to predict where the field will be in ten years. (p. 73)

Now, a decade later, the designation OT itself has faded, but the distinctions have not. In fact, in the most recent review of the literature, Weick and Quinn (1999) organized their report according to *episodic* change (discontinuous, transformational, and revolutionary) and *continuous* change (continuous improvement, transactional, and evolutionary). We will return to their review later in this chapter.

Organization Models

As noted earlier, Friedlander and Brown (1974) provided a framework or approach for understanding organization change, or OD (see Figure 6.1). They referred to two primary approaches to organization change: people, or human-processual, and technology, or techo-structural. They were categorizing targets of intervention (people and technology) and two outcomes of these interventions, human fulfillment and task accomplishment.

Some years later, in a more elaborate attempt to diagram the way planned organization change occurs, Porras (1987) provided a model that is grounded in open system theory, that is, environment (input), organization (throughput), organizational performance, and individual development (output), with a feedback loop connecting output back to input. The organization part of his model (throughput) consists of organizational members' behavior and the work setting (context).

Porras further delineates within the work setting part of his model's four components, what he calls "streams," or four basic dimensions: (a) organizing arrangements (e.g., goals, strategies, structure, and systems), (b) social factors (primarily culture but also including social patterns and networks and individual attributes), (c) technology (tools, equipment, machinery, job design, and technical systems), and (d) physical settings (space, ambiance, interior design, etc.). In the reviews of the literature that Porras and his colleagues provided (Porras & Robertson, 1992; Porras & Silvers, 1991), this model was used to organize their analytical summaries. See Figure 6.2 for a diagrammatic summary of the model.

Porras's model is essentially a description of how input from the external environment gets transformed into output-organizational performance and individual development. The model also highlights what, for Porras, are the primary elements and dimensions of an organization: the work setting elements (social factors, physical setting, etc.) and the member elements (cognitions and behaviors). With respect to output, he distinguishes between the performance of the organization and individual development, as opposed to, say, individual performance. One could argue, however, that organizational performance includes both unit (group, team, and department) and individual performance. These in turn, affect or produce organizational performance.

In a sense, then, this model by Porras is a description of how organizations operate and what the key elements are in that operation. The model adds to the array of like models in the field of organization development and change. See, for example, Burke (1994). The reason for coverage of the Porras model is to establish a backdrop or context for his thinking about how organization change occurs.

Organization Change Theory

Before plunging into the various change ideas and theories, let us consider what an adequate theory should include. Whetten (1989, in press) has proposed that a "complete" theory contains four elements:

1. *What* (constructs): factors that should logically be considered as explanatory parts of what is being considered, for example, if organizational, such factors as strategy, culture, performance, and so on.

2. *How* (linkages): how the factors under *What* relate to one another, typically portrayed in the form of boxes and arrows; what comes before what (strategy before structure), and what causes what.

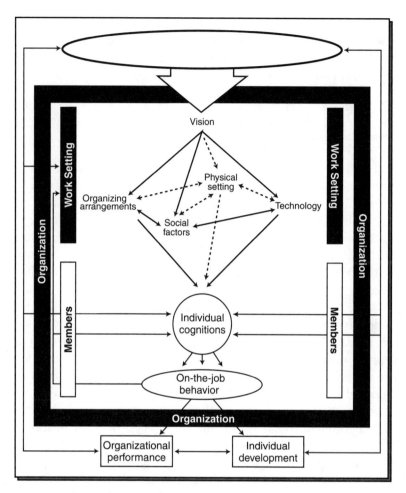

Figure 6.2. A change-based organizational framework

SOURCE: Modified and reproduced by special permission of the Publisher, Consulting Psychologists Press, Inc., Palo Alto, CA 94303 from **Handbook of Industrial & Organizational Psychology, Second Edition Volume 3** by Marvin D. Dunnette and Leaetta M. Hough, Editor. Copyright 1992 by Consulting Psychologists Press, Inc. All rights reserved. Further reproduction is prohibited without the Publisher's written consent.

3. *Why* (conceptual assumptions): the logic underlying the theory or model. As Whetten (1989) put it, "The soundness of fundamental views of human nature, organizational requisites, or societal processes provide the basis for judging the reasonableness of the proposed conceptualization" (p. 491).

4. The fourth element in Whetten's (1989) criteria set includes the combination of *Who/Where/When:* "These temporal and contextual factors set the boundaries of generalizability, and as such constitute the range of the theory" (p. 492).

These elements and criteria for what should be included in a complete theory can guide our review of the theories and models that follow.

In their review of the organization development and change literature, Porras and Silvers (1991) stated at the outset,

> Planned change that makes organizations more responsive to environmental shifts should be guided by generally accepted and unified theories of organizations and organizational change—neither of which currently exists. (p. 51)

They followed with a new model/theory of planned change that proposes a process of how organization change occurs. The framework begins with organizational interventions that are intended to affect certain variables, which in turn affect individual behavior and ultimately improve organizational performance and enhance individual development. This model (see Figure 6.3) relies on Porras's previous organizational model (see Figure 6.2) but is now cast in terms of change processes.

Porras elaborates further on his perspective about the change process in a slightly later work (Porras & Robertson, 1992). He is clearly on target when declaring that for organization change to occur, organizational members must "alter their on-the-job behavior in appropriate ways. This assumption is rooted in the belief that behavior is significantly influenced by the nature of the setting in which it occurs" (Porras & Robertson, 1992, p. 724). Moreover, the schema presented in Figure 6.3 is a straightforward and rather linear depiction of how organization change occurs. The process begins with some intervention that is intended to affect an organization's vision, purpose, and mission (an OT intervention) and/or an intervention that is aimed at changing aspects of the work setting (an OD intervention). These interventions in turn affect organizational members' thought processes or mental sets that may occur at any one level or at multiple levels—alpha, beta, and/or gamma changes; and thus, behavior is changed, which then leads to improved performance and enhanced individual development. This theoretical framework by Porras is fairly easy to understand and has a certain logical flow to it; that is, A leads to B, which in turn affects C, and so on.

Moreover, with this theory, Porras meets Whetten's criteria for a "completeness" reasonably well. The *what* (constructs) are there (vision, work setting, performance, etc.), the *how* (linkages) are in place,

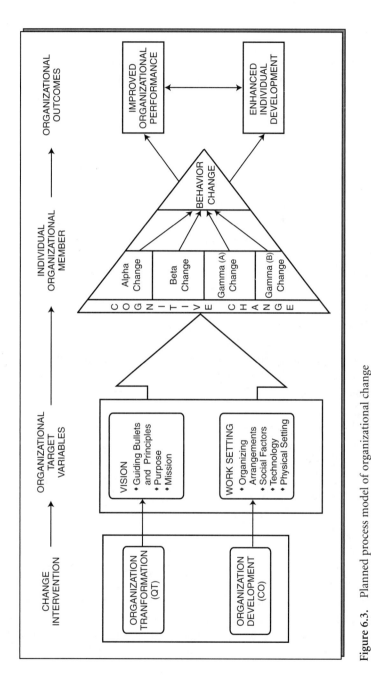

Figure 6.3. Planned process model of organizational change

SOURCE: J. I. Porras and R. C. Silvers, Organization development and transformation, 1991, *Annual Review of Psychology,* 42, pp. 51-78. With permission, from the *Annual Review of Psychology,* Volume 42 © 1991 by Annual Reviews www.annualreviews.org.

and the *why* is explicated. Also, the boundaries of the theory are fairly clear: This addresses how change occurs within an organization.

It is not likely, however, that organization change occurs in this manner. First, assuming that organizational members, who are human beings, after all, plan (or simply react to events from the organization's external environment) and implement organization change, we must account for how this very human process takes place. Although cognitive change can precede behavior change, most of the time, particularly the more emotional the situation is, it is the other way around; that is, behavior comes first, then cognition. We act and *then* attribute meaning to that action.

Second, we must account for what happens at the larger, more complex organization level, the social effect—how organizational members collectively *react* to events and how they interact with one another.

So, a problem here for organization change is being able to establish the causal linkages between vision (thought) and action (behavior). We want this attributed causation to ensure commitment and in turn, implementation of the new vision (mission, purpose, and goals). The argument now to be made is that it is preferable to promote, if not induce, the action desired to cause movement, for example, a training and development program, a multirater feedback process, a new business strategy, or installation of new work procedures and processes, rather than to provide an elaborate plan and rationale for change and expect the appropriate behavior to follow. Yes, one needs to have a change plan, but the implementation thereof is key and should move on the more desired behavior and less on the rationale and "thoughts."

To summarize in a practical way: The initiation of organization change begins with a vision of the future. This is a cognitive process. But we should not assume that this thought process will then generate the necessary behavior for the organization change. Although it is a necessary first step, the vision, or cognition, is not sufficient for change. Behavioral movement in the direction of the vision is required. It is best to begin with the vision (it is difficult to get there if we don't know *where* we're going) but not to *concentrate* on it. We concentrate on the behavior needed. As movement in the vision direction occurs, the appropriate attribution will gradually be made to explain why the direction makes sense. Even though organizational executives make pronouncements such as "We've got to change people's mental sets around here!" the change in mental set comes *after* behavior has occurred in the direction desired for the new mental set.

It may be that this argument sounds a bit illogical, but let us now consider some evidence that supports the idea of behavior change first, then change in mental set.

In the area of research and theory, considerable evidence now strongly suggests that William James, more than a century ago, was largely correct. He stated that emotional behavior precedes emotional experience (James, 1890):

> Our natural way of thinking about these coarser emotions is that the mental perception of some facts excites the mental affection called the emotion, and that this latter state of mind gives rise to the bodily expression. My theory, on the contrary, is *that the bodily changes follow directly the perception of the exciting fact, and that our feeling of the same changes as they occur IS the emotion.* Common sense says, we lose our fortune, are sorry and weep; we meet a bear, are frightened and run; we are insulted by a rival, are angry and strike. The hypothesis here to be defended says that this order of sequence is incorrect. . . . and the more rational statement is that we feel sorry *because* we cry, angry *because* we strike, afraid *because* we tremble. (p. 449)

It should be noted that at about the same time, more than a century ago, Danish physiologist C. G. Lange independently suggested much the same idea (Lange, 1885/1922). And as we may recall from our introductory psychology course, this idea became known as the James-Lange theory. Is this idea mere speculation or illogical theory?

Approximately seven decades after the James-Lange theory had been proposed, the social psychologist Stanley Schacter decided to test the idea. The theory, at the time, was controversial, and many believed it to be wrong. In a series of ingenious studies with college students, Schacter (1959) put the theory to the test. He injected adrenaline in the arms of experimental group participants and a saline solution in the control group participants. Adrenaline causes a rise in emotional energy. But what is the emotion exactly? Schacter hypothesized that he could *determine* what the emotion would be. The further two conditions of the study were to "cause" either anger or euphoria with the experimental groups. His results provided considerable validation for the theory. Compared with the control groups, the experimental groups behaved significantly more as Schacter's hypothesis predicted. In other words, an emotion was induced, but the attribution as to which emotion the subject experienced came *after* the inducement and the enacted behavior. Since then, supportive evidence has mounted. See, for example, a summary article by Laird and Bresler (1990).

In the same vein as the James-Lange theory, there is also growing evidence to suggest that the actual causes of our behavior are rarely conscious to us. Causation stems far more from our unconscious. We, of course, attribute causation via a conscious process, but this process is perceptual. The real causes are a result of intricate mechanisms that occur in our brains, of which we are unaware. In a comprehensive article regarding this theoretical perspective and put in the context of challenging the notion of "conscious will," Wegner and Wheatley (1999) summarized their premise by stating,

> The experience of will is a result of the same mental processes that people use in the perception of causality more generally. Quite simply, it may be that *people experience conscious will when they interpret their own thoughts as the cause of their action.* This idea means that people can experience conscious will quite independent of any actual causal connection between their thoughts and actions. (p. 480)

In other words, we *perceive* a causal link between our thoughts and actions. Our "will is not a psychological force that causes action" (Wegner & Wheatley, 1999, p. 481).

To perceive a causal link, Wegner and Wheatley (1999) posit that three criteria must be met: (a) priority, (b) consistency, and (c) the lack of other possible attributed causes. First, we must have the thought shortly before the action. (Studies show that if 30 seconds or more elapse, the causal link is less likely.) Second, the thought should be compatible with the action (Wegner & Wheatley, 1999):

> When people do what they think they are going to do, there exists consistency between thought and act, and the experience of will is enhanced. When they think of one thing and do another—and this inconsistency is observable to them—their action does not feel as willful. (p. 485)

Third, the thought should be the only apparent cause of action. "A basic principle of causal inference is that we tend to discount the causal influence of one potential cause if there are others available" (Wegner & Wheatley, 1999, p. 486).

In related work by psychologist John Bargh and his colleagues, a strong case is made that the ability to control our behavior consciously and intentionally is of course possible, but actually quite limited. Most of our daily psychological lives function through nonconscious means, what has been referred to as "automaticity" (Bargh & Chartrand, 1999).

In summary, first, to account for how the linkage typically occurs for organizational members between vision/mission (concepts, cognitions) and action (behavior), we must not assume that this is primarily a conscious, deliberate, and rational process. It is primarily the opposite. With a set of values and goals declared, we then quickly move to action: behavior that enacts these values and implements these goals without assuming that organizational members have made the linkages. As appropriate movement (behavior) continues over time, the proper attributions can eventually be made, for example, "We are doing this because we believe it is the right (value) thing to do." Behavior is followed by cognition. It should also be noted that this manner of theorizing is not unlike the thinking of Karl Weick, a contemporary organizational scholar. See his award-winning book on "sensemaking" (Weick, 1995).

Second, to account for what happens at the larger, more complex organization level, we must rely on theory and concepts that are non-linear, such as the work of Svyantek and others (e.g., Svyantek & Brown, 2000). Executives trying to bring about change often talk about how "messy" the process is or how little control they have ("Once we started this change effort, it seemed to take on a life of its own") and how difficult it is to sustain ("For every step forward we take, we seem next to fall back two—resistance is a very powerful thing!").

At the organization level, then, we must think in terms of attractors, the concept from nonlinear complexity theory, in terms of organizational culture (norms and values) and what gets systematically reinforced, so that we can strengthen some attractors and eliminate others. It is also useful to think of organization change as a series of "loops"—taking initiatives and then looping back to correct details missed on the first attempt or loop (see Chapter 1). It's messy and nonlinear but at the same time, realistic. In fact, Beer, Eisenstat, and Spector (1990) identified a number of false starts in the change effort at General Products. As Weick and Quinn (1999) pointed out, "This suggests that change is not a linear movement through . . . stages, but a spiral pattern of contemplation, action, and relapse and then successive returns to contemplation, action, and relapse before entering . . . maintenance and then termination stages" (p. 373).

Current Thinking Regarding Organization Change and Research

We will end this chapter in the same way that we began, that is, by considering the latest review article on organization change and development. The first of this genre was the review by Friedlander and Brown (1974). Throughout this chapter, subsequent reviews have been highlighted. The latest one is the *Annual Review of Psychology* chapter by Weick and Quinn (1999). Their review is less a summary of the research literature since the Porras and Silvers (1991) chapter and more one of describing and commenting on recent thinking about the nature of organization change. Weick and Quinn organized their chapter according to what they consider to be the two primary categories of organization change: episodic and continuous. These two ways of conceptualizing organization change were addressed in the previous chapter, that is, revolutionary versus evolutionary change in organizations. Their definition of episodic change is clear and useful (Weick & Quinn, 1999):

> The phase "episodic change" is used to group together organizational changes that tend to be infrequent, discontinuous, and intentional. The presumption is that episodic change occurs during periods of divergence when organizations are moving away from their equilibrium conditions. Divergence is the result of a growing misalignment between an inertial deep structure and perceived environmental demands. This form of change is labeled "episodic" because it tends to occur in distinct periods during which shifts are precipitated by external events such as technology change or internal events such as change in key personnel. (p. 365)

On the other hand, according to Weick and Quinn (1999), continuous change is "ongoing, evolving, and cumulative" (p. 375). They go on to clarify,

> The distinctive quality of continuous change is the idea that small continuous adjustments, created simultaneously across units, can cumulate and create substantial change. That scenario presumes tightly coupled interdependencies. When interdependencies loosen, these same continuous adjustments, not confined to smaller units, remain important as pockets of innovation that may prove appropriate in future environments. (p. 375)

By gleaning ideas and research results from the literature, Weick and Quinn (1999) concluded that episodic change arises as a result of inertia (entropy in open system theory terms) and an organization's inability to respond to external environmental changes adequately. Continuous change is driven, they argue, "by alertness and the inability of organizations to remain stable" (p. 379); but as Pascale, Milleman, and Gioja (2000) pointed out, this alertness and fighting equilibrium is rare.

Weick and Quinn (1999) also provided a new way of applying Lewin's three-stage model of the change process. They state that episodic change follows (or should follow) the stages as Lewin (1958) originally conceptualized, that is, unfreeze-movement-refreeze, whereas continuous change, to be effective, is more like freeze-rebalance-unfreeze. To *freeze* continuous change is to find the patterns in day-to-day life in the organizations and to reinforce them. To *rebalance* is to change the patterns so that fewer restraints and barriers are present and the continuous change can flow more freely. To *unfreeze* after the rebalancing is to innovate and find new ways of ensuring continuous change. These new ways evolve from habits of continuing to look for means of improving the manner in which work gets done and of continuing to strengthen the critical interdependencies of organization members. An example of this notion about continuous change is provided in Chapter 4, in the case of the professional services firm.

This differentiated way of considering organization change is likely to endure. The mounting evidence is impressive that change in organizations does indeed take one, but rarely both, of these two paths.

Summary

In a sense, this chapter has focused on reviewing the reviews of organization change research and theory over the past quarter of a century. Earlier, the lament was about not having enough or the right kind of research to draw any significant conclusions. Later, the argument was made that organization change research followed the wrong model—that is, normal science (Beer & Walton, 1987). Action science would be better. Then Porras argued, quite appropriately, that we had no adequate theory about how organization change actually works, and he proposed a framework and process (see Figure 6.3) as a remedy (Porras & Silvers, 1991). Two problems arise from Porras's proposed model/theory. One is its linearity and the other is his proposed sequence of the process, that is, cognition preceding behavior. Theory and research were cited as support for considering organization change more in terms of complex nonlinearity and in terms of behavior typically preceding thought, attribution, meaning, and related cognitive concepts.

Finally, it seems quite clear today that a highly useful way to understand, if not lead and manage organization change more effectively, is to consider whether the change is, or needs to be, episodic or continuous.

To end on a pithy statement: To assume that change in organizations is or can be rational is irrational.

7

Conceptual Models
for Understanding
Organization Change

In the previous chapter, organization change was considered as either discontinuous (revolutionary, or transformational) or continuous (evolutionary, or transactional). This kind of distinction can be useful in helping us understand and diagnose the nature of the required organization change. As a result, one is in a better position to know what types of action to take. If the required change is discontinuous ("a big leap"), then we need to concentrate on the organization's interface with its external environment, on the organization's mission, goals, and strategy, and probably on the organization's culture as targets for change. If, on the other hand, the required change is not as revolutionary and more resembles continuous improvement, then our focus may be on targets in the organization such as the reward system, information technology, work flow processes, or management practices.

The purpose of this chapter is to consider additional categorical concepts for understanding organization change more thoroughly, namely, content, or *what* to change, and process, or *how* to bring about the change. In Chapter 5, we considered the phenomenon of resistance to change. A link between the concepts and ideas presented there and in this chapter can be expressed as follows: The *content* of resistance is the threat of loss, and the threat of loss of control is *process*. In this chapter, we also consider (a) organizational change process frameworks in terms of both theory and practice and (b) a select group of 10 "mini-theories" about organizational behavior that are germane to organization change.

Content: What to Change

What to change usually (not always) begins with the organization's leaders being confronted with some event or shift in the organization's external environment. Examples include an economic downturn, the bursting forth of a new technology (e.g., from analog to digital), an announcement of a merger between two competitor organizations, the passage of new legislation, or some new mandate by a political leader, as in the case of Prime Minister Thatcher's decision to change British Airways (BA) from a government-owned airline to a public-owned corporation. Such modifications in the organization's external environment then cause senior executives and their constituents to consider what to change about their organization to meet the new challenges and to survive as an organization. This may mean a change as significant as changing the organization's mission, purpose, and raison d'être or as straightforward and less complicated as discontinuing certain products and/or services without changing the overall mission and purpose.

A useful perspective regarding what to change comes from the management guru and business/organizational observer and philosopher, Peter Drucker. In his 31st article written for the *Harvard Business Review,* Drucker (1994) argued that highly successful companies that do the right things often end up doing them "fruitlessly," and decline ensues. This "paradox," as Drucker called it, set the stage for his articulation of what he labeled "the theory of the business." This theory is a set of assumptions about how a given business can succeed in a particular environment and marketplace. According to Drucker, these assumptions "shape any organization's behavior, dictate its decisions about what to do and what not to do, and define what the organization considers meaningful results" (p. 96). Notice that in this quotation, he used the word *what* three times. In times of trouble for a business, Drucker was arguing that *what* to change is the theory of the business—the fundamental beliefs and assumptions about what causes what and how success is defined. Companies therefore get into trouble when "The assumptions on which the organization has been built and is being run no longer fit reality" (Drucker, 1994, p. 95). Drucker went on to cite IBM, General Motors, and Deutsche Bank as examples.

According to Drucker (1994), a theory of the business has three parts:

1. Assumptions about the external environment of the organization, such as society and its structure, the market, the customer, and technology

2. Assumptions about the organization's mission, purpose, and raison d'être

3. Assumptions about the organization's core competencies, that is, the skills and abilities required to accomplish the mission

Drucker (1994) followed with his four specifications of, or criteria for, a valid theory of the business:

1. The three assumptions listed above must fit reality.

2. All three assumptions must fit or be congruent with one another.

3. The theory of the business must be known and understood by all organizational members.

4. The theory needs to be tested constantly.

Although Drucker (1994) did not label his ideas as such, it should be clear that he was addressing transformational or discontinuous change. His argument was that tinkering with the organization when its theory of the business is out of sync with what is going on in the external environment will inevitably lead to business failure. Also implied in Drucker's thesis is that organizations that have experienced considerable success in the past (his examples of IBM and General Motors) tend to hold on to their assumptions and theory entirely too long, that is, persisting when reality has already changed.

A recent study by Audia, Locke, and Smith (2000) supports this implication quite dramatically. Moreover, the title of their article begins with "The Paradox of Success." Their research consisted of two studies. One was archival, based on data from the airline and trucking industries over a 10-year period, and the other was a laboratory experiment. Their studies showed the following (Audia, Locke, & Smith, 2000):

> That greater past success led to greater strategic persistence after a radical environmental change, and such persistence induced performance declines. The laboratory study also demonstrated that dysfunctional persistence is due to greater satisfaction with past performance, more confidence in the correctness of current strategies, higher goals and self-efficacy, and less seeking of information from critics. (p. 837)

In summary, the content of change can consist of a variety of possibilities. Again, we can use the discontinuous category of change compared with the continuous category to differentiate content. With discontinuous change, our content is associated more with transformational factors, such as the external environment, mission, purpose, and strategy, or in Drucker's (1994) language, the fundamental assumptions or theory of the business. With continuous change, our content is concerned more with day-to-day operations and transactions, and the focus would therefore be on factors such as products and services, work flow processes, organizational structure, and information technology. The model by Porras and Robertson (1992) presented in Chapter 6 provides examples of the content for organization change: vision, technology, physical setting, organizational arrangements (structure), and on-the-job behavior. The organizational models covered in the following chapter also provide further examples of content: purposes, rewards, helpful mechanisms, leadership, tasks, informal organization (culture), mission, and strategy.

Finally, it is interesting to note that the more successful an organization has been in the past, the more senior managers seem to hold on to the business content that got them to their current level of success—in spite of radical changes in their organization's external environment. General Motors' insistence on business as usual when the Japanese were encroaching on their territory is a case in point. It is no doubt safe to conclude that change comes the hardest for organizations (and individuals, for that matter) that have experienced success in the past. The values of staying in touch with one's external environment and listening to criticism cannot be overemphasized when it comes to change that is needed for future success and survival.

Process: How to Change—A Theoretical Framework

In an attempt to integrate the pluralistic quality of theory about organization change, Van de Ven and Poole (1995), using the key words *change* and *development,* conducted a computerized literature search across disciplines and turned up over 1 million articles. They reviewed about 200,000 titles and read about 200 of the articles. They identified 20 different theories of development and change and clustered them into four "ideal-type" development theories, or four primary schools of thought. These four are useful in that they help us understand better, at least broadly speaking, the primary ways to consider process: the *how,* and sometimes the *why* as well, of organization change. We will now briefly summarize the four primary theories or schools of thought that Van de Ven and Poole identified, that is, life cycle, teleological, dialectical, and evolutionary theories.

Life Cycle Theory

This school of thought states that an organization "follows a single sequence of stages or phases, which is cumulative (characteristics acquired in earlier stages are retained in the later stages) and conjunctive (the stages are related such that they derive from a common underlying process)" (Van de Ven & Poole, 1995, p. 515). Change is inevitable; life cycle theory rests on the metaphor of organic growth: In other words, an organization is like a living organism. Although an organization may undergo change as it passes through its phases, perhaps in both form and function, its identity nevertheless is maintained throughout the process.

Although Van de Ven and Poole (1995) classified Greiner's model of organization development as both life cycle and dialectical, his model is easy to understand in life cycle terms. Greiner (1972) posited five stages in an organization's life cycle: creativity (the start-up phase), direction (more focus needed), delegation (as organization grows larger), coordination (with differentiation of functions, integration is then required), and collaboration (working together more effectively as a total entity). As Van de Ven and Poole (1995) described the other critical ingredient of the Greiner model, "Each of these stages culminates in a different dialectical crisis (of leadership, autonomy, control, red tape and "?" [Greiner's symbol for not knowing what this stage would be], which propels the organization into the next stage of growth." (p. 530).

Others have proposed life cycle models of organization development and change, for example, Adizes (1979) and Kimberly and Miles (1980), but Greiner's remains popular with managers because his framework is easily understood. The Greiner model is popular with managers also because it seems to relate closely to their experiences.

Teleological Theory

Rooted in the philosophical doctrine of teleology, this form of organization development assumes that an organization is purposeful and adaptive. Accordingly, the development of an organization is toward a goal or some end state. As Van de Ven and Poole (1995) pointed out,

"Proponents of this theory view development as a repetitive sequence of goal formulation, implementation, evaluation, and modification of goals based on what was learned or intended by the entity" (p. 516). So, even though goals may be reached, new ones are set, usually as a function of changes in the external environment. Establishing an organizational mission statement, creating a new vision, planning a different strategy, or simply listing a set of goals are all examples of application of this school of thought. The point is this: Organizations change as goals and purposes change. The process is ongoing and iterative; in other words, an organization is never static or in permanent equilibrium.

Dialectical Theory

The basic assumption with this school of thought is that organizations exist "in a pluralistic world of colliding events, forces, or contradictory values that compete with each other for domination and control" (Van de Ven & Poole, 1995, p. 517). Organization change occurs as two different points of view collide and some resolution is reached. The desired resolution is a creative synthesis of the two opposites, or at least the two sufficiently different positions. As Van de Ven and Poole (1995) stated, "There is no assurance that dialectical conflicts produce creative syntheses" (p. 517). In the business world, acquisitions and hostile takeovers often represent resolutions that are not necessarily creative. A creative synthesis is usually mutually beneficial, but this kind of outcome is quite rare. So, organization change that occurs as a consequence of a dialectical process may be good or bad.

Evolutionary Theory

As might be expected, this school of thought assumes that organization change proceeds, as in biological evolution, according to a continuing cycle of variation, selection, and retention among organizations competing for resources in a designated marketplace or environment. "Competition for scarce environmental resources between entities [organizations] inhabiting a population [particular environment] generates this evolutionary cycle" (Van de Ven & Poole, 1995, p. 521). Organization change, then, is explained in terms of an ongoing, evolving process. As in other theories, the organization is never static; there is no permanent equilibrium. It's as if organizations have no choice but to change. As in biological entities, evolution is constant. Again, a living

Table 7.1   Four Process Schools of Thought for Organization Change

	Life Cycle	Teleological	Dialectic	Evolutionary
Key metaphor	Organic growth	Purposeful cooperation	Opposition, conflict	Competitive survival
Event progression	Linear and irreversible sequence of prescribed stages	Recurrent, discontinuous sequence of goal setting, implementation, and adaptation of means to reach end state	Recurrent, discontinuous sequence of confrontation, conflict, and synthesis	Recurrent, cumulative and probabilistic sequence of variation, selection, and retention

organism is the primary metaphor for understanding an organization according to this theoretical perspective about process.

Borrowing a couple of dimensions (metaphor and event progression) from Van de Ven & Poole (1995, Table 1, p. 514), we summarize these four process schools of thought in Table 7.1.

Van de Ven and Poole (1995) proceeded to argue quite logically and persuasively that although these four schools of thought may seem discrete, in reality, they are not. By considering interplay among these schools and examining underlying assumptions, the authors developed "a framework of 16 possible explanations of organization change and development" (Van de Ven & Poole, 1995, p. 534). Of these 16 explanations or theories, 4 are the original ones—life cycle, teleological, dialectic, and evolutionary. The remaining 12 combinations of 2 being together form, for example, an "organizational punctuated equilibrium theory" (Tushman & Romanelli, 1985); a theory combining 3 of the original 4 explanations, for example, Weick's (1979) book on *The Social Psychology of Organizing*, or perhaps a theory that uses all 4: human development progressions (Riegel, 1976). Van de Ven and Poole further argued that these schools of thought, although historically important and helpful to our greater understanding of organization change and development, are largely linear in nature; and organizational researchers have treated seemingly random patterns of change as "noise" and "error" distributions that "mess up" their experiments. Van de Ven and Poole (1995) conclude that a major extension of their framework of 16 explanations of organization change and development "is to develop and study nonlinear dynamics systems models . . . [and to examine] chaos as an alternative explanation" (p. 535). This conclusion, of course, relates to themes we address in Chapters 4 and 6.

Process: How to Change—Practice Frameworks

In this section, we move from a more macro, theoretical way of considering the change process to a more applied, practice-oriented way of considering the change process. In other words, the focus is more specifically on the *how,* the actual steps involved, the sequence of these steps, and related interventions. The general flow of this section will be from simple to more complex.

Early in the process of initiating organization change, it is important to determine as clearly as possible how ready people in the organization are to accept and implement the change. Another way of expressing this question of degree of readiness for change is to consider if and/or how resistant to the proposed change people who will be directly affected may be. A way of assessing this degree of readiness is to conceptualize the potential according to what the social and psychological costs may be. David Gleicher's formula for determining these costs is referred to by Beckhard and Harris (1977) as follows:

$$C = (ABD) > X$$

Where C = change, A = level of dissatisfaction with the status quo, B = clear desired state, D = practical first steps toward the desired state, and X = the cost of change. In other words, there has to be enough dissatisfaction with the current state of affairs (A) for someone to be mobilized for the change. The various subsystems need to have clear enough goals (B); otherwise the "cost" (X) is too high. For each subsystem, there needs to be some awareness of practical first steps (D) to move, if movement is to take place. (pp. 25-26)

Both clarity of change direction and motivation are necessary for acceptance and commitment on the part of organizational members.

We will now proceed to more specificity regarding the process of change implementation.

Lewin's Three Steps

During the World War II era, Kurt Lewin (see Chapters 2 and 3 for other references to his work) and his associates (Lewin, 1947) conducted a number of studies as part of a larger effort at changing food habits in line with war needs at the time, that is, to influence people to eat less desirable but cheaper foods (whole wheat bread instead of white, beef briskets and organs instead of steak, etc.). After 4 years of studies and action research projects, Lewin concluded that to be successful, the change process needed to follow a three-step procedure: (a) unfreezing, (b) moving, and (c) freezing at a new level (or refreezing). The first step is to *unfreeze* the present level of behavior. This step, according to Lewin, can take many forms and needs to be tailored as much as possible to the particular situation. To reduce prejudice, for example, this first step of unfreezing might be catharsis (Allport, 1945) or participation in a series of sensitivity training sessions (Rubin, 1967). At the organizational level, the unfreezing step could be one of presenting data to organizational members that show a sizable gap between where they are and where they need to be to meet growing demands, for example, in their marketplace, where customer service is slipping dramatically. The second step involves *moving* toward the new desired level of behavior. With respect to the organizational gap example, moving might take the form of (a) training managers to behave differently toward their subordinates in order to improve customer service (see Schneider, 1980, for research related to this example) or (b) implementing action plans for changing work processes or improving information systems. The *refreezing* step establishes ways to make the new level of behavior "relatively secure against change" (Lewin, 1947, p. 344). This step could include installing a new reward system to reinforce the new, desired behavior (Lawler, 1977) or restructuring certain aspects of the organization so that new accountability arrangements and new ways of measuring performance are put into place.

Lewin's Three Steps Expanded: Schein

Schein (1987) has appropriately pointed out that although Lewin's steps may convey discrete actions, the opposite is true. Schein states that the steps (he calls them *stages)* overlap and the process is more elaborate and complicated than a mere three steps. He stayed with three stages, but within each one, he expanded and elaborated.

Stage 1: Unfreezing. Creating motivation and readiness to change. There are at least three ways of unfreezing an organization, according to Schein (1987):

- Disconfirmation or lack of confirmation: Demonstrate a need for change by, for example, surfacing organizational members' dissatisfaction by showing that the customer base is eroding and something must be done to stem the tide, or by providing information about radical change in the organization's external environment that threatens the survival of the enterprise.

- Induction of guilt or anxiety: When organizational members are faced with data that show a gap between what is and what would be better, they are likely to be motivated by guilt feelings and general anxiety to reduce the gap and to take action toward goals that would make things better.

- Creation of psychological safety: Creating disconfirmation and inducing guilt and anxiety are not enough to accomplish the unfreezing stage, however. Schein contends that for people to move to the second stage and actually change, they must believe that doing so will not cause feelings of embarrassment, humiliation, or loss of face or self-esteem. Organizational members need to feel worthy and psychologically safe, that is, to have no fear of retribution or punishment for embracing the change.

Stage 2: Changing. This stage involves "cognitive restructuring," according to Schein (1987). What he meant is that organizational members need to see things differently than before and as a result of this different view, must act differently. Two processes are necessary to accomplish this stage:

1. Identification with a new model, mentor, leader, or even a consultant to "begin to see things from that other person's point of view. If we see another point of view operating in a person to whom we pay attention and respect, we can begin to imagine that point of view as something to consider for ourselves" (Schein, 1987, p. 105).

2. Scanning the environment for new, relevant information. Has this kind of change worked in other organizations? Are we in danger of reinventing the wheel? Can we learn from others' experiences? Action involved here may mean inviting outsiders with relevant experience to visit us and share their stories or a select group of organizational members attending relevant conferences to gain new information about this kind of change. Or it could take the form of sending the top executive team to Japan to study their experiences with quality improvement and related initiatives, as was the case with SmithKline Beecham in the early days of their merger (Bauman, Jackson, & Lawrence, 1997).

Stage 3: Refreezing. As indicated earlier, this stage involves the integration of the change for organizational members and for Schein (1987), has two parts:

1. Personal and individual: helping the organizational member feel comfortable with the new behavior that is required to make the change succeed, that is, to link the new behavior with one's self-concept. Schein noted that this process

requires considerable practice: trying out the new behavior, getting feedback, and then being rewarded when one gets it right.

2. Interpersonal: making sure that the new behavior fits well with others who are significant in the organization and that these other significant individuals (organizational members that one works with closely) are comfortable with the new behavior from the "changed" person. In other words, "If I change, you will also need to change if we are to work together effectively in the future."

Phases of Planned Change

Ronald Lippitt, a protégé of Lewin's, also elaborated on the three-step procedure (Lippitt, Watson, & Westley, 1958). Working with his two colleagues, Lippitt expanded the three steps to five phases. Supporting Schein's point, some 30 years later, Lippitt and his colleagues thought that *phase* was a better term to use, because overlap occurs across the three steps. The five phases are as follows:

1. Development of a need for change (unfreezing)

2. Establishment of a change relationship between the change agent (consultant, usually external to the organization or perhaps an internal organizational member who is championing and leading the change effort) and the client organization

3. Working toward change (moving)

4. Generalization and stabilization of change (refreezing)

5. Achieving a termination in the relationships, that is, ending the "change contract" between the consultant-change agent and the client organization

Lippitt, Watson, and Westley (1958) wrote an entire book about these five phases, and the simple listing above gives only a flavor, not the depth, of their thinking. For more specificity regarding their five phases, see their original book, or summaries provided by Burke (1994) and by Hornstein, Bunker, Burke, Gindes, and Lewicki (1971).

Organization Change as a Transition

Many practitioners and scholars have written about the concept of transition as a way of understanding the process of organization change. For our purposes, that is, considering the more applied ways of thinking about change, we will briefly consider two models that are based on this idea of transition.

Beginning with what they call "demand system," meaning forces in the environment that initiate the process of organization change, Beckhard and Harris (1987) described their transition model as involving the following:

> Three distinct conditions: the *future state*, where the leadership wants the organization to get to; the *present state*, where the organization currently is; and the *transition state*, the set of conditions and activities that the organization must go through to move from the present to the future. (p. 29)

These authors pointed out that organization change and the leading and managing thereof "is not a neat, sequential process" (Beckhard & Harris, 1987, p. 30). After the demand system has been delineated, the next step is to define the need for change and then to determine whether to change. If the choice is to change, Beckhard and Harris defined their process for bringing it about, defining the future state, assessing the present state, and—where most time and energy is spent— working on getting from the present to the future, the transition state. *Transition management,* as Beckhard and Harris labeled it, is a process of conducting activities such as planning a "road map" for the change effort. This involves determining where to intervene first, choosing transition technologies, such as pilot program, educational interventions, and confrontation meetings (Beckhard, 1967), and creating transition management structures, for example, a parallel structure for change purposes that operates alongside the traditional structure. See, for example, Miller (1978).

A second transition model comes from the popular writings of William Bridges (1980). His model is an individual one, not one for organizations (see Chapter 5 for this perspective on Bridges), but can be easily applied to organization change. Moreover, his three phases are not unlike Lewin's three-step procedure. The first phase for Bridges is *endings,* the process of letting go of the past and of the previous ways of doing things. Bridges emphasized the need for people to achieve some closure about the past and to celebrate what was good about it. Bridges labeled the second phase as the *neutral zone,* a period of time in which the individual is neither in the past nor in the new phase. This phase is experienced as a state of limbo and emotional disconnection and as ambiguous and often anxiety provoking. There are individual differences regarding the time it takes for people to let go of the past and embrace the new, but it is a phase the leaders of change need to be sensitive to and not rush people through. Bridges calls the third and final phase *new beginnings,* the time when organizational members start to focus on new goals and priorities, begin to try the requisite new behaviors, and are psychologically prepared to move ahead. Again, patience on the part of change leaders is needed, because as people try new behaviors and skills, mistakes will be made and corrective action will be required.

Although simple in concept, the transition models of Beckhard and Harris and Bridges nevertheless illustrate the complexities of large-scale organization change. Together, these models help us to be clearer about the importance of understanding organization changes at multiple levels all at the same time.

In summary, it should be recognized that these process models of organization (and individual) change, beginning with Lewin in the 1940s, are sequential—steps, stages, or phases—and they are helpful for planning and managing a change effort. This sequential planning in linear and causal terms can be useful: If we do A, B is likely to follow; if Y happens, it will likely be a consequence of X. This mode of thinking helps us to make sense out of complex, seemingly unrelated organizational behavior. Taking this way of thinking too literally, however, will often result in errors of judgment and being blindsided by unanticipated outcomes. We must bear in mind, therefore, that as organization change actually occurs, it is not sequential and is far more complex, ambiguous, and even "messier" than the models convey. Recall that in Chapter 1, the point was made that the implementation of organization change is nonlinear and often unpredictable. Also, as we discuss in Chapter 6, it is useful for us to be as clear as possible as to whether the change requires large-scale, radical, and discontinuous initiatives or whether instead, the change is more continuous, involving partial improvements to the organization, not major surgery. Although we need to think and plan these sequential ways even for discontinuous change processes, these models may be more directly applicable for continuous improvement initiatives because the latter do not, as a rule, take the form of punctuated equilibrium, but move along in a smoother, linear way.

We now move from models to theories. The models we have covered have addressed process and, although somewhat simple, they were fairly comprehensive in scope. The theories we will now cover address change in more circumscribed or limited ways. These theories address both the content and process of organization change but are partial, not comprehensive, statements. These "mini-theories" do not in all cases concern organization change per se, but they do inform us about the what and the how, the content and the process.

Mini-Theories Related to Organization Change

The purpose of this section is to provide brief coverage of 10 theories from psychology and organizational behavior that are applicable to organization change and development. The choice of the theories presented is selective. Other theories could have been covered. The intent is to show how theory can be applied to organization change via these selections. The intent is not to attempt an exhaustive listing of theories that might be applicable. For a broader coverage of these theories, see Burke (1994).

We begin with theories that address primarily the individual, then cover those that are more interpersonal and group focused, and conclude with theories that emphasize the larger system.

Individual Emphasis

Need Theory: Maslow/Herzberg

Although both Maslow (1954) and Herzberg (1966) based their theories on individual needs, they differed in two primary ways. Maslow's hierarchy of needs addressed motivation per se, whereas Herzberg's focused more on job satisfaction. The second difference is that Maslow's hierarchy was represented as a single continuum, from basic, creature comfort needs to self-actualization, whereas Herzberg posited two continua—one addressing dissatisfaction, from high to low, and the other addressing job satisfaction, from low to high. Herzberg's two-factor theory stated that so-called hygiene or maintenance factors, adequate versus inadequate (e.g., fringe benefits, good supervision, etc.), contributed to dissatisfaction; and motivator factors (e.g., degree of autonomy on the job, recognition, opportunity to achieve, etc.) contributed to job satisfaction. The *content* for applying Maslow's theory would be extent of motivation, and for Herzberg, it would be degree of job satisfaction. The *process* focus for both theories would be enriching individuals' jobs, that is, providing more autonomy, recognition, and achievement opportunities, and empowering employees by giving them more authority and decision-making responsibilities.

Expectancy Theory (Cognitive): Vroom/Lawler

The focus here regarding motivation is more on extrinsic behavior and less on internal or intrinsic needs. The theory is based on three assumptions (Lawler, 1973; Vroom, 1964):

1. People believe that their behavior is related to certain outcomes—the performance-outcome expectancy.

2. Outcomes (rewards) have different values for different people; for example, some are more attracted to money than others are.

3. People relate their behavior to certain probabilities of success—the effort-performance expectancy. "If I try harder, will the increased effort pay off for me?"

Thus, as stated in Burke (1994),

> People will be highly motivated when they believe that their behavior will lead to certain rewards, that these rewards are worthwhile and valuable and that they are able to perform at a level that will result in the attainment of the rewards. (p. 39)

The *content* for applying expectancy theory is both motivation and rewards, particularly the degree of effort put forth by organizational members, whether the reward system is the right one for most people and whether people see a strong link between their efforts and the rewards they receive. The *process* focus could be on changing both the way organizational members' performance is measured (i.e., attempting to ensure that people see the link between their behavior and how performance is measured) and the reward system, to ensure that organizational members (a) value the rewards they may receive and (b) see the link between their performance and the rewards they receive. To ensure that these processes work optimally, it is imperative that organizational members believe that the measuring and reward processes are administered in a fair and just manner.

Job Satisfaction: Hackman and Oldham

Grounded in both need and expectancy theories yet more specific and targeted, Hackman and Oldham's (1980) *content* emphasis is on three primary psychological states that affect employee satisfaction:

1. Experienced meaningfulness of the work itself

2. Experienced responsibility for the work and its outcomes

3. Knowledge of results, that is, performance feedback

The *process* focus, therefore, is on work and job design, that is, designing jobs and roles for organizational members that enhance these three psychological states and in doing so, increasing motivation and perhaps performance as well. *Perhaps* is inserted in this latter phrase because performance is often based more on ability than on motivation.

Positive Reinforcement: Skinner

B.F. Skinner was not exactly an organizational theorist, but he did indeed address organizational issues and the application of his empirically based theory when he wrote the book *Walden Two* (Skinner, 1948). Key to understanding Skinner and his work is to understand his emphasis on control, that is, control of one's environment. *Walden Two* describes a utopian community designed and operated strictly according to Skinner's principles of operant behavior and schedules of reinforcement. This book is fictional, of course, but is very clearly an application of Skinnerian theory and research. More recently and certainly not fictional, Skinner's principles were applied in a business setting, Emery Air Freight, in the early 1970s (see "At Emery Air Freight," 1973). His principles were applied carefully and as "close to the letter" as possible, and as a result, Emery realized an annual savings of $650,000.

The content for *change,* then, is the reward system, particularly the application of incentives on a partial positive-reinforcement basis. The *process* focus is on the work environment, with the intent of controlling the conditions of how employees are rewarded. The initial determination is to clarify the performance behaviors desired and then to administer positive reinforcement accordingly.

Group Emphasis

The Group as the Focus of Change: Lewin

Field theory is the succinct way of labeling Lewin's contribution. Borrowing concepts from physics, Lewin (1951) explained individual behavior as an interaction between a person's needs and personality and the field of forces impinging on the individual from the external environment. The key in this explanation is the matter of perception, how the individual perceives these forces—especially in terms of whether the forces are perceived to be imposed or induced or whether they are "owned" by the person, that is, directly affecting his or her needs. Forces that are perceived to be induced are usually resisted, whereas those that are owned by the individual are embraced. Lewin (1958) also distinguished between driving forces and restraining forces: *drivers* push an individual toward new behavior (e.g., higher productivity), and *restraining forces* inhibit new behavior. A driving force may be strong supervision toward greater productivity, and a restraining one may be a group norm that expects organizational members to conform to a certain level of productivity and perform no higher.

Content, for application of Lewin's theory, would be an analysis of perceived forces in the work environment and what people perceive the norms and values to be. The nature and degree of conformity to group standards (norms) represent Lewinian content as well. The *process* focus would be on (a) changing group norms, (b) reducing restraining forces instead of increasing driving forces (the latter increases resistance, after all), and (c) increasing owned forces and decreasing imposed forces. And finally (Burke, 1994),

> Adherence to Lewinian theory involves viewing the organization as a social system, with many and varied subsystems, primarily groups. We look at the behavior of people in the organization in terms of (1) whether their needs jibe with the organization's directions, usually determined by their degree of commitment, (2) the norms to which people conform and the degree of that conformity, (3) how power is exercised (induced vs. own forces), and (4) the decision-making process (involvement leading to commitment). (p. 43)

Changing Values Through the Group: Argyris

The value base for Argyris (1971) is largely represented by McGregor's (1960) theory Y, as opposed to theory X. By theory X, McGregor meant that managers hold certain assumptions about people in work organizations: that they are inherently lazy, require structure and direction, and given too much freedom, will not work responsibly. Theory Y assumptions, on the other hand, hold that people are not lazy, want to do a good job, do not require close supervision, and prefer work that is meaningful and challenging. Argyris contended that many managers and executives espouse Y values but behave according to X beliefs. This inconsistency between words and actions, particularly on the part of organizational leaders, causes mistrust, lower commitment, and poor morale on the part of employees, Argyris argued. He has written widely on such topics as the relationship of individual personality and organizational dynamics, organizational intervention theory and method, and organizational learning; but a core, if not *the* core, of his work is the degree of congruence between what he calls *espoused theory* and *theory in action* (Argyris & Schön, 1982). Argyris has often worked with top organizational executive groups and attempts to apply many of Lewin's principles regarding such areas as induced versus owned forces. See the previous section on Lewin, "Group Emphasis."

The *content* for Argyris (1971) are values, at least espoused values in the organization, the substance of decisions, and whether these decisions, when enacted, are congruent with spoken beliefs and values on the part of the top executive group. Argyris's *process* focus is on actual behavior of executives. The process may involve, for example, the recording of an executive group's meeting, analyzing the content of the meeting (problems discussed, decision debated and then made, etc.), and then reporting his analysis back to the group. This analysis often emphasizes the degree of congruence between statements and arguments made and subsequent action taken. Argyris used the theory Y, theory X concepts, and values of McGregor and his frame of reference. The overall change goal, then, is to reduce the gap between words and deeds.

The Group Unconscious: Bion

Originally trained as a psychiatrist and then as a psychoanalyst, Bion (1961) held the theory that a group has an unconscious as an individual does; this "collective unconscious," as he refers to it, operates parallel to the conscious group, or the work group. The work group has the purpose of task accomplishment, whereas the unconscious, or "basic assumption group," as he calls it, has the purpose of destroying the group leader. Bion's main issue, therefore, is authority: who has it and especially how it is exercised. The collective unconscious assumes that authority is to be resisted, destroyed, and then replaced with a new leader who will get it right—which according to Bion, never happens. The same dynamic continues regardless of the individual players. As long as the work group is dominant over the basic assumption group, productive outcomes can be realized. But if the group members wander from the task, frequently fight among themselves, form subgroups that are unintegrated with the total group, and overly defer to the leader instead of assuming task responsibility themselves, then the basic assumption mode has become dominant and the group will fail at task accomplishment.

The *content* for Bion is purely and simply the collective unconscious, that is, issues of authority. The *process* focus is to reduce the effect of the basic assumption mode and enhance the work group mode by staying focused on the task and being aware of the passage of time.

The Larger-System Emphasis

Participative Management—The One Best Way: Likert

Likert's main contributions are his linking-pin idea of management hierarchy and his four-system model of organizations (Likert, 1967). The latter is more relevant to our coverage.

Likert, perhaps best known for his agree-disagree, 5-point scale, "the Likert scale," categorized organizations according to management approach and declared four main categories (1967):

System 1   Autocratic management: top-down and exploitative.

System 2   Benevolent autocracy: not exploitative but still top-down. "We at the top know best and we will take care of you as long as you do your job."

System 3   Consultative management: Managers ask their people for their opinions, ideas, and suggestions but reserve the right to make the final decisions.

System 4   Participative management: Decisions involving policy and affecting large numbers of people are made in groups by consensus.

Likert (1967) then used seven behavioral functions within organizations to further describe and differentiate his four systems: leadership, motivation, communication, interaction and influence, decision making, goal setting, and control. The *content* for Likert was quite specific and clear: the four systems, or management approaches, and how they are manifested or practiced within each of the seven functions. Likert was just as specific and clear about *process*, which was the use of survey feedback methodology. His "Profile of Organizations" (1967), later called "Survey of Organizations," is a diagnostic questionnaire organized in terms of the questions surveyed according to the seven functions across the four-system models (i.e., management approaches). Answers by organizational members are profiled according to the four systems in two ways: what the respondents perceive the current situation to be and what they believe their ideal responses would be. Usually, the respondents' profiles are centered around System 2 or 3 regarding their current perceptions, and the more ideal is typically clustered around System 4. In other words, a gap between what is and what should be is established. Organizational members' motivation, it is contended, is quite naturally a desire to reduce the gap.

Likert (1967) not only argued that there is one best way to manage—according to System 4—and established what he considered to be the relevant *content,* he also posited one best *process,* that is, survey feedback. In an organization change effort, then (Burke, 1994),

> Likert's approach is highly data-based, but the diagnosis is largely limited to the functions he deems important. Once the survey data are collected, they are given back in profile form to organizational family units—to a boss and his or her team. . . . Although organizational change agents may be uncomfortable with Likert's one best way and may prefer an approach that is more contingent and perhaps more flexible, they can be very sure of the direction and the objectives of the change effort. (p. 48)

It All Depends: Lawrence and Lorsch

Unlike Likert, Lawrence and Lorsch are contingency theorists: There is no one best way for management, for strategy, for structure, or for how to deal with systems and processes in the organization. It all depends. Depends on what? you might reasonably ask. The one word that captures their point of view is *interface,* and they focus primarily on three forms (Lawrence & Lorsch, 1967): (a) the organization's relationships with its external environment, (b) relationships of units within the organization, and (c) the relationship, or implicit contract, between the organizational member and the organization.

The main contribution that Lawrence and Lorsch (1967) have made is their replication in the United States of a study conducted by Burns and Stalker (1961), in the United Kingdom. The respective studies showed that the most effective internal structure or organization design for a business-industrial enterprise depended on how stable or dynamic (rapidly changing) the organization's external environment or marketplace was. Moreover, how units within the organization should relate with one another, that is, degree and nature of information exchange, cooperative behavior, and how conflict should be handled, again depended on the nature and characteristics of the organization-environment interface. These interfaces in turn affected the individual-organization relationship, for example, how permanent and secure one's job might be, as opposed to having to change jobs and/or having to learn new skills.

If an organization's environment were rapidly changing, as in a high-tech industry, then the internal structure would need to be more decentralized than centralized so that many more organizational members would be in a position to monitor and keep up with changes in technology, what customers want, and changes in government regulations. If the external environment is not as volatile, then a more centralized internal structure may be more effective, that is, decisions being made at the top more than on a unit-by-unit basis.

Lawrence and Lorsch (1967) further argued that highly differentiated organizations, those that are structured largely by function or by highly separate business units, are likely to experience considerable conflict between functions, such as marketing versus manufacturing or between separate business units (the so-called silo effect). Thus, a premium is placed on managing and resolving conflict.

To summarize, the *content* for Lawrence and Lorsch (1967) are the interfaces and the nature and characteristics of these relationships, beginning with the environment-organization interface. The *process* would emphasize internal restructuring, conflict management and resolution, and how all of the above affect the relationship between management and the employee, the implicit set of expectations between these two parties within the organization.

The Organization as a Family: Levinson

Educated and trained originally as a clinical psychologist, with a lacing of Freudian psychoanalytic theory, it is not surprising that Levinson views an organization much like a nuclear family. His claim (Levinson, 1972) is that organizations replicate family dynamics with, for example, the CEO as father and ego-ideal, the head of human resources as mother, the nurturer, and the remaining executives who report directly to the CEO as siblings, with the requisite behavior of "sibling rivalry." It is also not surprising to learn that much of Levinson's consulting experiences have been with family-owned businesses.

Levinson (1972) believes that an organization has a personality (we might call it "culture"), just as an individual has a personality, and that the health or effectiveness of an organization, not unlike a person, depends on how well the various parts of the personality (id, ego, and superego, in Freudian terms) are integrated. Levinson refers to this process as "maintaining equilibrium."

For organization change and improvement, the relevant *content* for Levinson (1972) consists of first, the behavior of the top executive group, diagnosed according to family dynamics that are viewed through the lens of psychoanalytic theory; second, how the top-family dynamics affect and are replicated throughout the organization; and third, how integrated the various parts of the organization's personality are. Levinson (1975) also pays considerable attention to the levels of stress in an organization, especially among executives, and how stress is dealt with. Further content is what organizational members do with their energy, that is, the balance of energy directed toward goal accomplishment compared with that directed toward dealing with stress.

Levinson's *process* would be to conduct a "clinical history" of the organization, much as a physician or therapist would do with a patient, and then work with the top executive team, especially the CEO, to ensure better integration of the organization's personality and to direct as much energy as possible toward the task and less toward dealing with stress.

Summary

The 10 theories from psychology and organizational behavior that were selected for this chapter are those most applicable for organization change and development. These mini-theories address only certain aspects of organization change, and none are truly comprehensive. It is likely that at some stage in the future, a more comprehensive theory will emerge from domains such as cell biology, chaos theory, and/or nonlinear complex systems theory. But until that day, we must rely on combinations of theories that alone are unsatisfactory, but together can enhance our understanding.

Table 7.2 is an attempt to succinctly summarize the 10 theories covered in this section of the chapter.

The Content and Process of
Strategic Change in Organizations

At a more macro level of theory and research regarding organization change, Rajagopalan and Spreitzer (1997) reviewed the literature on strategic change and classified their findings into two schools of

Table 7.2 Summary of Primary Psychological and Organizational Behavior Theorists According to Their Perspectives, Content, and Process/Applications

Perspective	Theorist	Content Emphasis	Process/Application
Individual	Maslow; Herzberg	• Individual motivation • Job satisfaction	• Career development • Job enrichment
	Vroom; Lawler	• Individual expectancies and values • Individual motivation and rewards	• Performance measurement • Reward system design
	Hackman & Oldham	• Job satisfaction and psychological states regarding work	• Job and work redesign • Job enrichment
	Skinner	• Individual performance • Reward system	• Work environment • Incentive systems and reward system design
Group	Lewin	• Field of forces • Norms and values	• Reducing restraining forces • Changing conformity patterns • Increasing owned, decreasing imposed forces

(Continued)

Table 7.2 (Continued)

Perspective	Theorist	Content Emphasis	Process/Application
	Argyris	• Espoused values • Decision substance • Congruence of words and actions • McGregor's theory X, theory Y	• Analyzing content of executive meetings • Changing executive behavior toward greater congruence
	Bion	• Group unconscious • Issues of authority	• Reducing the adverse effects of the group unconscious and enhancing the work group mode
Larger system	Likert	• Management style and approach (four system model)	• Survey feedback • Moving toward participative management (System 4)
	Lawrence & Lorsch	• Organizational interfaces, especially external environment and internal structure	• Changing structure • Conflict management and resolution between organizational units
	Levinson	• Behavior of top executive group from perspective of family dynamics and psychoanalytic theory • Organizational personality (culture)	• Clinical history of organization • Integrating disparate parts of organizational personality • Stress management

thought regarding the research domains and the methodologies that researchers used: the *content* school and the *process* school. The former refers to antecedents and consequences of strategic change, the *what*, and the latter focuses on the role of managers, or *how* they seemed to have implemented strategic change. Rajagopalan and Spreitzer (1997) went on to point out that although these two schools of thought are related, they "have evolved independently with little theoretical or empirical synergy, resulting in theoretical and practical gaps in researchers' understanding of strategic change" (p. 48). These authors further classified the 59 studies that they reviewed from the 1980s and 1990s into four research and theoretical perspectives. The four categories represented their attempt to reduce the theoretical and practical gaps in understanding. In other words, they found the content-process distinction to be overly simplified. Rajagopalan and Spreitzer (1997) identified three distinct "theoretical lenses: the rational, learning, and cognitive lenses" (p. 50). Their fourth classification was various combinations of these three, which they appropriately labeled "multi-lens studies."

All three lenses, or perspectives, are alike in that they consider both content and process and are concerned with an organization's alignment with its external environment. In this regard, Rajagopalan and Spreitzer (1997) cast their perspectives well within the larger open system theory framework and stated, at least implicitly, that for survival, an organization is dependent on its external environment. Briefly defined, the three lenses, or perspectives, are as follows:

- Rational: This school of thought focuses more on content than on process and assumes that the external environment can be viewed objectively; that is, there are facts out there that can be obtained, classified, and acted on. Sequential planning and somewhat linear thinking also characterize this perspective.

- Learning: This perspective makes a different assumption about the external environment, that it is dynamic, changing and uncertain. Objectivity is very difficult. Although the change process (emphasized more than content) takes the form of a series of iterative actions that are evolutionary, not discontinuous, these actions are not linear or sequential. Managers must take change steps, learn from the consequences of these steps, and then take the next change step according to what was learned from the preceding steps.

- Cognitive: Like the learning perspective, this school of thought focuses more on process than content and focuses on *managerial cognitions,* such as core beliefs, causal maps, and knowledge structures. Managerial actions regarding strategic change are studied via this lens. Then, attributions are made retroactively as to what managers were apparently thinking to have caused such actions.

As part of the conclusions from their analysis of the 59 studies, Rajagopalan and Spreitzer (1997) stated,

> The rational lens perspective reflects a crucial aspect of the reality facing managers, namely, that changes in strategies must match the requirements of a firm's environmental and organizational contexts in order to be successful. . . . The learning and cognitive lens perspectives provide value to the rational lens perspective because they help researchers to understand (a) *why* different firms respond differently to a similar context (because of different cognitions and actions) and (b) *how* firms can maximize the effectiveness of their adaptive responses (through different managerial actions aimed at the environment and/or the organization). (p. 70)

This synopsis does not do justice to the depth of Rajagopalan and Spreitzer's work. Nevertheless, the point of the brief summary is twofold: First, their review of the strategic change literature demonstrated that content and process are intertwined. Discussing content as separate from process is like attempting to explain behavior as driven by either nature or nurture. It is not possible to explain causes of behavior as being one or the other. Conceptual distinction in this case may serve as an analytical and theoretical convenience but does not reflect reality. Second, a contribution that Rajagopalan and Spreitzer have made was to show us a little more clearly what the reality of strategic change is; in other words, strategic change in organizations is not exactly obvious, cannot be explained adequately from a single perspective, and is not a linear process (see Chapter 6).

Strategies for Effecting Change in Human Systems

In this final section of the chapter, we will consider, again briefly, broad strategies for change. In the previous section, with the summary of Rajagopalan and Spreitzer's (1997) work, the term *strategic* was used. Strategic, for this review, referred to the organization's strategy, that is, how the organization implemented its mission. Strategic therefore concerned content, although most of the studies they reviewed addressed both content and process.

Strategies for change covered in this final section refer more exclusively to process, or how change is implemented. Our coverage relies on the classic work of Chin and Benne (1985), because their thinking represents a broader and more comprehensive perspective than we have considered thus far and because it is an appropriate way to conclude and integrate the wide-ranging content of this chapter.

It should be noted initially that Chin and Benne (1985) discussed strategies for change genotypically and in the context of *planned* change: a conscious, deliberate attempt to change an individual, a group, an organization, or community. They grouped their strategies into three categories. The first one, and, they argued, the one most frequently used, was what they called *empirical-rational* strategies. They labeled the second *normative-reeducative* and designated the third group of strategies as *power-coercive*. What follows is a definition of each of these three groups of strategies for effecting change.

Empirical-Rational Strategies

The fundamental assumption underlying this group of strategies is that people are rational and that they will follow their rational self-interest once it is made apparent to them. As Chin and Benne (1985) put it,

> A change is proposed by some person or group which knows of a situation that is desirable, effective, and in line with the self-interest of the person or group, organization, or community which will be affected by the change. Because the person (or group) is assumed to be rational and moved by self-interest, it is assumed that he (or they) will adopt the proposed change if it can be rationally justified and if it can be shown by the proposer(s) that he (or they) will gain by the change. (p. 23)

There are six strategies within this empirical-rational group, according to Chin and Benne (1985):

1. Basic research and dissemination of knowledge through general education: the strategy of knowledge building and general education to widely spread the results of studies so that thinking people will understand, approve, and act in accordance.

2. Personnel selection and replacement: The difficulty of getting knowledge into practice may be due to certain people occupying positions of responsibility who do not take appropriate action. In other words, the wrong people are in these positions and need to be replaced. This strategy comes from industrial psychology.

3. Systems analysts as staff and consultants: In this case, we have experts who deliver knowledge in a rational and systematic manner (often via computers, which is even "more" rational), the assumption being that their expertise is unique, highly technical, and specialized; therefore, they know best. This strategy is represented by traditional management consulting.

4. Applied research and linkage systems for diffusion of research results: Chin and Benne used the words *applied research;* we could also use *action research.* In any

case, what is meant here is the use of sound research methodology, data gathering, and analysis in the service of promoting change. The research conducted is highly targeted, and the changes are data driven. The assumption is that these kinds of data will be accepted for change because the methodology is steeped in the scientific method.

5. Utopian thinking as a strategy of changing; Perhaps the best example of this strategy has already been mentioned in this chapter, that is, Skinner's *Walden Two* (1948). The point is that utopian thinking is an effort to extrapolate from science to a future and better vision for society, community, or an organization.

6. Perceptual and conceptual reorganization through the classification of language: Enemies of a rational-empirical strategy are superstitions and myths. One way to counter this type of enemy is to purify language. Experts here are people disciplined in semantics. The assumption is that experts in semantics can "see more correctly, communicate more adequately and reason more effectively and thus lay a realistic common basis for action and changing" (Chin & Benne, 1985, p. 31). For example, Hayakawa (1941), a prominent semanticist of his time, sought ways of clarifying and correcting the names of things and processes, according to Chin and Benne (1985).

Names associated with this group of strategies include Thomas Jefferson, Horace Mann, Henry Murray, E.L. Thorndike, Frederick Taylor, B.F. Skinner, and S.I. Hayakawa.

Normative-Reeducative Strategies

Change agents adopting this group of strategies would accept the premise that human beings are rational and intelligent. But as important—if not more so—is the assumption that people conform and are committed to sociocultural norms. Undergirding these norms are individual beliefs, attitudes, and values. Thus (Chin & Benne, 1985),

Change in a pattern of practice or action, according to this view, will occur only as the persons involved are brought to change their normative orientations to old patterns and develop commitments to new ones. And changes in normative orientations involve changes in attitudes, values, skills, and significant relationships, not just changes in knowledge, information, or intellectual rationales for action and practice. (p. 23)

An application of this strategy would be the T-group, or sensitivity training. Further assumptions state that people are more active than passive in the attempts to satisfy needs and that our interaction with the environment is transactional, that is, seeking information and gratification from the environment and attempting to influence the interactive process.

There are two primary strategies within this normative-reeducative group, and they have the following in common:

- The client system is heavily involved in the change process—change is *not* imposed.
- The problem the client is facing is not always assumed to be a technical one but may have more to do with norms, values, and attitudes, thus requiring reeducation.
- Nonconscious factors may need to be surfaced.
- Applying methods and concepts from the behavioral sciences is primary.

These are the two primary strategies within this group:

1. Improving the problem-solving capabilities of a system. Chin and Benne (1985) stated that organization development (OD), as based on the thinking and practice of Kurt Lewin, was the major representation of this strategy. Also, later, the work of Argyris and Schön (1978) introduced the concept of organizational learning with their ideas of *single-loop learning,* or fixing problems, and *double-loop learning,* or fixing problems plus learning more about the problem-solving process. Double-loop learning, then, is much like what Chin and Benne were describing with this change strategy.

2. Releasing and fostering growth in the persons who make up the system to be changed. Those who promote this strategy tend to view the individual as the basic unit within an organization, group, or community. That individual's growth and development take precedence. The work of Maslow, summarized earlier in this chapter, and McGregor's theory Y and theory X have been highly influential. Also, the sensitivity training (T-group) movement has been a significant lever for their strategy of change. In addition to Maslow and McGregor, other names associated with the normative-reeducative strategy include John Dewey, Sigmund Freud, Kurt Lewin, Warren Bennis, Eric Trist, Carl Rogers, Rensis Likert, Chris Argyris, and Bradford, Benne, and Lippitt of the NTL sensitivity-training era.

Power-Coercive Strategies

This group of strategies is based on the use of power in whatever form it may take: political, nonviolent resistance, and so on (Chin & Benne, 1985):

The influence process involved is basically that of compliance of those with less power. . . . Often the power to be applied is legitimate. . . . thus the strategy may involve getting the authority of law or administrative policy behind the change to be effected. (p. 23)

The source of power in the rational-empirical approach is knowledge, but here, the sources are more likely to be political and economic sanctions for lack of compliance to the proposed change. Chin and Benne (1985) describe three strategies within this group:

1. *Nonviolence:* Names that immediately spring to mind are Mohandas Gandhi and Martin Luther King Jr. Coercion is the prime lever, but conducted nonviolently, often dividing the opposition via moral conviction, perhaps combined with economic sanctions (e.g., boycotting certain commercial enterprises).

2. *Use of political institutions:* Coercion here does not necessarily involve oppression, provided a democratic process can be sustained. A recent example of this strategy was the use of both state (Florida) and federal courts to resolve the Bush versus Gore presidential election. This form of change, even though enacted via law and legislation, can nevertheless feel oppressive to those being affected.

3. *Changing via the recomposition and manipulation of power elites:* Chin and Benne (1985) cite Karl Marx as a classic example of this strategy, in that he believed strongly in a classless society and in overcoming the power of the ruling class. This strategy is largely economically based and dependent on large numbers of people organizing, as in unions, to become a power of production in society.

In addition to Marx, representative others included within the power-coercive group of strategies are C. Wright Mills, Bayard Rustin, and Saul Alinsky. For more specific coverage of these three broad strategies of change by Chin and Benne, see the volume by Hornstein et al. (1971).

Summary

The theme of this chapter has been the content-process distinction regarding organization change, with *content* referring to the *what,* or substantive, aspects of change (we found Drucker's, 1994, "theory of the business" instructive) and *process* referring to the *how*, or ways that change occurs or can occur. With respect to the latter, Van de Ven and Poole (1995) discussed four theories regarding the change process. Their coverage discussed how organization change happens through the lenses of life cycle, teleological, dialectical, and evolutionary theories or schools of thought, whether or not the change is deliberate and planned. They noted that although these four theories are useful to our understanding, they overlap, and in reality, organization change more often than not is explained via multiple theoretical lenses.

We then moved from theory to practice and considered different (but again overlapping) frameworks for understanding how change can occur. These frameworks, beginning with Lewin's (1958) three steps and the elaborations of Schein (1987) and Lippitt, Watson, and Westley (1958), address *planned* change, or deliberate initiatives.

Returning to theory again, this time summarizing mini-theories from the behavioral sciences that are relevant to but not necessarily directed toward organization change, we considered the 10 theories from both the content elements of each one and the process for change advocated, or at least implied.

The work of Rajagopalan and Spreitzer (1997) addressed both content and process, but they argued that the distinction, although useful for helping us understand strategic organization change more thoroughly, was, after all, not reflective of reality. They discussed three theoretical perspectives—rational, learning, and cognitive—and showed how these distinctions can be integrated for a deeper understanding of strategic change.

Finally, to help integrate much of the chapter, we considered the broad conceptual framework regarding process and planned change developed by Chin and Benne (1985). It is not obvious as to how Van de Ven and Poole's (1995) four developmental theories fit within Chin and Benne's framework. The former, though theoretical, is largely descriptive and explanatory, whereas the latter, which is also descriptive, is, however, about planned change and therefore has an advocacy component to the explanations. In a sense, both the Van de Ven and Poole and the Rajagopalan and Spreitzer contributions explain and enrich our understanding. Chin and Benne also seek explanation and understanding, but their understanding has more to do with the choices of change agentry when the objective is to deliberately bring about change in an organization, group, or community. With regard to the broad strategies of Chin and Benne, the practice frameworks of Lewin and others fit largely within the normative-reeducative group of strategies. Rajagopalan and Spreitzer's rational school of thought is similar to the rational-empirical group of strategies; their learning school of thought is similar to the normative-reeducative group of strategies; and their cognitive school of thought is similar to some combination of rational-empirical and normative-reeducative strategies.

8

Integrated Models for Understanding Organizations and for Leading and Managing Change

In the previous chapter, we considered organization change from a *content* perspective, *what* to change, and from a *process* perspective, *how* to bring about the change. These perspectives were addressed both theoretically, for example, Van de Ven and Poole (1995), and from the standpoint of what research has to tell us, for example, Rajagopalan and Spreitzer (1997).

An additional perspective regarding content and process can be made by returning briefly to a comparison of management consulting, as it is described at the end of Chapter 2, with the kind of organization change consulting implied so far in this book. What has been implied will become much more explicit in the remaining chapters. The point to be made here is that management consulting tends to be content focused—on *what* needs to be changed. The process of *how* to bring about the change is either ignored or left to others, especially the client, to implement. Effective consulting for organization change must focus on *both* content and process. The organizational frameworks examined in this chapter help to integrate content and process as we consider organization change in a more applied manner. In the title for Chapter 7, the term *model* was used, meaning conceptual model, in other words, frameworks and ways of thinking that emanate from theory.

A brief recap: In Chapter 6, we reviewed the organization change literature and in so doing, began to introduce the notion of an organizational model with the framework provided by Porras and Robertson (1992). In Chapter 7, we considered conceptual frameworks about organization change in terms of content and process. And now in the present chapter, we address organizational models per se.

In this chapter, the notion of a model is considered more in terms of "a representation of," that is, a graphic depiction of an organization. Theoretical concepts help us to understand organization change in a more profound way, for example, Gersick's (1991) use of *deep structure* as a means of distinguishing between fundamental and superficial changes in an organization. Organizational models as used in this chapter help us map and choreograph organization change in both content, or what to emphasize, such as organizational mission and purpose (see coverage of Drucker's theory of the business in the beginning section of Chapter 7), and process, or how to think through a planned change effort (see Lewin's three steps in Chapter 7, for example).

With the present chapter, we are gradually shifting from how to think about organization change to how to think about doing it. Referring once again to chapter titles, this time the modifier *integrated* is used. The organization models covered in this chapter address content explicitly and process either explicitly or implicitly. Our primary purpose is to present integrated models that help us to know more about what to change and how to do it. Application of theory and concepts is the raison d'être of this chapter and chapters that follow.

What Is an Organizational Model?

The first definition of *model* in dictionaries is something like a "standard to emulate, to imitate, or with which to compare." Additional definitions often include a "copy" or a "subject for an artist." But the usual second definition is the one meant here, that is, a "representation, to show the construction or appearance of something." By model, then, we mean a representation of an organization that more often than not is metaphorical in nature. One of the most commonly used metaphors is an organism, that is, any organization being depicted as an open system (see Chapter 3) that, like an organism, has input and output. The throughput is what the organization (organism) does with the input to produce an output, transforming input to output. With the organism, input is oxygen and other ingredients from the external environment being used and transformed into energy as well as waste. With the organization, it is money, people, and materials from the external environment being used and transformed into products and services that are thrust back into the external environment. Other metaphors for organizations have been a machine, brain, culture, political system, and psychic prison (Morgan, 1997).

Organization and organization change models were discussed in Chapter 6. A brief recap should remind us. With respect to the latter, early work by Friedlander and Brown (1974) provided a framework for understanding organization change that was based on two primary approaches: human-processual and techno-structural. Integrating these two approaches was the challenge, according to Friedlander and Brown.

Porras (1987) has provided an example of the former, an organization model grounded in open system theory and metaphorically based on an organism (see Chapter 6). Porras's model consists of four components: organizing arrangements, such as goals; social factors, such as culture; technology, such as tools; and physical settings, such as space. These four components plus organizational members' behavior form the throughput dimensions of his model.

The remainder of this chapter will be devoted to examining models like the one by Porras, that is, organizational models that integrate content and process and either imply or explicitly address ways of implementing change.

Why Use an Organizational Model?

An organizational model can be useful in a number of ways (Burke, 1994):

- *An organizational model can help to categorize.* When observing and/or collecting data about activities and behavior in an organization, we are faced with myriad informational bits, in the thousands, if not millions. Because we cannot deal with everything, what should we select out or pay attention to? A model can help to "chunk" and categorize the bits and pieces into a more manageable set of, say, 10 or 12 components instead of thousands.

- *An organizational model can help to enhance our understanding.* If we find that serious organizational problems exist with our model in, say, three of the categories but not in the remaining components, then we know more readily where we should take action than we might otherwise have chosen.

- *An organizational model can help to interpret data about the organization.* Assume that, in our model, we have the two categories of strategy and structure. As it turns out, most organizational models do include these two components. Suppose further that from data we have about the organization, we recognize that a serious problem exists with the structure, such as the hierarchical arrangement or decision-making authority, and we need to do something soon about this problem. We know from research (Chandler, 1962) that for optimum organizational effectiveness, there must be a strong link between the organization's strategy (i.e., how the mission and purposes are to be accomplished) and the structure. First, we must achieve clarity about strategy and then let this clarity help us to determine what the structure should be. Borrowing from the world of architecture, it means that form (structure) should follow function (strategy). So, we would not attempt to correct the structure until we were clear about what the organization's strategy would be for now and into the future. To concentrate only on the structure without due consideration initially of the strategy would fix nothing; in fact, it would make matters worse. An organizational model with these two components that are linked and in the proper order—strategy before structure—can help us to interpret our data appropriately and make the right decisions.

- *An organizational model can help to provide a common, shorthand language.* Instead of making statements such as "Well, it's the way we do things here; it's our beliefs and values," and so on, we can simply say "culture," and we will quickly know what we mean. A model, therefore, can help us to be more efficient with language.

- *An organizational model can help to guide action for change.* If an organizational model is arranged in such a way that (a) certain dimensions under certain conditions are more important or carry more leverage or "weight" than other dimensions and (b) an order or sequence of dimensions or organizational elements and/or functions is at least implicit, if not obvious, then change direction can become clear. That is, priorities about what to tackle first and what comes next, and so on, can establish a road map and implementation strategy for the overall change effort. The model described in the next chapter provides this kind of help.

An organizational model can indeed be useful, but there are at least two important caveats:

1. A model is only as good as the components selected and the arrangement of these components, that is, how each part relates to each of the others. As we know, organizations consist of many components. We need to categorize myriad parts into a workable number and decide which components are the most important.

2. Gareth Morgan (1997) stated the second caveat eloquently:

Metaphor is inherently paradoxical. It can create powerful insights that also become distortions as the way of seeing created through a metaphor becomes a way of *not* seeing. (p. 5)

Organization Models and Organization Change

By way of introduction to this main body of the chapter, it should be noted that many organization models exist. Most organizational theory textbooks provide one or more models. Mintzberg (1989), for example, like Morgan (1997), describes a variety of approaches: the entrepreneurial, machine, diversified, professional, and innovative organizations, and he has his own version (see Mintzberg's chapter on "Deriving Configurations"). Most of these models are descriptive and do not address organization change as such.

Many current models are based on the earlier thinking of Harold Leavitt (1965). His diamond-shaped organizational systems model helped to set the stage for thinking about organizations as interdependent *multivariate systems* (see Figure 8.1).

Although Leavitt's (1965) model was primarily descriptive, he did consider change by noting first that the four major components, *task* (the organization's purpose, e.g., to provide a service, to manufacture a product, etc.), *people* (those who carry out the task), *technology* (tools, computers, etc.), and *structure* (work flow, decision-making authority, communications, etc.) all interacted and were interdependent with one another. Second, Leavitt pointed out that change in any one of the components would result in change among the other three.

Leavitt's (1965) early version, although grounded in systems thinking—interdependence and each component affecting the other three—was not based on *open* system theory, at least not in its entirety. The model represents only throughput, or the transformation process, with no accounting for input or output.

The following three models are based on open system theory and come from the world of organization development, meaning that they

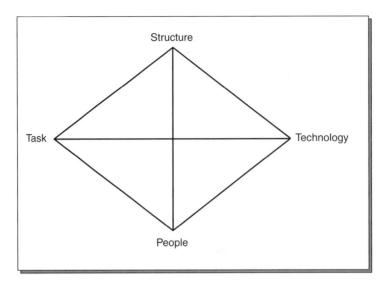

Figure 8.1. Leavitt's organizational systems model

address *what* to diagnose for change and consider, at least to some degree, how to intervene so that organization change can be implemented. These models represent an integration of content and process and have evolved from both practice and theory. Each author of these models has spent time and energy as an organizational consultant, and most have also taught graduate students in business schools and therefore have spent time and energy as academics. Thus, the models are grounded in both theory/research and change-consulting practice.

Weisbord's Six-Box Model

Marvin Weisbord (1976) must be more intuitive than most people, because he preferred a visual way of presenting his model. He relied on the organism metaphor as well as another one—the air traffic controller's radar screen. The six "blips" on the screen tell us which organizational components are the most important and by the intensity of the blips, where trouble spots might be. Weisbord was quick to clarify, however, that we must pay attention to the screen (organization) as a whole and avoid focusing too much on one particular box in the model (see Figure 8.2).

As the figure shows, the boxes are surrounded by a circle that represents the external environment, with arrows pointing in both directions,

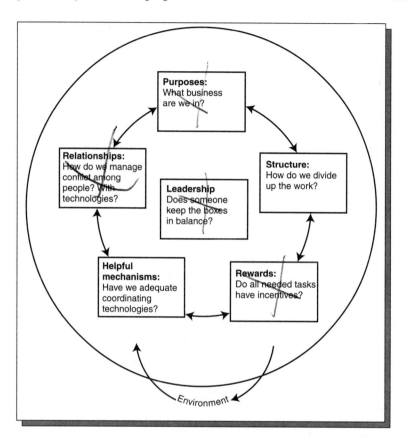

Figure 8.2. Weisbord's six-box organizational model
SOURCE: M. R. Weisbord, "Organizational Diagnosis: Six Places to Look for Trouble With or Without a Theory, 1976, *Group and Organization Studies, 1,* pp. 430 447. Reprinted by permission.

that is, the input and output representations. Weisbord (1976) is a proponent of understanding organizations both from the formal and informal perspectives. In other words, there is the formal system represented by, say, the structure—and the informal system imbedded in the organizational culture. But Weisbord stated that there are informal and formal aspects of each of the six boxes. So, for example, the structure box has its formal dimensions, the organization chart depicting lines of authority and accountability, and also has its informal dimensions, unspoken rules about how authority is actually exercised. Diagnostically, Weisbord argued, the extent of the gap between the formal and informal is highly important, and the action to be taken (the process side) is that of reducing the gap. Otherwise, the organization will remain more ineffective than effective.

To understand more clearly what Weisbord meant by or how he defined each box, it is instructive to consider the primary questions he asked about each one. The boxed questions in Figure 8.2 give us the general idea for each organizational component in the model. More specifically, Weisbord's (1976) primary question(s) for each box are as follows:

- Purposes: How clear are organizational members about the organization's purpose and mission? How supportive are they of the organization's purpose and mission?

- Structure: How adequate is the fit between the organization's purpose/mission and the internal structure that is designed to serve that purpose? (This question is similar to the strategy-structure link mentioned earlier.)

- Rewards: What are the similarities and differences between what the organization formally rewards and punishes and what organizational members actually believe they are rewarded or punished for doing?

- Helpful mechanisms: Which processes and procedures in the organization (planning, budgeting, information systems, etc.) actually help organizational members do their work, and which of them hinder more than help?

- Relationships: For this box, Weisbord was concerned with three categories: between individuals; between and among groups, units, and departments, and so forth; and between the person and the requirements of his or her job. He argued that, diagnostically, first, one should consider the quality of these relationships, and then one should consider the adequacy of the models for managing and dealing with conflict.

- Leadership: This box is at the center of the model because Weisbord believed that organizational leaders' jobs are to watch for blips on the radar screen regarding each of the other five boxes and to maintain a balance among them.

To summarize, Weisbord (1976) believed that regardless of the particular wording for these organizationally diagnostic questions, they need to be asked on two levels:

1. How large is the gap between the formal and informal dimensions of the organization, that is, the degree of fit between the individual and the organization?

2. What degree of discrepancy is there between "what is" and "what ought to be," that is, the congruence between the organization and its external environment?

Some of the strengths of Weisbord's six-box model are simultaneously its weaknesses: Although categorizing the many organizational dimensions into six boxes helps to simplify and provide quick understanding, organizations are far too complicated to be represented by only six categories. A strength of the model is the prominent position of the *leadership* box in the middle, signifying the coordinating function. If there are negative blips on this part of the radar screen, we know that we have serious issues. It is also clear that the *purposes* box links most directly with both the *relationships* and *structure* categories, but how does *purposes* link to the other boxes? The *leadership* box does imply a causal linkage to all the other five boxes, but no other causal linkages are suggested.

Weisbord's six-box model can be helpful for rapid and simple diagnostic purposes. It is also useful for client organizations that have little sophistication about systems thinking and the larger complexities of organizational dynamics. But when a deeper and more complicated diagnosis is required, these six boxes are simply not sufficient.

The Nadler-Tushman Congruence Model

Nadler and Tushman (1977) developed their model at about the same time Weisbord was creating his, and they made the same assumptions: that an organization is an open system and therefore is influenced by its environment (inputs) and also shapes its environment, at least to some extent, by its outputs. The Nadler-Tushman model will be presented according to the open system framework, starting with inputs, then outputs, and finally, the bulk of the model, which they refer to as the transformation process, or the throughput (see Figure 8.3 for a depiction of the model).

Inputs

Nadler and Tushman (1977) viewed inputs to the system as relatively fixed. The four they cited are the *environment,* the *resources* available to the organization, the organization's *history,* and *strategies* that are developed and then evolve over time. These inputs help define how people in the organization behave, and they serve as constraints on behavior as well as opportunities for action.

As we know from the works of Burns and Stalker (1961) and Lawrence and Lorsch (1967), the extent to which an organization's environment is relatively stable or dynamic significantly affects internal operations, structure, and policy (see Chapter 7). For many organizations, a very

Figure 8.3. The Nadler-Tushman congruence model for diagnosing organizational behavior

SOURCE: D. A. Nadler and M. L. Tushman, "A Diagnostic Model for Organization Behavior," 1977, in *Perspectives on Behavior in Organizations,* edited by J. R. Hackman, E. E. Lawler, and L. W. Porter, pp. 85-100, New York: McGraw-Hill. Reprinted by permission of McGraw-Hill.

important aspect of environment is the parent system and its directives. Many organizations are subsidiaries or divisional profit centers of larger corporations, such as colleges within a university or hospitals within a larger health care delivery system. These subordinate organizations may operate relatively autonomously with respect to the outside world (having their own purchasing operations, for example), but because of corporate policy, they may be fairly restricted in how much money they can spend. Thus, for many organizations, we must think of their environments in at least two categories: the larger parent system and the rest of the outside world—government regulations, competitors, and the marketplace in general.

Resources within the Nadler-Tushman model include capital (money, property, equipment, and so on), raw materials, technologies, people, and various intangibles, such as company name, logo, or brand, which may have a high value in the company's market.

An organization's history is also input to the system. The history determines, for example, patterns of employee behavior, policy, the types of people the organization attracts and recruits, and even how decisions are made in a crisis. Recall from Chapter 6 the example of two banks with highly similar backgrounds. When they merged after some

150 years of independence, their respective histories had shaped two entirely different corporate cultures. History is an important variable in the understanding of any organization.

Although strategy is categorized as an input in the model, Nadler and Tushman set it apart. Strategy is the process of determining how the organization's resources are best used within the environment for optimal organizational functioning. It is the act of identifying opportunities in the environment and determining whether the organization's resources are adequate for capitalizing on these opportunities. History plays a subtle but influential role in the strategic process.

Some organizations are very strategic; they plan, for example, the rational perspective regarding strategic change delineated by Rajagopalan and Spreitzer (1997; see Chapter 7). Other organizations simply react to changes in their environments or act opportunistically, rather than according to a long-range plan that determines which opportunities will be seized and which will be allowed to pass, similar to the learning perspective described by Rajagopalan and Spreitzer. As Nadler and Tushman (1977) pointed out, however, organizations have strategies whether they are deliberate and formal or unintentional and informal. Rajagopalan and Spreitzer made the same point.

Outputs

Shifting to the right side of the model (Figure 8.3), we will consider outputs before covering the transformation process. Thus, we shall examine the organization's environment from the standpoint of both how it influences the system and how it becomes influenced by the system's outputs.

For diagnostic purposes, Nadler and Tushman (1977) presented four key categories of outputs: system functioning, group behavior, intergroup relations, and individual behavior and effect. With respect to the effectiveness of the system's functioning as a whole, the following three questions should elicit the necessary information:

1. How well is the organization attaining its desired goals of production, service, return on investment, and so on?

2. How well is the organization using its resources?

3. How well is the organization coping with changes in its environment over time?

The remaining three outputs are more directly behavioral: how well groups or units within the organization are performing; how effectively these units communicate with one another, resolve differences, and collaborate when necessary; and how individuals behave. For the last output, individual behavior, we are interested in matters such as turnover, absenteeism and, of course, individual job performance.

The Transformation Process

The components of the transformation process and their interactions are what we normally think of when we consider an organization: the people, the various tasks and jobs, the organization's managerial structure (the organization chart), and all relationships of individuals, groups, and subsystems. As Figure 8.3 shows, four interactive major components compose the transformation process, changing inputs into outputs.

The *task component* consists of jobs to be done and the inherent characteristics of the work itself. The primary task dimensions are the extent and nature of the required interdependence between and among task performers, the level of skill needed, and the kinds of information required to perform the tasks adequately.

The *individual component* consists of all the differences and similarities among employees, particularly demographic data, skill and professional levels, and personality-attitudinal variables.

Organizational arrangements include the managerial and operational structure of the organization, work flow and design, the reward system, management information systems, and the like. These arrangements are the formal mechanisms used by management to direct and control behavior and to organize and accomplish the work to be done.

The fourth component, *informal organizational,* is the social structure within the organization, including the grapevine, the organization's internal politics, and the informal authority-information structure—whom you see for what.

Congruence as the Concept of Fit

As Nadler and Tushman (1977) pointed out, a mere listing and description of these system inputs, outputs, and components is insufficient for modeling an organization. An organization is dynamic, never static, and the model must represent this reality, as the arrows in Figure 8.3 do. Nadler and Tushman went beyond depicting relationships, however. Their term *fit* is a measure of the congruence between pairs of inputs and especially between the components of the transformation process. They contend that inconsistent fits between any pair will result in less than optimal organizational and individual performance. If, for example, an organization's strategy is to become a global corporation and a part of "formal organizational arrangements"(structure) includes a division of international operations rather than international emphasis being a structural aspect of all units within the organization, then we have a lack of fit, or incongruence. Nadler and Tushman's hypothesis, therefore, was that the better the fit, the more effective the organization will be.

Nadler and Tushman (1977) recommended three steps for diagnosis:

1. Identify the system: Is the system for diagnosis an autonomous organization, a subsidiary, a division, or a unit of some larger system? What are the boundaries of the system, its membership, its tasks, and—if it is part of a larger organization—its relationships with other units?

2. Determine the nature of the key variables: What are the dimensions of the inputs and components? What are the desired outputs?

3. Diagnose the state of fit. This is the most important step, involving two related activities: determining fits between components and diagnosing the link between the fits and organization outputs.

For their model, then, Nadler and Tushman (1977) argued that one must concentrate on the degree to which the key components are congruent with one another. It should be noted that measuring these degrees of congruence is no easy undertaking. The process requires considerable data gathering and analysis.

For diagnosing the link between fits and outputs, the organizational change agent must focus the outcome of the diagnoses of the various component fits and their behavioral consequences on the set of behaviors associated with system outputs: goal attainment, resource usage, and overall system performance. Considering the component fits, or lack thereof, in light of system outputs helps identify critical problems of the organization. As these problems are addressed and changes are made, the system is then monitored for purposes of evaluation through the feedback loop.

In summary, the Nadler-Tushman model is comprehensive and sophisticated—thus the reason for more space being devoted to the coverage of their framework. Although mostly descriptive, their model does suggest certain cause-effect linkages, that is, the idea of congruence. Little or no congruence between, for example, strategy and structure would produce poor organizational performance. Moreover, incongruence between the external environment and strategy would also suggest a causal relationship with performance. The point is that many other congruencies or incongruencies could be emphasized. There are many possibilities. What would help, but are not provided in the Nadler-Tushman model, are ideas for determining which organizational dimensions are more central or "weightier" than which other dimensions. Their category of "Formal Organizational Arrangements" consists of quite a number of components, such as structure, job design, formal policies and systems, and goals/objectives. Some of these, such as goals, for example, might be more central than others. Finally, no means are suggested for determining when congruence is in place or for determining what levels of congruence/incongruence produce desirable or undesirable effects.

Perhaps being influenced by thinking associated with chaos and non-linear complex systems theory (see Chapters 3 and 6), Nadler and Tushman (1989) more recently began to question their own congruence position. To use their words,

> While our model implies that congruence of organizational components is a desirable state, it is, in fact, a double-edged sword. In the short term, congruence seems to be related to effectiveness and performance. A system with high congruence, however, can be resistant to change. It develops ways of insulating itself from outside influences and may be unable to respond to new situations. (p. 195)

Tichy's TPC (Technical, Political, Cultural) Framework

Although similar to the other two models, particularly the Nadler-Tushman framework, Tichy (1983) focused much more explicitly on organization change. In fact, his nine components should be seen less as "boxes" in a model and more as "change levers." Figure 8.4 displays these levers in a certain order that Tichy considered important for organization change.

Briefly, the nine change levers are as follows:

1. External interface, or the organization's external environment (input)

2. Mission

3. Strategy (Tichy combined mission and strategy in the model, but he considered them distinct levers)

4. Managing organizational mission/strategy processes (that is, realistically engaging the relevant interest groups)

5. Task (change often requires new tasks)

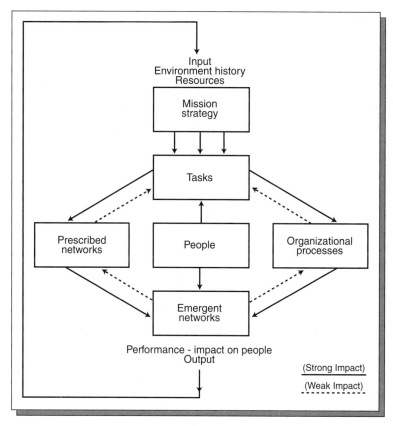

Figure 8.4. Tichy's framework
SOURCE: N. M. Tichy. *Managing Strategic Change: Technical, Political, and Cultural Dynamics.* © 1983 by John Wiley & Sons, Inc., New York. Reprinted by permission of John Wiley & Sons, Inc.

6. Prescribed networks (more or less, the formal organizational structure)

7. Organizational processes (communicating, problem solving, and decision making)

8. People

9. Emergent networks (more or less, the informal organization)

Managing as such is not shown in the model. Tichy considered management as pervading the entire framework. He assumed "that organizational effectiveness (or output) is a function of the characteristics of each of the components of the model, as well as a function of how the components interrelate and align into a functioning system" (Tichy, 1983, p. 72).

The TPC in Tichy's (1983) thinking provides the more unique aspect of his framework. Technical, political, and cultural represent the three primary systems that cut across the nine levers. Tichy considered these three systems to be the dominant ones for understanding organizations in general and organization change in particular. The technical system is based on science and hard data and therefore represents a highly rational perspective. The political system is based on power dynamics and the fact that in organizations, some groups and individuals are more powerful than others. With respect to change, the primary behavior representing this perspective is negotiation. The cultural system concerns shared values and norms, or "cognitive schemes" as Tichy called them. These schemes are what link people together and constitute the organization's culture. Consistent with Lewinian thinking (see Chapter 7), culture change occurs, according to Tichy, by developing new norms and perhaps values. Dealing with only one or two of these systems instead of all three simultaneously will lead to ineffectiveness as far as organizational performance is concerned. All three must be realigned for successful change. Tichy, therefore, saw these three systems as intertwined metaphorically as three strands of a rope. The three systems or perspectives can be understood separately, but for effective change to occur, all must be managed together. Overlaying these three systems with the change levers produces a matrix like the one shown in Figure 8.5.

Tichy (1983) argued that these systems must be aligned with levers and each with every other one for effective change to occur. For diagnostic purposes, data must be collected for each cell of the matrix. These data need to be informative regarding the degree of change required for proper alignment. Across the matrix, the alignment is *within* a system, and down the matrix, the alignment is *between* systems. An illustration of the former, within, might be a case of new technology arising in the external environment and the organization's holding on too long to its own technology, which may be rapidly reaching obsolescence. An illustration of the latter, between, might be a case of attempting cultural change toward a more trusting set of values when the political system in the organization is based in part on "Information is power," and it is best to share this form of power very sparingly.

To summarize, Tichy's model includes most of the variables that are critical to understanding and especially changing organizations. The TPC rope is a unique feature of his framework and adds to our

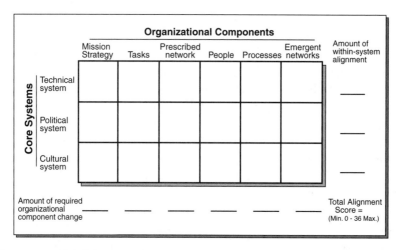

Figure 8.5. Tichy's TPC matrix
SOURCE: N. M. Tichy. *Managing Strategic Change: Technical, Political, and Cultural Dynamics.* © 1983 by John Wiley & Sons, Inc., New York. Reprinted by permission of John Wiley & Sons, Inc.

understanding of what to consider in and how to think through the implementation of a large-scale change effort in an organization.

There are some limitations, however. The *people* component in Tichy's model is barely mentioned. Moreover, issues at the individual level of organizational analysis have a lower priority than group and organizational levels. To be fair, Tichy (1983) did admit this omission in his book by stating that he skimmed over the psychological aspects of change. Also to be fair, the cultural and political strands of the TPC rope do address people issues, but at a more macro level than at the level of, say, job-person match (congruence) or local work unit activities, such as self-directed work group dynamics and teamwork. Finally, the previous criticism of too much emphasis on congruence potentially having an adverse or dampening effect on organization change could also be true for Tichy's argument regarding the high degree of importance of alignments.

A Comparison of the Three Models

The models by Weisbord, Nadler-Tushman, and Tichy have more in common than in difference. All three are based on the open system theoretical way of thinking and consequently include the external environment (input), the bulk of each model being the throughput (or transformation process) and performance (outputs). With Weisbord (1976), the output was accounted for merely by an arrow pointing to outside the circle; Nadler-Tushman (1977) actually used the term *outputs* and referred to them at three levels, individual, group, and organization; and Tichy (1983) used both terms, *performance* and *output*. All three models refer to organizational direction in one way or the other—purpose, mission, or strategy—and all three account for structure and people. Tichy is unique with his systems rope metaphor, and Weisbord is the only one to make leadership and rewards explicit. Culture looms large in Tichy's model, whereas Nadler-Tushman did include an informal organizational component, and Weisbord used relationships, which he would probably argue accounts for culture. Tichy was simply much more explicit about it because he considers culture to be critical to organization change. And finally, as noted before (Burke, 1994),

> With regard to explanation, Weisbord argues that leadership is critical, Nadler and Tushman advocate congruence (but not too much of it), and Tichy espouses alignment. The Weisbord and Nadler-Tushman models present more of a contingency viewpoint, whereas Tichy takes a strong normative stance. Tichy's strategic rope, consisting of technical, political, and cultural strands, must indeed be a braided rope; that is, the strands must be aligned, the three systems, as he labels them, must be aligned with his key levers (organizational components), and the levers themselves must be aligned with one another. (p. 70)

Summary

Organizational models can be useful in helping us to understand the dynamics of action taken and organizational members' behavior in organizations. Because actions and behavior cover such a wide array of data, categorizing this enormous universe into more manageable chunks helps us to transform the data into useful information. Models, then, help us to be more efficient and to be more rational as we attempt to understand and change an organization.

But any organizational model has its limitations. How can we be certain that the categories of our model are the primary and correct ones? And even if our components make sense and are widely accepted, what is missing and perhaps overlooked?

The models covered in this chapter and the one by Porras described in Chapter 6 were all born from a combination of practice and theory/ research. Thus, from the standpoint of organization change, these models do provide "best guesses" so far about what is important to consider. But they do, nevertheless, represent selectivity; that is, they are all based on the same organism metaphor (as noted, there are other useful metaphors), and they conform more to Chin and Benne's (1985) normative-reeducative strategy for change than to either their empirical-rational or power-coercive strategies (see Chapter 7). Recall that a primary example of a normative-reeducative strategy for change is organization development (OD). The models covered in this chapter as well as the one by Porras and Robertson (1992) from Chapter 6 all evolved from the field of OD.

This chapter does not complete our coverage of organizational models. After all, as the author of this book, I have not had my say! The next chapter is my statement about organizational modeling and change. The Burke-Litwin model (Burke & Litwin, 1992) is presented next and represents an attempt not only to provide a descriptive model of what is important to consider in understanding an organization but also to take a position about organizational performance and change. The Burke-Litwin model is therefore a statement about cause and effect, and the perspective taken is a normative rather than a contingent one.

9

The Burke-Litwin Causal
Model of Organization
Performance and Change

The organization models we have considered thus far, the one by Porras covered in Chapter 6, and by Weisbord, Nadler-Tushman, and Tichy in Chapter 8, integrate content and process, at least implicitly, but they are more about organizational functioning than change. The exception is Tichy's technical, political, cultural (TPC) framework. His model addresses change: the importance of alignment for organization change to be effective. But Tichy is not explicit about cause and effect and neither are the authors of the other organization models. How does the political system in Tichy's TPC affect or influence the cultural system and vice versa? How does the alignment of the technical system with the lever of mission/strategy affect performance, and more particularly, how does it shape change? These questions are not addressed.

The purpose of this chapter is to respond to some of these kinds of questions by first explaining the Burke-Litwin model and second, by attempting to validate the framework with brief coverage of related research and theory.

Background

My colleague in the derivation of the Burke-Litwin model, George Litwin, conducted research in the 1960s on organizational climate (Litwin & Stringer, 1968; Tagiuri & Litwin, 1968) that established the groundwork for what later became our overall organizational framework (Burke & Litwin, 1992).

In graduate school at the University of Michigan and later as a professor at the Harvard Business School, Litwin was influenced by the works of Atkinson (1958) and David McClelland, respectively.

McClelland was a need theorist and believed that human needs could be aroused by manipulating the environment. Although we all may have some degree of need to achieve, McClelland (1961) showed from his research that such a need could be increased and enhanced. Litwin wanted to demonstrate this phenomenon organizationally and from the standpoint of leadership. He hypothesized that different styles of leadership could create different organizational climates (environment) that would appeal to (arouse) different motives or needs. Working with MBA students in a laboratory setting, Litwin created three separate organizations led by distinctly different leaders, one being a power-oriented leader to arouse followers' need for power, a second being an achievement-oriented leader having a strong task focus with challenging goals, and a third being an affiliation-oriented leader to arouse relationship and interdependent needs. His study showed that performance and morale differed significantly across the three laboratory organizations, with the achievement leader having both the highest performance and the highest morale (Litwin & Stringer, 1968).

Based on this early work, Litwin (Litwin, Humphrey, & Wilson, 1978) developed an abbreviated organizational model with climate as the centerpiece. He defined organizational climate as a set of psychological priorities of a given (usually) work environment that are based on the collective perceptions of the people in that environment. The nature of a climate is determined by a number of organizational variables, not just management or leadership approach. These other variables for Litwin et al. (1978) included norms and values (culture) and management systems (policies and procedures). Figure 9.1 depicts this early version of Litwin's model.

Note that Litwin et al. (1978), in addition to climate affecting motivation, also included the outcome variables of organizational performance and employee health and retention. Also, it should be noted that the importance of this early research and theory development regarding organizational climate was the cause-effect position that Litwin took, that is, the linkage of psychological and organizational variables. His empirically testable claim was that the better work unit climate, the greater the likelihood of high organizational performance.

In other words, this kind of thinking and research set the stage for how we developed the Burke-Litwin model. One final point before we proceed to a description of the model: Although there is overlap between climate and culture (in any organization, rarely, if ever, is a single variable discrete), we do make a distinction (Burke & Litwin, 1992):

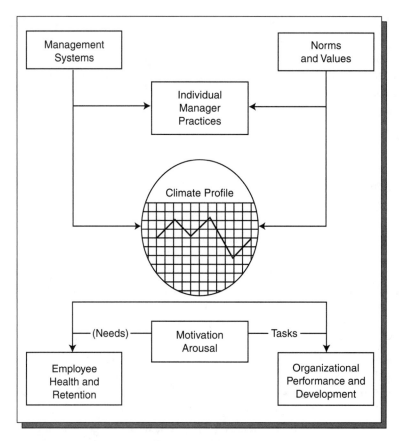

Figure 9.1. Organizational-climate system
SOURCE: G. H. Litwin, J. W. Humphrey, and T. B. Wilson, Organizational Climate: A Proven Tool for Improving Performance, 1978, in *The Cutting Edge: Current Theory and Practice in Organization Development,* edited by W. W. Burke (p. 190), La Jolla, CA: University Associates.

> Climate is defined in terms of perceptions that individuals have of how their local work unit is managed and how effectively they and their day-to-day colleagues work together on the job. The level of analysis, therefore, is the group, the work unit. Climate is much more in the foreground of organizational members' perceptions, whereas culture is more background and defined by beliefs and values. The level of analysis for culture is the organization. Climate is, of course, affected by culture, and people's perceptions define both, but at different levels. (pp. 526-527)

Schneider (1985) has made similar distinctions between climate and culture in organizations. Moreover, although there are similarities, understanding the differences between culture and climate is one of the keys to understanding organization change more thoroughly.

The remainder of this chapter is devoted to, first, a description of the model, and then to coverage of research and theory that supports the primary tenets of the model.

The Model

As noted earlier, the Burke-Litwin model has its roots in the organizational climate studies conducted by Litwin and his colleagues during the latter part of the 1960s. Further development of the model did not occur until the late 1970s and 1980s, when Burke and Litwin began their collaborative work in the arena of organizational change consulting, first, with Citibank, as the financial enterprise was known back then, and later, with British Airways (BA) beginning in 1985.

The model as conceived today actually emerged from practice, that is, as a consequence of trying to understand more about how to bring about change at BA. This case is introduced in Chapter 4. The organization change of BA at the time was initiated by a decree from the prime minister of Great Britain, Margaret Thatcher. BA, the nation's flagship airline, (a) was not exactly efficiently run, (b) had evolved from the Royal Air Force of World War II and was therefore managed rather bureaucratically and in a top-down military manner, and (c) ended each year financially in the red, with the government thus having to make up the deficit. Thatcher decided to put a stop to this way of doing business and declared that BA would have to survive on its own as a private corporation, publicly owned, with stock traded on both the City of London and the New York Stock Exchanges. The decree was finally enacted in February of 1987. Thus, BA, in order to survive, had to change. Every nook and cranny of the organization was affected, especially at the outset BA's mission, business strategy, leadership, and organizational culture. The theory of the business (Drucker, 1994; see Chapter 7) had to be altered significantly, primarily from conceiving of BA as *the* nation's airline, with all the requisite rights and privileges to a commercial enterprise that must serve customers to survive. This story of change at BA, with all its complexities, could easily take up additional pages. The change, after all, took time (about 5 years), was quite dramatic and dynamic, and was deemed successful by a variety of measures and independent sources. For more, see Burke (1994), Burke and Trahant (2000), Georgiades and

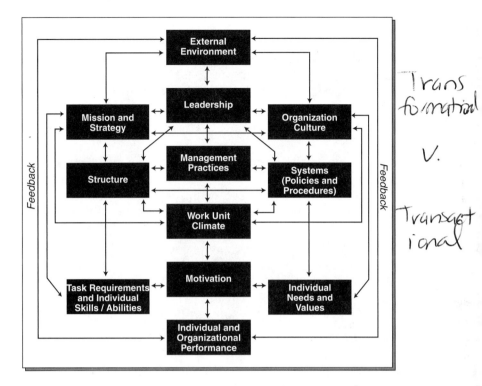

Figure 9.2. The Burke-Litwin model of organizational performance and change
SOURCE: From the Burke-Litwin model of organizational performance and change.
©1987, 1992 by W. Warner Burke, Associates, Inc.

Macdonell (1998), Goodstein and Burke (1991), and Litwin, Bray, and Brooke (1996).

As we proceed with a description of the model, the influence of the change at BA and our consequent learning can easily be discerned. The criticality of an organization's external environment, for example, cannot be overestimated. For BA, at the time, the external forces impinging on the enterprise were in no small way represented by the persona of Margaret Thatcher. For most organizations, the external environment is not as dramatic, but just as important nevertheless for understanding organization change. The overall model is depicted in Figure 9.2.

As can be seen, the model conforms to the open system way of thinking, in which the external environment box serves as the input dimension and the individual and organizational performance box serve as the output dimension. The remaining boxes represent what we consider to be the primary throughput dimensions. To complete the picture (metaphor), the feedback loop connects the input with the output. Note that the arrows for the feedback loop go in both directions, meaning that organizational outcomes—products and services—affect the external environment, for example, customer satisfaction, and that forces in the external environment can affect performance directly (depending on how performance is defined and measured), for example, a change in government regulations or company stock price being affected by Wall Street trends.

As noted above, the 12 boxes that compose the model represent our choices of what we consider to be primary for organizational under-standing and analysis. Although we made our own choices, we have definitely been influenced by the thinking of others. One can easily see overlap with the Weisbord, Porras, Nadler and Tushman, and Tichy models. And like some of these authors, we have accounted for dimen-sions at the larger-system level with such variables as mission, strategy, leadership, and culture, at the group or local work unit level with climate, and finally, at the individual level with individual needs and values, task requirements and individual skills, and motivation.

The arrows that connect the boxes and go in both directions signify the open system principle of multiple impact, that is, a change in any one category or box will eventually affect all the remaining boxes. To portray the model as close to reality as possible, there would be arrows, or linkages, between each box and all the other boxes. Figure 9.2 depicts some of the more important linkages rather than attempting to show every possible connection. The clutter of displaying all connections would look rather daunting, if not messy. But daunting and messy is no doubt closer to reality. Moreover, our two-dimensional display is limi-ted. Closer to reality would be a display of the model in the form of a hologram. Circular arrows would depict reality much more accurately. Yet our model predicts cause, so some directions are more important or weightier than others when it comes to planning and implementing successful organization change. A quick example can be provided by comparing the linkage between the culture and systems boxes. Although the arrow connecting the two is bilateral, culture probably has a stronger influence on systems than the other way around. Evidence for a strong linkage between the two boxes has been provided by Kerr and Slocum (1987). Their research showed that an organization's reward system (a subdimension of the larger systems box) is a manifestation of its culture and that the reward system can be used, perhaps should be used, to facilitate change in an organization's culture. In other words, their study supports the notion of linkage and its bidirectional nature. With our display of culture above the systems box (and therefore carrying more "weight," or influence) we are going farther than the Kerr and Slocum study, that is, beyond mere linkage, and stating that culture, especially the aspects of beliefs and values, helps to *determine* the type of reward system senior managers deem appropriate. Therefore (Burke & Litwin, 1992),

> Displaying the model the way we have is meant to make a statement about organizational change. Organizational change, especially an overhaul of the company business strategy, stems more from environmental impact than from any other factor. Moreover, in large scale or total organizational change, mission, strategy, leadership and culture have more "weight" than structure, management practices, and systems: That is, having organizational leaders communicate the new strategy is not sufficient for effective change. Culture change must be planned as well and aligned with strategy and leader behavior. These variables carry more weight, because changes in them (e.g., organizational mission) affect the total system. Changing structure, on the other hand, may or may not affect the total system. It depends on where in the organization a structural change might occur.
>
> We are not necessarily discussing at this stage where one could *start* the change, only the relative weighting of change dynamics. When we think of the model in terms of change, then, the weighted order displayed in the model is key. (p. 529)

Transformational and Transactional Dimensions

Key to understanding change according to the model is the top half compared with the bottom half. Borrowing language and concepts from James McGregor Burns (1978) and his distinction between two primary forms of leadership—transformational and transactional—we have conceived of the model similarly. Burns classified *transformational leaders* as being those who bring about change; they never leave a situation the way they found it, and the "situation" (organization, community, nation, etc.) will be different as a consequence of this kind of leader being in charge. He classified *transactional leaders* as being those who see the leader-follower relationship as just that, a transaction: "If you do such and such for me, I'll see that you (follower) get rewarded" (promotion, bonus, time off, etc.). This latter form of leadership may involve change, but not change that is sweeping or transformational in nature (change in the *deep structure* of the system; see Chapter 4). Transactional leaders are more interested in maintaining the status quo,

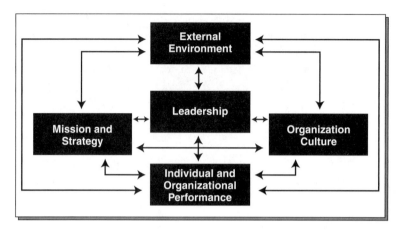

Figure 9.3. The transformational factors

but if change is necessary, they would argue that it should be gradual and evolutionary, not sudden and revolutionary.

The categories or boxes in the top half of the model—external environment, mission and strategy, leadership, and culture—are referred to as the *transformational factors.* Changes in these boxes are likely to be caused by direct interaction with external environmental forces and will as a consequence require significantly new behavior from organizational members. Figure 9.3 is a display of these transformational factors. It is similar to Burns's conception of transformational leadership, but, of course, in an organization context, a change in any of these boxes or organizational dimensions means that the entire organization or system is affected and that the change is discontinuous and revolutionary in nature (see Chapter 6), that is, affecting the deep structure of the system and requiring visionary leadership.

The remaining boxes or organizational dimensions in the lower half of the model are what we refer to as the *transactional factors.* These dimensions build on the original thinking and climate research of Litwin and his colleagues (see Figure 9.1). These factors concern more of the day-to-day operations (transactions) of the organization, and with respect to change, we would use terms such as *continuous improvement, evolutionary,* and *selective,* rather than *sweeping.* Figure 9.4 is a depiction of the transactional factors in the model.

As noted above, the transformational/transactional distinction regarding organization modeling and change comes from theory about

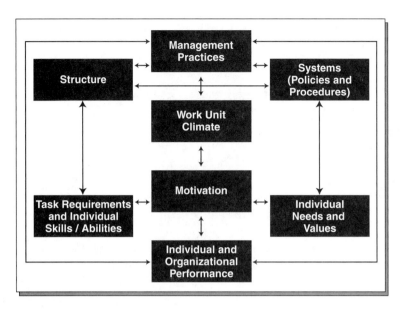

Figure 9.4.   The transactional factors

leadership. This theory stems from several sources, perhaps the first being Zaleznik's (1977) distinction between a leader and a manager, and one year later, Burns's (1978) similar distinction, though phrased differently. Transformational (Burns) is very much the same as Zaleznik's *leader,* and transactional (Burns) is very similar to Zaleznik's *manager.* Burke (1986) combined these two ideas about leadership and hypothesized that each leader (transformational) or manager (transactional) could empower others effectively, but the behaviors would differ depending on whether one was acting as a leader or as a manager. With respect to our organizational model and staying with the transformational (leader) and transactional (manager) distinctions, transformational change is more closely linked with leadership and transactional change is more closely associated with management. Organization transformation requires a change leader (see Chapter 11) who personally identifies with the change that is needed and sees no distinction between the organization's new mission and his or her mission. Transactional change requires managers who see their jobs as that of constantly focusing on improvement and quality rather than on an overhaul of the total system.

With this transformational-transactional distinction serving as a backdrop, what now follows is a brief definition of each box in the model.

External Environment. Forces or variables outside the organization that influence or will shortly influence organizational performance. These forces include variables such as customer behavior and satisfaction, marketplace conditions (the extent of competition for commercial enterprises, for example), political circumstances, government regulations, world financial and economic conditions, and changing technology. For more elaboration on how the external environment influences an organization, see Pfeiffer and Salancik (1978).

Mission and Strategy. Briefly, *mission* concerns what the organization "is all about," its purpose, its raison d'être, and its primary goals. The organization's *strategy* concerns the *how*, or implementation, that is, how the mission is to be accomplished. Of late, the term *vision* has emerged as a popular organizational and leadership concept. Vision is more associated with the leadership category in the model, but a quick word of distinction here between mission and vision is warranted.

Mission is current, or the present, and concerns ultimate purpose. It is cerebral, meaning that the statement of mission is carefully and logically crafted, with key words carrying significant weight, for example, "to serve." Mission is tied directly to the core competencies of the organization and provides an answer to the question: If this organization did not exist, what difference would it make? Vision addresses the future and concerns aspirations and desired outcomes. Though not irrational, vision nevertheless is emotional and often reflects passion that organizational members feel, especially leaders. Vision statements can be lofty and imply challenge and a "stretch" for the organization over the next 3 to 5 years. Vision, therefore, is more about leadership, and mission is more about purpose.

Part of the following chapter is devoted to the Dime Bank's change story. As an example of an organizational vision, their statement follows (Dime Savings Bank, 1997):

Our Vision

The Dime will be the preeminent super-community bank in the greater New York area and a high-performance mortgage banking and consumer financial services company in select markets throughout the United States. We will be a leading provider of diversified financial products and services to individuals, families and businesses, creating profitable relationships with our customers and communities. Extraordinary customer service and the highest ethical standards will be our defining characteristics. We are committed to delivering customer satisfaction, achieving employee partnership, and demonstrating superior financial performance.

For research on the nature and importance of corporate mission statements, see Pearce and David (1987), and for an in-depth treatment on how strategy links to the external environment, internal structure, and corporate culture, see Porter (1985).

Leadership. Although this category is usually associated with the behavior of senior executives, and appropriately so, leadership is, after all, exercised throughout an organization. In any case, the primary association here is with providing *direction,* whether it comes from the chief executive officer or from a first-line supervisor. Also by leadership, we mean persuasion, influence, serving followers, and acting as a role model, and we do not mean command and control, domination, and serving edicts instead of followers. As the model shows (Figure 9.2), leadership and management practices are in separate boxes. Although there is definitely overlap between the two (thus, the boxes are juxtaposed), we believe that there are sufficient differences to warrant separateness. Leadership is about vision; change; using one's intuition, influence, persuasive and presentation skills; and rewarding people via personal praise and providing opportunities to learn new skills. Management is about role, task accomplishments, setting objectives, and using the organization's resources (for example, budget or information systems) efficiently and effectively, and rewarding people via extrinsic factors such as money, titles, and promotions. For more specifics regarding this distinction, see, for example, Bennis and Nanus (1985), Burke (1986), Burns (1978), and Zaleznik (1977).

Culture. Although not very scholarly sounding, the popular definition, namely, "the way we do things around here and the manner in which these norms and values are communicated" (Deal & Kennedy, 1982) is quite appropriate for quickly describing what organization culture actually means. The *way* means the norms we conform to and the values we believe in. *Culture,* then, embodies rules that we follow, both explicit and implicit. *Explicit* rules (norms), for example, are what the human resource manual states about issues such as mode of dress and hours of work. *Implicit* rules are followed but never discussed, informal rules of behavior or codes of conduct that are not written down but govern much, if not most, behavior in organizations, for example, conforming to an implicit norm of subordinates telling their boss what they believe he or she wants to hear, rather than telling the truth. The history of an organization is also important to understanding culture, particularly knowing about the values and customs of the founder(s) (Schein, 1983). For one of the more definitive sources for understanding organization culture, see Schein (1992).

Structure. We normally think of structure as the "organization chart," the diagram of boxes with titles and people's names in them, with lines that connect them—solid lines of connection, with the occasional addition of dotted lines to complicate matters even further. With respect to definitional words, *structure* refers to the arrangement of organizational functions (e.g., accounting, manufacturing, human resource management, etc.) and/or operational units (e.g., the western region, customer service for product group X, Goddard Space Flight Center within NASA, etc.) that signify levels of responsibility, decision-making authority, and lines of communication and relationships that lead to implementation of the organization's mission, goals, and strategy. For one of the classic articles about structure, see Duncan (1979), and for more current coverage, see Galbraith (1995).

Management Practices. This category addresses what managers do each workday to carry out the organization's strategy. *Practices,* in this case, refer to a particular set of specific behaviors. An example of a management practice might be "to encourage direct reports and associates to take initiative regarding innovative approaches to various tasks and projects." In practice, two different managers may "encourage direct reports and associates" to the same degree, but how each one does it behaviorally and specifically may differ. One manager may challenge; the other may use highly positive remarks and "pats on the back." Although he used the term *competency* instead of *practice,* Boyatzis (1982) is an early contributor to this line of research and thinking; for additional examples, see Burke and Coruzzi (1987) and Luthans (1988).

Systems. We are concerned here with policies and procedures that are designed to help and support organizational members with their job and role responsibilities. This category in the model is akin to one of Weisbord's six boxes, the one labeled *helpful mechanisms*. Included within this *systems* box are subcategories such as information systems and technology, sometimes referred to as MIS (management information systems), the organization's reward system, and a variety of control systems: performance appraisal, the setting of goals and the budget process, and human resource allocation. In other words, the systems category within the model covers a lot of territory. Sources that help to explain what is meant by some of these subcategories include Lawler (1990) on reward systems; Flamholtz (1979) on control systems; Beer, Spector, Lawrence, Mills, and Walton (1984) on managing human resource assets; and Kraemer, King, Dunkle, and Lane (1989) on MIS.

Climate. To recap what we mean by this category, *climate* is the collective perceptions of members within the same work unit. These perceptions include the following:

- How well they are managed, in general
- How clear they are about what is expected of them in the workplace
- How they feel their performance is recognized
- How involved they are in decision making
- Whether they believe they are managed according to standards that are challenging and fair
- How much support they feel from fellow work unit members
- How effectively they believe they work with other units in the organization

For more on climate, see the references by Litwin and the edited book by Ashkanasy, Wilderom, and Peterson (2000).

Task Requirements and Individual Skills/Abilities. The short version of this category is job-person match: the degree to which there is congruence between the requirements of one's job, role, and responsibilities and the knowledge, skills, and abilities (competence or talent) of the individual holding the job. For more on what we mean by this category and its importance to individual motivation and productivity, see Burke and Pearlman (1988).

Individual Needs and Values. This is the category on the other side of the *motivation* box from *task requirements and individual skills/abilities,* meaning that these two categories influence motivation significantly.

Both boxes have to do with congruence. In this latter case, *needs and values* concern the extent to which one's needs are met on the job: for example, the need for security or achievement and the degree to which there is congruence between what the individual organizational member believes is important, worthwhile, and valuable and what the organization stands for, such as its purpose, values, and how people in and out of the organization (including customers) are treated. The arrow connecting *culture* with this box represents this linkage and potential for congruence between the individual and the organization. Moreover (Burke & Litwin, 1992),

> [Most] behavioral scientists believe that enriched jobs enhance motivation and there is evidence to support this belief, yet as Hackman and Oldham (1980) have appropriately noted, not everyone has a desire for his or her job to be enriched. For some members of the workforce, their idea of enrichment concerns activities off the job, not on the job. As the American workforce continues to become even more diverse, the ability to understand differences among people regarding their needs and values with respect to work and job satisfaction increases in importance. (p. 533)

For more about individual needs and values in organizations, see Meglino and Ravlin (1998) and Sagie and Elizur (1996).

Motivation. For all living humans (and for animals as well), being motivated is a natural state. If Freud is correct about dreams, we are constantly motivated, even while asleep. With respect to the workplace, however, we must be more specific, and in this context, we are concerned with certain needs being aroused—in the language of McClelland (1961), the need to achieve, to affiliate with others, and perhaps to have a need for power. These aroused feelings are not random but are directed toward goals that when reached, will help to satisfy our needs, and these needs will persist until some degree of satisfaction has been attained. A primary function of organizational leaders and managers, therefore, is to establish the proper goals, that is, goals that are organizationally important and will respond to individual needs for ends such as achievement, meaningful work, reasonable autonomy on the job, recognition, and so on.

As noted above, job-person match and congruence between the goals and values of the organization and the individual's needs and values contribute significantly to workplace motivation. For brief summaries of relevant theory and research regarding workplace motivation, see

Chapter 7 and the section on mini-theories related to organization change with individual emphasis. And finally, for a definitive statement on the nature of work motivation with supportive theory and research, see Katzell and Thompson (1990).

Individual and Organizational Performance. To be more complete, we should note that *group,* or work unit, should be added to the description of this category in the model; *output,* in the language of open system theory, refers to the outcomes and results of all the throughput activities that in turn are responses to the external environment (input). Also, as indicated by the feedback loop directly connecting the external environment with performance, depending on how performance is defined and measured, the external environment may directly affect performance, for example, stock price in the case of a publicly owned corporation. In general, however, performance is defined and measured by indices such as productivity, customer satisfaction, quality of product and/or service, profit and/or earnings per share, and so forth. A deeper understanding of performance, especially at the organizational level, can be found in the writings of Cameron and Whetten; see, for example, Cameron (1980) and Cameron and Whetten (1982, 1981).

More recent work that reflects a unique approach to measuring performance and one that has caught the imagination of and is used by many corporations is the contribution by Kaplan and Norton (1996). Their "balanced scorecard" concept and related measurements have broadened the corporate "bottom-line" notion from merely financial indices to measures of customer satisfaction, innovation, and internal business practices.

Given that a definitional overview has been provided, we will now consider evidence in support of our normative stance, that is, the causal assumption underlying the model.

Support for the Model's Validity

Recall that a fundamental premise of the model is that planned change should follow the flow from top, or external environment, to bottom, or performance. Although the arrows connecting the boxes travel in all directions—down, up, and laterally, to reflect open system theory fundamentals—those pointing downward are presumed to carry more causal weight. The earlier example of culture influencing systems is a case in point. The following coverage of research and theory in support of the premise of the model is therefore selective, that is, it emphasizes studies that demonstrate the downward weighting. Thus, concerning organization change, the premise is that external environment has the greatest impact. Then, inside the organization, the transformational factors (mission/strategy, leadership, and culture) have the greatest impact. Next in importance come the transactional factors as they are serially portrayed in the model.

The Influence of the External Environment

First, it should be noted that two excellent sources for defining the *texture*, describing the causal nature of and understanding the linkage between the external environment and organizations, are Emery and Trist (1965) and Katz and Kahn (1978, chap. 5). Second, the Burke-Litwin model is an attempt to represent reality; it is not reality as such, however. After all, human beings in the organization are the reality, with their decisions and daily activities. To put things in boxes is only a depiction and an overly simplified one at that. Thus, the immediate box in the model affected by the external environment is leadership, the senior executives and primary decision makers for the organization. These executives in turn determine the mission and strategy, or at least change these variables. These executives also shape the organization's culture—but not entirely. The work of Hofstede (1991) shows that organizational culture is influenced by societal norms and values. In any case, much of reality can be described as what influences the thinking and feelings of senior executives, and their consequent decisions in turn help to shape the two boxes on either side of leadership in the model (see Figure 9.2). Collins (2001), for example, has shown via his concept of "Levels 1 to 5" of leadership, particularly levels 4 and 5, how a CEO can significantly influence the ultimate performance of a corporation. So, with respect to organization performance and change, leadership does indeed matter. For more evidence, see the comprehensive article by Hogan, Curphy, and Hogan (1994).

With respect to strategy, Prescott (1986) provided evidence for how external environment influences this box and in turn influences performance. Executives' perceptions of their organization's external environment have been shown to directly and causally affect their decision making regarding strategy (Miles & Snow, 1978). Regarding the impact of environment on organizational culture, we can once again refer to

Hofstede's (1991) research, which demonstrated the powerful influence of national origin, with its customs and mores, on individual behavior. And if we consider a more limited perspective, that is, industry group, as representing environment, then Gordon's (1985) study of utility companies and financial institutions showed that corporate culture is directly affected by industry category.

The Transformational Factors

Mission and strategy, leadership, and culture are the transformational factors that most immediately and directly respond to external environmental dynamics. Mission and strategy are together because both concepts concern direction, goals, and objectives for the organization and its various units, with mission being the *what* and strategy the *how.* The order (mission, then strategy) is important for reasons of common sense (How could strategy be implemented effectively if the mission were not articulated?). Furthermore, at least one study indicates that mission does influence strategic decisions that in turn affect performance (Pearce & David, 1987). Moreover, although Figure 9.3 does not reflect it, an arrow should directly connect mission and strategy with culture (yet leadership is the most important conduit between the two boxes), because mission statements usually either explicitly or implicitly include values and philosophy. These statements represent and reflect the organization's culture (Wilkens, 1989).

As to the influence of strategy, three additional studies are worthy of note. First, Chandler's (1962) classic study demonstrated the importance of strategy *preceding* structure; that is, the more successful companies in a given industry determined strategy *before* designing or changing the internal organizational structure. Chandler's criterion for success was a company's financial performance. In the model, therefore, strategy carries more weight than structure.

More recently, an analysis of 262 large companies over a span of 28 years showed the "reciprocal relationship between strategy and structure. However, our results support the original conception of a hierarchical relationship between the two—strategy is a more important determinant of structure than structure is of strategy" (Amburgey & Dacin, 1994, p. 1427). A third study, a meta-analytic analysis by Miller and Cardinal (1994) of 26 previously published studies suggested that strategic planning positively affects performance. What is interesting about this analysis is the link between strategy and performance and the speculation about the mediating variables between the two. Of course, the underlying assumption of the Burke-Litwin model is that those mediating variables are the transactional factors that lead to climate, to motivation, and so on, and finally, to performance.

As already noted regarding the leadership factor, there is ample evidence that senior executives in leadership positions influence organizational performance. Also, an early study by Fleishman (1953) showed how supervisors are influenced by their managers' approaches and styles. Thus, the leadership box precedes the management practices category in the model. Finally, two studies about 30 years later showed that leadership accounted for more variance in organizational performance than did other variables (Weiner & Mahoney, 1981) and that leadership was significantly related to improved organizational performance over time (Smith, Carson, & Alexander, 1984).

The Transactional Factors

The remaining categories (boxes) in the model leading to performance and change are in the transactional domain. These categories—structure, systems, management practices, work unit climate, individual needs and values, task requirements and individual skills/abilities, and motivation—when compared with the transformational factors, represent organizational dimensions and activities that are characterized as more day-to-day operations, incremental regarding change, and are more related to foreground (work unit climate) than to background (culture).

With respect to structure, Joyce and Slocum (1984) showed that this category in the model had a direct impact on climate, as did management practices, another primary variable in the study. In an earlier study, Schneider and Snyder (1975) essentially demonstrated the same outcome. Lawrence and Lorsch (1967, 1969) have shown that structure influences management practices, and Galbraith (1973, 1977) has demonstrated that structure directly affects task requirements as depicted in the model. As noted before (Burke & Litwin, 1992),

> Regarding the impact of *systems,* perhaps the most important subsystem of the policy and procedures (systems) box is the organization's reward system. The belief that "people do what they are rewarded for doing" is practically a cliché. Demonstrating this relationship of rewards and behavior in the workplace is not as obvious and straightforward as one might presume, however. Witness the pay-for-performance controversy for a case in point. There is evidence, nevertheless. (p. 537)

Bullock and Lawler (1984), for example, have shown linkages down the middle of the model between management practices, climate, motivation, and performance in their research on gain sharing (a participative incentive process). Deutsch (1985) has shown a linkage between reward systems and individual needs and values, as has Jordan (1986).

Another subsystem of the policy and procedures box is human resource management (HRM), or the HR system. In a large-scale study of 293 U.S. firms, Huselid, Jackson, and Schuler (1997) showed that at least for large companies, HRM effectiveness had a positive impact on performance. Multiple measures of performance were used by these researchers, including indices of financial, productivity, and market value. Interestingly, they compared technical HRM effectiveness, for example, strong capabilities in areas such as recruiting, selection, performance measurement, training, and compensation/benefits administration, with strategic HRM effectiveness, capabilities, and activities, that is, "designing and implementing a set of internally consistent policies and practices that ensure a firm's human capital contributes to the achievement of its business objectives" (Huselid et al., p. 172). This means, for example, strategic use of compensation for purposes of organization change instead of simply administering compensation to remain competitive in the labor marketplace. Huselid et al. (1997) further found that, although it was less commonly practiced among the organizations they studied, strategic HRM was a stronger predictor of positive organizational performance than was technical HRM effectiveness.

And finally, another major subsystem in the policy and procedures box is the MIS, or sometimes simply referred to as IT (information technology) or IS (information system). One of the leading experts in this arena is Zuboff (1988). Her work has demonstrated rather dramatically the impact that IT has on worker behavior in general and on motivation and performance in particular.

Directly in line between leadership and climate is the category of management practices. Even though it was defined earlier, for more comprehensive coverage of what we mean by management practices, including numerous examples, see Burke, Richley, and DeAngelis (1985). With respect to research, the work of Schneider is the most relevant here. In a series of studies, he has shown a clear and direct connection between management practices and climate (Schneider, 1980, 1990a; Schneider & Bowen, 1985, 1995).

While covering the history and background of the Burke-Litwin model earlier in the chapter, we noted that the work of Litwin and his colleagues has demonstrated the impact of climate on motivation and in turn on performance. Independent of this earlier work, Rosenberg and Rosenstein (1980) have also shown that climate, with particular emphasis on participation, influences productivity positively.

Motivation in the model can perhaps best be understood as an intervening or mediating variable, because in research studies, motivation is sometimes treated as an independent variable (example, the hypothesis might be that highly motivated workers are more productive) and at other times, as a dependent variable (for example, when job satisfaction or morale is used as a surrogate). In any case, what is important from the perspective of the model are the two categories (boxes) on both sides of motivation, *task requirements and individual skills/abilities* and *individual needs and values.* With this perspective, we are considering motivation as an intervening category, with performance as the ultimate dependent variable or outcome. A premise of the model is that these two boxes significantly influence motivation: If the job and the person do not match well, motivation will suffer; if individuals' needs on the job and values regarding work and the workplace are incongruent with the organization's culture, areas such as the reward system and motivation will suffer. With respect to research regarding the impact of job-person match (task requirements and individual skills/abilities), Burke and Pearlman's (1988) chapter provides considerable evidence for this aspect of the model, as does the research by Hunter and Schmidt (1982). Hackman and Oldham's (1980) work provides some of the clearest support for the impact of individual needs and values on motivation and so do the research outcomes in the study by Guzzo, Jette, and Katzell (1985).

Referring again to the work on organizational climate by Schneider (Schneider, 1980, 1990a); Schneider & Bowen, 1985, 1995), support for the hierarchical relationship of climate, motivation, and performance in the middle of the Burke-Litwin model comes from their research with "front-line" people in service businesses, such as tellers and loan officers in banks or ticket agents and cabin crews in an airline (regarding the latter, see Burke, 1994, and Goodstein & Burke, 1991, for the BA case example). How these front-line employees are treated by their supervisors has a direct effect on customer satisfaction. In bank branches, for example, where these service employees were managed more participatively as opposed to bureaucratically (following procedures strictly), customer satisfaction was significantly higher. In other words, the managers' practices of participation created a climate that positively influenced motivation and in turn performance, which then had a positive impact on customer satisfaction.

Finally, recall that when changing the transformational factors in the model (external environment, mission/strategy, leadership, and culture), the consequent organization change is more likely to be discontinuous (episodic and revolutionary) and affecting the deep structure (Gersick, 1991) of the total system. Changing the transactional factors (structure, systems, and climate) is more likely to result in continuous improvement: incremental and evolutionary organization change.

Summary

The goal of this chapter was to provide an organizational model or framework that would help to explain open system theory in action and to provide a way of thinking about planned organization change. Background about and a brief descriptive overview of the model was covered, followed by the section on support for the model's validity. It should be noted that the studies cited in this latter chapter section were selective. Other studies could have been included that both support and call into question some of the underlying assumptions of the model. However, the main point is that evidence exists to support the model's validity. To be fair, it should be noted that the evidence cited comes from a variety of sources and regarding the model, is somewhat piecemeal. An ideal test of the model's validity would be research that simultaneously examines the effect of all boxes in the model across an array of different organizations.

Although not always a test of the entire model, some "simultaneous examinations" have been approximated. A study by Bernstein and Burke (1989) demonstrated support for parts of the model and Fox's (1990) research in a hospital "demonstrated that leadership, culture, and management practices predicted significant variances in employees' perceptions of work unit climate and organizational performance [with] leadership and culture [being] clearly the two strongest indicators" (Burke & Litwin, 1992, p. 540). A longitudinal study of a large British corporation by Anderson-Rudolf (1996) and a more recent employee survey analysis within a major global corporation (Alexander, 2002) have both demonstrated support for the model's assumptions. With a description of the model and some preliminary support for its validity now in place, in Chapter 10, we take one more step; that is, we examine how to apply the model for purposes of organization diagnosis and change.

The application of the model that follows in the next chapter, with two case examples, is an attempt to demonstrate some primary benefits of its use. Two such benefits are the diagnostic quality and guidance for change interventions. Using an organizational survey based on the model, key strengths in the organization are identified, as well as issues that need attention. With respect to the latter, actions required (interventions for further change) are easily flagged. Recall an earlier statement from Chapter 8 arguing that an organizational model is only as good as the factors selected to compose the model and the relationships of these factors (boxes) with one another. The following chapter, applying the Burke-Litwin model, illustrates these kinds of qualities.

10 Application of the Burke-Litwin Model

In the preceding chapter, preliminary validity of the Burke-Litwin model was covered. That coverage leads us to conclude that the model represents organizational reality to some degree and that practitioners can apply it with a reasonable amount of confidence. Moreover, the proof of any organizational model is its degree of usefulness for (a) adequately understanding current organizational dynamics (diagnosis) and (b) helping to steer change in such a way that performance of an organization will be improved. In other words, a useful model should help us understand and guide the process that it models, in this case, organization change. One way of determining whether a model does what it purports to do is to test it in real-life situations. The two cases of organization change described in this chapter provide support for the Burke-Litwin model's heuristic value.

What follows, therefore, are two case examples of the model's application. The primary purpose of this chapter, then, is to demonstrate the usefulness of the Burke-Litwin model and to make it "come alive" and provide a means for action and change by describing actual organizational examples.

In both examples, multiple organizational surveys were conducted over time. Questionnaire items for the surveys were based on the 12 categories of the model, starting with external environment and concluding with performance. For an excellent source on the use of organizational surveys as tools for assessment, research, and as interventions for change, see the work by Kraut and his colleagues (Kraut, 1996).

Case 1: Dime Bancorp, Inc.

Dime Bancorp is the holding company for The Dime Savings Bank of New York, a regional financial enterprise serving customers and businesses through some 90-plus branches, primarily in the greater New York City metropolitan area. Due to an acquisition in 1997, Dime also provides financial services and mortgage banking via more than 200 offices throughout the United States. Dime currently is the result of a merger between the Dime Savings Bank and Anchor Savings Bank in January 1995. Our case begins with this merger. First, a little history.

Background

Dime was founded in 1859 as The Dime Savings Bank of Brooklyn. With a minimum deposit of a dime, the founder, William Edwards, encouraged all New Yorkers, even the most humble, to save. In 1862, the Dime was the first bank to offer banking by mail, permitting depositors fighting in the Civil War to send money to their families in the North.

Interestingly, Anchor was founded at about the same time, also in Brooklyn. Anchor also encouraged savings and focused on the local community as its primary market. Over the years, both Anchor and Dime grew by way of mergers and acquisitions that led to regional expansion and a broader range of services to individual customers and businesses.

With the merger of Dime and Anchor in January 1995, it seemed at the time that with such similar histories and resemblances in terms of size, revenues, customer base, and so on, one might assume that the two organizational cultures would be alike. In fact, the opposite was true: The two cultures were highly *dissimilar!* This conundrum was in part explained, however, by the idea of *attractors,* referred to in the brief coverage of non-linear complex system theory in Chapter 6. Recall that attractors are patterns of behavior with the dual characteristics of "sensitivity to initial conditions" and "stability." The former characteristics suggests that early history regarding the founding of an organization is highly significant; that is, initial behaviors in the organization's start-up phase that receive positive feedback become reinforced and stabilized quickly. These initial behaviors are quite specific, if not unique, to the situation at the time, therefore distinct in nature, likely to be undetectable at the time, and become entrenched over time as a consequence of consistent reinforcement. These small, undetectable behaviors loom large later and account for highly differentiated cultures, even though on the surface, due to more macro similarities, one would assume likeness, not dissimilarity. Apparently, early in the development and growth of the Anchor Bank, attention to detail was rewarded. Their culture some 150 years later reflected this emphasis. Dime, on the other hand, was more concerned with the bigger picture and becoming a "presence" in the greater New York City area. This difference between the two banks, though perhaps minor over a century ago, was highly significant at the time of the merger.

The respective CEOs of Dime and Anchor were quite aware of the differences in culture and therefore sought consultative help with the merger. The merger occurred because the two CEOs and their respective boards of directors realized that their piece of the financial services pie was shrinking, and that proceeding alone, as in the past, was probably not wise to ensure a successful future for their businesses and for their stakeholders. Commercial banks were dominant (and still are), while savings banks were fighting hard for new business. Thus, an intent of the merger was to become less savings and more commercial.

Once the merger became official and the two companies were one enterprise, three major initiatives were undertaken. First, a strategic planning process was launched to better understand how the resources of the two former companies could now be deployed to gain market share rather than losing share, which had been true for each of the two prior to the merger. Second, an organization-wide opinion survey was conducted (a) to determine the state of morale, (b) to assess employee understanding of the company's strategy, its new culture, leadership, organizational structure, and so on, and (c) to establish an internal benchmark for future survey comparisons and to track trends and progress. The third early initiative was to draft a new mission statement for the merged organization. Each of the two companies had a mission statement, but these were discarded, and a task force consisting of 15 employees who represented the two merged banks and comprised a cross section of the organization was formed to draft the new mission statement. This task force tapped another 100 or so employees to get opinions and suggestions about what the mission content should be. After many drafts, they presented their statement to the top executive team and got further feedback and suggestions. The final version was then presented to the board of directors and was unanimously approved. This third initiative was highly involving of many people in the organization and consequently led to strong commitment to the new mission statement.

Organizational Survey

The initial organizational survey revealed that most employees at all levels were positive about the merger, supported leaders at the very top of the organization, believed in the mission statement, and understood the overall business strategy, but were not very clear about the newly merged organizational culture and structure and were critical in general of several systems elements (such as information systems and compensation), and of leadership and management. As a consequence of these survey outcomes, a number of actions were taken. Changes were made to strengthen the information system (new management, updated software, etc.), the reward system was improved, some of the organization's structure was changed, and a major initiative was launched to improve leadership and management, starting with the top 125 executives and managers.

The CEO was highly supportive of these change efforts deriving from the survey and served as a role model for leadership and change. Working closely with an external consultant who had been involved from the beginning, the CEO and the head of human resources authorized, planned, and implemented a major effort to clarify the organization's culture and to develop and train managers in both leadership and management skills. Using the mission statement as a primary source, five values were extracted that seemed to represent the desired culture. In other words, corporate values were implicit within the mission statement. These values were then tested throughout the organization and eventually, a sixth one was added. The six values served as content guides for determining a set of practices that were behavioral manifestations of these values. These 36 practices, 6 per value, were then used in a questionnaire for the purpose of providing feedback for the top 125 people in the company. A 2 1/2-day leadership program was conducted for these top managers, and this feedback was the central element. Prior to the program, each participant rated himself or herself on the 36 practices and simultaneously were rated by their respective bosses, peers, and subordinates. Other questionnaires were used as prework as well. During the program, all participants received this multirater feedback and could compare how they viewed themselves with how the other three rating sources perceived them on the same set of behavioral practices, the primary content of which was leadership. Six months later, these 125 top people participated in another 2 1/2-day program, but this time the focus was on performance and project management. Multirater feedback was integral to this second program as well, coupled with a "Time 2" assessment of the earlier 36 leadership practices to see how these top managers were doing. The 125 also received intensive coaching on the feedback they received.

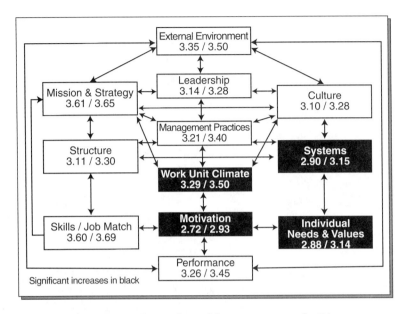

Figure 10.1.   1996/1998 Burke-Litwin model summary scores for Dime

At about the same time that the leadership development program was launched, a second organization-wide survey was conducted using approximately 90% of the questions asked at Time 1, so that comparisons could be made and trends determined. Based on ratings via a 5-point Likert scale, the results showed that out of 125 questions asked at both Time 1 and Time 2 (about 2 years later), except for two items, which remained about the same, all ratings were higher at Time 2. Significant improvements had been made over the 2-year period, at least "in the eyes" of the employees (see Figure 10.1).

Combining data from both the second survey and summaries of these multirater norms, that is, no individual being identified, trends and further problem areas could be discerned. For example, it became clear from these data that further work had to be done with helping managers do a better job in coaching and developing their subordinates. A further next step in this organizational change effort was to cascade down to the next levels of management in the 2 1/2-day programs on leadership and management.

As can be seen from Figure 10.1, the survey items of both Time 1 and Time 2 and the results reported to the managers and employees of the bank were organized according to the Burke-Litwin model. Further

Figure 10.2.   1998 Predictive model for Dime

statistical analyses within the framework of the model were conducted. For example, a regression analysis performed using the Time 2 results (1998) appeared to be associated with the respondents' perceptions of organization performance. To be clear, the performance category was assessed by survey questions such as "To what extent does the bank provide high quality customer service?" and "To what extent is the bank currently achieving the highest level of employee performance of which it is capable, given its existing resources and technology?" So, their responses are *perceptions* regarding organizational performance, not performance measurements per se. Referring to Figure 10.2, it can be seen that employees' responses to questions in the four model categories of business environment, mission and strategy, individual needs and values, and motivation had the strongest statistical relations with

Figure 10.3. 1998 Predictive model for Dime

perceived organizational performance. Figure 10.3 provides a more detailed picture.

The specific items in the figure that have a plus sign (+) in parentheses following the abbreviated survey statement indicate an above-average score on the survey (3.5 or greater); those that have a minus sign (-) indicate a below-average score (2.9 or less). All items listed in each of the four boxes (individual needs and values, motivation, mission and strategy, and the business environment) were positively correlated with perceived performance.

The message to the client went something like this: *The parts of the model that appear to be most positively related to employees' perceptions of how well the Dime is performing include their views of the bank's external business environment and their understanding of and commitment to the bank's mission and strategy.*

In other words, these transformational factors relate significantly and positively to perceived performance. These related perceptions could perhaps be reinforced even more so that a self-fulfilling prophecy could have more effect; that is, assuming that clarity about environment and mission/ strategy relates positively to perceived performance, strengthening these perceptions might eventually influence organizational performance positively. The categories related to morale are problematic, however. Lower-than-average ratings on individual needs and values, especially work-personal life balance and motivation (e.g., employees' perceptions of morale, empowerment, and control), may be contributing to a negative view of organizational performance and could be affecting performance adversely. It is therefore suggested that a thorough examination of people's jobs in the bank be undertaken. This examination would include consideration of the following:

- *Degree of workload: Are some employees overloaded in their jobs and others not, or is it true that most people are overworked and an increase in hiring is warranted?*
- *Feelings of empowerment and a related sense of having little control regarding changes in the bank need to be examined further; that is, do people have too much responsibility with too little authority?*

Working on these morale issues should improve motivation and, in turn, performance.

These exact words were not actually said to Dime employees, but the above statement does capture the message that was given. Of course, all the other items in the survey and the model categories were covered and explained. The regression analysis was conducted on the Time 2 results only. The important and exciting news was the increase from Time 1 to Time 2 in 123 of the 125 total survey items. Although it was not scientific proof that the desired changes at Dime were successful, the executives, managers, and employees believed nevertheless that positive change had occurred.

What has been briefly described, that is, from the original merger to these later action steps, spanned a period of more than 4 years. The financial services company continues to focus on organizational change and improvement and currently seeks growth of market share primarily via acquisitions of other similar businesses.

In summary, it should be clear that this case represents organization change that is more revolutionary than evolutionary in nature, because the emphasis of change was mission/strategy and culture. A compelling case for change as a consequence of the merger was made by the respective leaders of both companies, and a "disruption" ensued as a consequence. The change process today is more of a gradual, step-by-step continuous improvement effort. The organization's initial and continuing change process has been effective because of many factors; the main ones are as follows:

- The CEO's leadership, support for change, and modeling behavior
- Change initiatives carefully planned and driven by data
- An enlightened human resource leader and staff
- Strategic change expertise provided by external consultants
- Key changes made among the top 20 executives
- Significant acquisitions of additional businesses

Significant change over the 4-plus years described in this case has clearly been made. The fundamental nature of the business has changed somewhat in that the organization is making a deliberate effort to become more of a commercial and less of a savings bank. The merged culture is a bit more representative of one of the previous organizations than of the other, but it is a new culture nevertheless. Systems have been significantly improved with the introduction of new technology. Moreover, shifting demographics have caused change in managers' behavior, that is, to becoming more attuned and sensitive to individual differences.

The main objective of presenting the Dime case was to show how the Burke-Litwin model can be used in a change effort, especially linking the model to data collected with an organizational survey. Another objective was to provide an overview of the entire change effort at Dime so that our major theme of organization change can be continued. In the case of Dime, the initial change was transformational, and as shown by the survey data, the transformational factors in the model were the primary levers for change: external environment, mission and strategy, leadership, and more gradually, culture. As noted above, change continues today at the Dime, but for now the process is focusing more on the transactional factors and is more continuous than discontinuous. Should another major acquisition or merger occur in the near future, however, continuous will no doubt shift back to discontinuous.

Our second case comes from across the Atlantic, the British Broadcasting Corporation (BBC). The BBC case is quite different from the

Dime. For example, the Burke-Litwin model has framed four different surveys conducted in the organization during the 1990s. Moreover, the BBC is a nonprofit organization supported by a licensing fee collected from British citizens, quite a different mode of generating income. However, there is a similarity: The BBC, like the Dime, has a unique and venerable history.

Case 2: British Broadcasting Corporation (BBC)

Our case[1] begins in 1992, when John Birt, the deputy director general of the BBC, was about to become the director general (CEO, in corporate speak). Significant organization change often begins when a new leader takes over. Birt knew that he would need to be a change agent. Some background regarding the BBC and what the corporation was facing when Birt became director general will provide perspective for understanding the application of the Burke-Litwin model in this case.

Background

For more than 70 years, the BBC has been Britain's public service broadcasting agency and is widely regarded as a national asset. Its programs, both in television and radio, are viewed and listened to all over the world. The BBC is highly respected and admired worldwide, especially for its news broadcasting but also for its drama, comedy, music, and other arts productions. In fact, in a recent survey in which Americans were asked what they thought was the United Kingdom's finest exported product, the BBC won hands down.

Income for the BBC is generated from sales of its programs around the world, particularly in the United States, but the primary source of revenues comes from its license fee. British citizens who own a radio and/or television set are charged an annual fee of approximately $125 for the privilege of listening to and viewing BBC programs. And like the Public Broadcasting Service (PBS) in the United States, there are few commercials. But the similarity ends there. PBS in the United States has to raise funds for its broadcast services. The BBC's license fee may seem an imposition, but the service provided nationwide via two TV channels and five radio stations costs the British public per day less than the price of a daily newspaper or a stamp for sending a first-class letter.

In 1981, there were three television channels in the United Kingdom: the two BBC channels and ITV, an independent commercial station. There were four national BBC radio stations and 40 local ones, half of them operated by the BBC. Ten years later, Channel 4, another independent commercial TV broadcasting company, was available throughout the country; a fifth channel was being planned; and there were more than 70 licensed cable and satellite channels. BSKyB alone provided six channels. In the short span of a decade, much had changed in the BBC's external environment. Competition was now a huge reality. Moreover, because new technology was bringing about change, for example, from analog to digital, costs needed to be managed more carefully and new avenues for revenues needed to be explored. This was the external environment John Birt faced when he took over the reins of the BBC.

Originally educated as an engineer, Birt realized that he did not know what he needed to know about leading and managing change in a large, complex, and bureaucratic organization. So, he hired an external consultant (the author) first to tutor him about organization change and then to help him plan the changes he needed to make. The consultant used the Burke-Litwin model (naturally!) as the primary tutorial vehicle. Birt thought the model made sense, and he agreed to its use as the framework for bringing about change.

Table 10.1 shows most of the organization change initiatives that Birt and the BBC undertook over a period of about 7 years. As can be seen from the table, most of the boxes in the model were used as change levers. Incidentally, some of the language may need clarifying, for example, BBC *staff* refers to all employees, not staff in the sense of the more American distinction of line versus staff, as in the U.S. Army and other large bureaucratic organizations.

BBC Staff Surveys

Supported strongly by his human resource and training and development staff, Birt authorized a variety of assessments over the years of his directorship. A highly important measure has been the staff survey, having been conducted four times thus far. Through survey results, progress regarding the BBC change effort could be tracked and monitored. Typical of these kinds of assessments, there was good news from the survey results and news that was not so good. Figure 10.4 provides an overview of the four staff surveys from 1993 to 1997. What follows is a narrative about these four surveys, written primarily by Bob Nelson of the BBC. His language and perspective has been maintained. Moreover, to read it from the user's viewpoint is helpful. According to Nelson,

(Text continues on page 234)

Table 10.1 BBC Organization Change Initiatives and Purposes According to Burke-Litwin Model Categories

Burke-Litwin Model Category	Culture Initiative	Purpose/Goal(s)

Vision and mission	• "Extending Choice"—the BBC's role for the future:
	
	  – Inform the national debate (whatever the current debate might be).
	  – Express British culture and entertainment.
	  – Create opportunities for education.
	  – Communicate between the United Kingdom and abroad.
		• In addition to the BBC's public service role of providing high quality broadcasting services at minimum costs, this fundamental mission was *extended* to include the four roles, specified as the first and foremost change initiative.

Strategy	• Commercial policy development and creation of BBC Worldwide. • BBC 2005 (10-year strategy). • Program strategy review.	• To develop a new policy framework and organizational structure for commercial activities, compatible with "Extending Choice" and with regulatory constraints. • To take a long-term look at BBC's opportunities and threats and the likely consequences for programs, services, structure, systems, and policies. • Annual assessment regarding the four *extended* roles of the BBC.

(Continued)

Table 10.1 (Continued)

Burke-Litwin Model Category	Culture Initiative	Purpose/Goal(s)
Leadership	• Key senior appointments: 11% of top 120 positions filled from outside within 2 years.	• To bring to the BBC a critical mass who can lead change of the kind required and encourage the other "older hands" to do so as well.
	• Appropriate leadership behavior identified via research and used to develop relevant action.	• To make leadership behavior explicit by developing the competencies required to change the BBC culture.
	• Leadership development program.	• To encourage through training, feedback, and rewards the development of leadership behavior that is relevant, consistent with BBC values, and is more open and accountable.
Culture	• "Extending Choice" workshop.	• Via a 1-day event for 100 BBC staff at a time, give everyone an opportunity to understand more definitively what "Extending Choice" means and to have a say in where the BBC is going and how to get there.
	• Initial staff survey (1993).	• To establish internal benchmarks about where the BBC is perceived to be according to the Burke-Litwin model categories, especially the BBC culture.

(Continued)

Table 10.1 (Continued)

Burke-Litwin Model Category	Culture Initiative	Purpose/Goal(s)
Structure	• Resources directorate established (January 1993).	• To separate program making from resources provision in a single structure to reduce costs and clarify accountabilities.
	• Separation of commissioning from production.	• To clarify decision making and develop a clearer distinction between separate functions.
	• Redefinition of the role of the center (headquarters) on policy, strategy, performance, and compliance.	• To clarify responsibility and emphasize the importance of a continuing strategic drive and to create a policy framework.
Management practices	• Generation of a set of management practices that are relevant to "Extending Choice."	• To link behavior with purpose, vision, and goals.
	• Personal performance review: top 300 jobs by January 1994, and remainder during 1994-1995.	• To link measurement actions with clear strategies objectives and to reward achievement accordingly.
	• Corporate communications with staff.	• To encourage good practice regarding communicating with staff by making it a normal practice of management.

(Continued)

Table 10.1 (Continued)

Burke-Litwin Model Category	Culture Initiative	Purpose/Goal(s)
Systems (policies and procedures)	• "Producers' Choice": operational 1993, followed by market testing and best practices study (1994). This initiative provides program producers with a choice of whether to use internal resources (which has been the practice thus far) or to purchase them externally.	• To promote efficiency and value for money, to improve the understanding of the actual cost of individual programs, to develop accountability to a level that can influence the cost and quality of BBC resources and services, and to provide convincing measures of the BBC's relative efficiency in the marketplace.
	• Performance review (1993).	• To establish in every area of activity how well the BBC is performing against declared strategic aims and goals.
	• Producers' guidelines (1993).	• To clarify the BBC's editorial and ethical standards for program makers and the public.
	• Managers' guidelines (1994).	• To determine how BBC managers should behave in their relationships with staff and reach agreement with the recognized trade unions.

(Continued)

Table 10.1 (Continued)

Burke-Litwin Model Category	Culture Initiative	Purpose/Goal(s)
Climate	• Involvement initiatives by managers: "breakthrough," suggestion schemes, problem-solving teams (1993-1994).	• To encourage a process through which people will feel involved in their work and feel able to influence it.
Task requirements and individual skills/abilities	• Job evaluation system conducted by external consulting firm (1993-1994).	• To describe jobs in ways that enable scope, size, and nature to be determined with related grading.
	• Human resource planning process and training plans (1994).	• To assess the likely demand for jobs and supply of occupational skills in the future and develop training plans to tackle gaps between demand and supply.
	• Business education program (1993).	• To enhance management skills and knowledge in business practices and thus build a critical mass of relevant competencies for the BBC's future.

	1993	1994	1997	1999
External Environment	3.41	3.36	3.92	3.73
Mission / Strategy	3.08	3.22	3.45	3.10
Leadership	2.14	3.22	2.50	2.64
Culture	2.92	2.89	3.37	2.77
Managerial Practices	3.00	3.12	3.25	3.25
Structure	2.08	2.78	2.83	2.53
Systems	3.08	2.94	2.75	2.93
Work Group Climate	3.24	3.36	3.34	3.32
Job / Skill Match	3.26	3.23	3.27	3.42
Individual Needs/Values	3.32	3.25	3.19	3.12
Motivation	2.60	2.88	3.69	3.28
Performance	3.26	3.24	3.48	3.33

A Burke-Litwin Model Summary

- 1993
- 1994
- 1997
- 1999

Figure 10.4. The BBC staff survey results, 1993, 1994, 1997, 1999—A Burke-Litwin model summary

There have been four staff surveys. The first, in 1993, was a sample survey, those in 1995, 1997, and 1999 have been a full census of all staff. Overall, response rates have varied from the lowest at 35% (in 1999) to 46% (in 1993). The lowest response rate is still a "good" response for this kind of survey.

In each survey a large proportion of the questions have remained the same. In 1997 questions were added to merge a proposed communications survey with the Staff Survey, but overall the focus of the questions in all surveys has been driven by the Burke-Litwin model of organisational performance and change.

This model and the survey enable us to understand how staff perceive the relative impact and importance of sections in the model (e.g., strategy, structure, systems) for the BBC's overall performance as an organisation.

In 1993 staff understood little about the impact of the external environment. Competition, political and financial pressures and technology were generally a mystery. As a result, the culture was inappropriate to the environmental threats we faced, the strategy was in its infancy, organisational structure reflected an earlier broadcasting world and managerial behaviour was uninspiring.

By 1995, after extensive staff briefings, the publication of Extending Choice, and re-organisation, things were different. Staff were clearer about the competitive environment but had become concerned with "bureaucracy" and whether it was "safe to say what you think." It was clear that the behaviour of managers was key, and there was much discussion about "staff morale." Overall the results of the 1995 survey were "worse" than the 1993 survey.

In the 1997 staff survey, after extensive strategy work, programme reviews and management development activity, progress had been made. People were clear about the need for change, could identify with the BBC's aims and strategy, and were more positive about how managers behaved. There was also a clear view about the threats and opportunities posed by competition and technology. However, staff saw their leaders as out of touch, organisation structure as unclear, and systems as unhelpful.

The 1999 staff survey: For this fourth assessment the picture is a complex one. In some areas, after correction for untypical items in the 1997 survey, there has been little significant movement either way. However, overall the trend on many sections, especially the more critical ones, is an improving one. Figure 10.4 shows the overall pattern of responses from the four surveys. In summary, over the six years:

- perceptions of how leaders and managers behave has improved.

- awareness of the external environment and the BBC's mission and strategy have remained robust.

- motivation (the extent to which people feel driven to perform) is strong and improving. Pride, satisfaction, and enjoyment are all high.

- climate (the ways in which work-group members work together) and the match between jobs and skills are strong, with little movement over six years.

The work to explain the BBC's strategy, the continuing investment in management development activities, the programme strategy reviews and the "tribe" work and other initiatives have all clearly contributed to these results. We also know that changing staff perceptions, whilst driving large scale change, is a slow but gradual process.

This year, the key issues on which we need to focus are *leadership* (the ways in which people at all levels behave), *systems* (the organisational processes which support tasks), and *structure* (the ways in which work is organised).

Leadership behaviour is critical to organisational performance. Many of the questions in this section are prefaced with the phrase "the managers that I know . . ." so the behaviour applies to *all* managers at any level.

Two questions prefaced with the phrase "members of the top team of my directorate . . ." and asked in 1997 produced an improved response in '99 compared to '97. However, leadership overall is still a low scoring, if improving, item.

Three questions in the survey contributed to the low result:

- To what extent do any of the managers you know in the BBC persuade and influence others to work together toward a common goal? (2.9)

- To what extent do members of the top team of my directorate provide a clear sense of what needs to be done to move from where we are now to where we need to be? (2.5)

- To what extent do any of the managers you know in the BBC promote innovation and creativity despite the risks which may be involved? (2.6)

New staff (those with the BBC for less than one year), women at all levels, Afro-Caribbean staff and senior managers all rated leadership significantly more positively than others. Worldwide and World Service are smaller directorates than others, geographically more isolated, and also have sophisticated communication and briefing systems in place. Whilst lessons should be learnt from Worldwide and World Service practices, a systematic and sustained focus on leadership behaviour at all levels across the whole of the BBC will need to be developed if we are to continue an improved trend.

The section on *Systems* included IT systems, reward systems, commissioning and communications systems. However, the items with the most impact on our overall performance in this section and which lowered the overall score to 2.93 were all answers to the following questions:

- Internal and external communications are consistent. (2.7)

- Employees can always believe the information put out by the BBC. (2.9)

Analysis of the driving variables in the model identifies the *Systems* section as important, but we seem to have reversed a declining trend, when '93, '95 and '97 results are compared to '99.

A focussed and consistent initiative by managers at all levels to explain to staff in all directorates, face to face, could have a significant impact, albeit with a skeptical audience.

With respect to *Structure,* comparisons with the 1997 survey on this item are unreliable because only one question was asked. However in 1999 (at 2.53 overall) it was the lowest-rated item. Six questions were asked, four contributed most to the low result out of five in total.

- The way my directorate is organised helps achieve our directorate strategy and goals. (2.6)

- The way my department is organised helps me work effectively. (2.8)
- The current organisation of the BBC encourages staff to be flexible and responsive to change. (2.3)
- Group members are clear about objectives, performance standards, priorities, and deadlines. (3.0)

This section also contained the question which scored the lowest of all 107 items in the survey:

- The internal market helps the BBC achieve its purposes. (2.1)

All staff dislike the way in which the BBC, their directorate, and department is organised. They still see little relevance in the internal market and believe it works to the detriment of effective cross-directorate working.

Clearly the BBC's structure and the critical business systems which support it have delivered reduced cost, improved programme performance and clearer accountability, but we have not yet won staff over to this view. Moves to reduce the complexity of inter-departmental trading and to secure long-term partnerships will all help, but we need to work hard to explain the benefits.

Summary and Analysis: Much has changed since 1992/93, and to isolate independent drivers of change in staff perception is difficult. However, it is clear that when we focus on developing understanding, involving and explaining issues, we tend to get change. For example:

- Awareness about the external environment (financial, technological, and competitive issues) is much stronger. Our strategy work, and the debates in directorates about it, has had an impact.
- Manager development work over the last few years has focussed on the basics of managing; agreeing on clear objectives, creating a mission, rewarding performance, and demonstrating a commitment to training. All these basic managerial practices scored well, especially in Worldwide and World Service.
- People are clear about the BBC's public service aims and are still proud to work here. Teamwork is highly regarded; people believe they have the skills they need to do their present jobs.
- Worldwide and World Service have clear communication systems (World Service for some time) and clear management development programmes (particularly in Worldwide). They are both geographically isolated, and to a certain extent removed from the systems and business processes elsewhere, which have tended to lower the results generally. Both have new chief executives and cultures very different from the "mainstream" BBC. The most significant driver is likely to be that both have invested heavily in management development programmes, with strong top down commitment.

We perform better than U.K. companies using the same survey technique in the area of motivation, individual needs and values, and job-skill match; at about the same level of achievement on mission/strategy, culture and management processes; but not so well on leadership strategy and systems. Comparisons with U.S. companies are more complex, but again the motivation of our staff compares well.

Throughout all of this, leadership behaviour (the ways in which *all* managers behave) is key, particularly in the area of communication. Will "communication," despite all our efforts, ever improve? In 1976 a controller in the BBC was quoted by Prof. Tom Burns (Burns: The BBC, *Public Institution and Private World,* 1979, MacMillan):

I'm very worried about communication. You're up against a communication blockage. Heads of department don't find it difficult to communicate their own ideas, but they seem to find it very difficult to pass on information about the BBC generally. I don't think they are good at passing on what they could pass on with advantage. . . . I discover, when talking to junior people, that they either do not know what I myself have communicated to their seniors, or have seriously distorted view of it—to the point of mythology.

The messages we now have to communicate are more complex than those from the comparatively comfortable days of the 1970s. We have to continue to work at this.

Regarding action to be taken, the survey results are being progressively released to directorates and business units in a process which includes training key people to be able to interpret the results on directorates and work with them to develop specific action plans. To allow time for this process to be completed directorates will be asked, over the next three months, to formulate a detailed plan of action for discussion by December. These plans need to reflect the timescales and intentions of other projects which will have an impact on staff perception, e.g., the supplier strategy, the commissioning review and licence fee discussions.

Leadership development is key. Directorates will need to develop detailed plans for development work which will be supplemented by BBC wide initiatives. A complementary plan will be submitted to tackle this in the same timescale.

Work in hand to improve our Structures and Systems needs to continue, and we need to explain both more clearly. Whilst these are important factors to get right their impact on performance is through leadership and the ways in which managers behave. Managers at all levels need to find ways to make the systems work flexibly and collaborate across existing systems more effectively.

To conclude, very few organisations have such good data about how their staff feel on critical issues stretching back to the early 1990s. The message is very clear. When we focus on issues both in directorates and across the BBC the views of staff change. Our efforts to explain competition, financial pressures, and technology have all raised understanding of their impact and significance. Perceptions of leadership, managerial behaviour, and match between jobs and skills have all improved. Work group climate, culture and strategy are all holding well. Motivation is strong and improving.

While structure, systems and leadership are all improving, they are this year the important drivers if we want to change perception. The most critical of these and central to the model is leadership. Recent work in Worldwide and World Service on leadership behaviour confirms the significance of this section. An integrated and sustained programme to address leadership behaviour at all levels when the present uncertainties surrounding BBC Resources and Worldwide have been resolved would produce measurable results.

In summary, like the Dime, the BBC change effort, with multiple initiatives concentrating in the transformational categories of the Burke-Litwin model, was more revolutionary or discontinuous change than evolutionary or continuous change. As the years went by, and perhaps by 1997 or so, the BBC change effort became more continuous and less discontinuous.

Summary

The aim of this chapter has been to demonstrate the utility of the Burke-Litwin model for organization change. In both the Dime and BBC cases, the model framed the respective change efforts, beginning with due consideration of the external environment and then linking this information (external forces) with the transformational factors for internal change leverage. The *deep structure* (Gersick, 1991) of both organizations was affected—the merger and moving from a savings to a commercial bank in the Dime's case, and in the case of the BBC, launching a new vision/mission ("Extending Choice") and initiating such interventions as "Producers' Choice," "Performance Review," and the structural change of separating the resources directorate. These impacts on the deep structure and culture of both organizations represent revolutionary, discontinuous change.

In both of these cases, the CEO and director general were key ingredients of the organization change, for example, having a long-range view, spearheading and supporting an expansion of mission, energizing many people in their organizations to take up the banner of change, and changing executives at the top to get a better team effort. Also, significantly in each case, the CEO and director general relied on and put considerable trust in their human resources executives. They both had a sense of how important the human side of the organization change was and recognized their need for expertise and assistance with this critical aspect of the overall change effort.

These final comments provide a segue to the next chapter, which concerns the leadership role and function in organization change.

Note

1. This section was written with the help and approval of Bob Nelson, Controller, Development & Training of the BBC. In fact, the later section explaining the Staff Survey results over a six-year time span is in Bob's words. I am deeply grateful to him for this invaluable assistance.

11 Leading Organization Change

A psychologist friend and colleague, Dale Lake, years ago learned to fly an airplane, now a primary hobby for him. Flying in the copilot seat with him over and seemingly through the Colorado mountains was a thrill I will never forget. He told me at the time that a primary reason he loved to fly was the precision required and the joy of accurately navigating a chosen destination. He elaborated by saying that for him, flying served as an antidote to the lack of precision in psychology. The antidote for me is boating. Charting a course in the Gulf of Mexico, cruising through the water, and then seeing on the horizon a buoy or lighthouse at the place and time it was supposed to appear is highly satisfying and indeed fun. In planning the trip, one must take into account environmental factors such as tide changes, strength of the current, wind and other weather-related elements (e.g., potential for fog), as well as internal factors, such as engines (I prefer motors, not sails) and instruments (radar, radio, etc.). Are they in good working order?

Although not as precise, using an organizational model in the manner described in the previous chapter is not unlike charting the course and reading the navigational signs. The organizational model serves as a navigational chart that helps us to account for environmental factors both external and internal to the organization. And if we have (a) measures over time, which are automatically provided in boating and flying and in the organization are a matter of comparing a Time 1 with Time 2 measures, as in the Dime case, and (b) multiple time measures, as in the BBC example, then we can determine whether we are on course and if needed, which is usually the case, take corrective steps.

But who is the "royal we" in the above statement? Staying with the comparison for one more moment, the "we" is the pilot or the captain. Without this person at the controls or at the helm, the destination will never be reached. Without leadership, planned organization change will never be realized. The leadership box in the Burke-Litwin model is therefore critical. It is the leader who articulates and brings together the external environment with the organizational mission, strategy, and culture and then provides a vision for the future: the destination, the change goal(s).

The purpose of this chapter, then, is to define what leadership is, especially executive leadership, and explore the role of the organization change leader.

First, let us return to a phrase stated above: Without leadership, planned organization change will never be realized. This is a strong declaration. So, we will initially respond to the question that is implied here: Does leadership really matter? Evidence will be provided. Next, we will address a definition with an attempt to clarify the nature and characteristics of leadership. And, finally, taking the bulk of the chapter, we will discuss the role of the change leader in the context of phases of planned organization change.

Does Leadership Matter?

Before moving too far along with the assumption or implicit premise that leaders do indeed make a difference, perhaps we should pause for a moment and examine the assertion. There is, after all, a school of thought that embraces the argument that leadership is exaggerated and that leaders are not exactly influencing organizational performance. Some argue, as Zaccaro (2001) has noted, "that organizational performance is strictly a function of environmental characteristics and contingencies" (p. 5); for example, see Aldrich (1979), Bourgeois (1985), Lawrence and Lorsch (1967), and Romanelli and Tushman (1986). Others in this camp have argued that precedence plays a large role, and so do organizational culture and previous organizational decisions and activities (Miles & Snow, 1978; Starbuck, 1983).

These arguments questioning the influence of leaders are heavily dependent on definitions, the measurements and methods used, and the kinds of statistical analyses employed. In other words, some of their conclusions can be questioned as a function of methods. To be fair, however, leaders do not account for all or even most of the variance in explaining organizational performance.

But leaders do make a difference, especially in terms of organization change. Anecdotal evidence and common sense need to be considered. As Hogan, Curphy, and Hogan (1994) have pointed out in their answer to this question, "The fact that Lincoln's army was inert until Ulysses S. Grant assumed command and that some coaches [e.g., Phil Jackson in basketball and Bill Parcells in football] can move from team to team transforming losers into winners is, for most people, evidence that leadership matters" (p. 494). Interestingly, Hogan and his colleagues also reflect on the harmful side of leadership; that is, leaders can have a harmful effect, for example, Hitler and Stalin. And Hogan et al. also cite evidence from the consumer side—a manager's direct reports or a leader's followers—that leaders make a difference; for example, see Bass (1990), Hughes, Ginnett, and Curphy (1993), and Yukl (1998). Furthermore, as Hogan et al. (1994) noted,

> Conversely, reactions to inept leadership include turnover, insubordination, industrial sabotage, and malingering. R. Hogan, Raskin, and Fazzini (1990) noted that organizational climate studies from the mid-1950s to the present routinely show that 60% to 75% of the employees in any organization—no matter when or where the survey was completed and no matter what occupational group was involved—report that the worst or most stressful aspect of their job is their immediate supervisor. Good leaders may put pressure on their people, but abusive and incompetent management create billions of dollars of lost productivity each year. (p. 494)

For more on leaders' negative influence, see Dixon's (1976) book on military incompetence and more recently, Hornstein's (1996) book on "brutal bosses."

In addition to the report of Hogan et al. (1994), Zaccaro (2001) has cited convincing evidence that leaders do matter. For example, a study by Weiner and Mahoney (1981), which covered 193 companies across 19 years, showed that leadership accounted for about 44% of the variance in profits and 47% in stock price. Additional evidence can be found in studies by Barrick, Day, Lord, and Alexander (1991), Hambrick (1989), and Hitt and Tyler (1991). What has not been as clear from the literature is the impact of leadership on organization change. There are numerous cases that anecdotally support the argument that leadership matters in times of change; see, for example, Burke and Trahant (2000). But there has been little evidence that scientifically demonstrates the leader's impact. It seems reasonable to assume, nevertheless, that because there is mounting evidence that leaders affect organizational performance in general, surely they have an impact on organizational change in particular. We will proceed in this chapter, in any case, with the assumption that leaders have a significant influence on organization change, and the latter part of this chapter describes how this influence can occur.

On Defining Leadership

Defining and attempting to clarify leadership is a lot like trying to define and describe love. First, we know it when we see it and feel it, but finding accurately descriptive words for what we see and feel is not easy. Second, there may be as many and as diverse definitions for leadership as there are for love. Rost (1991), in his book on leadership, devotes two chapters just to definitions, a total of 58 pages. And finally, definitions and descriptions depend on who you are talking with and what your respective experiences have been. All of us have experienced leadership, good and bad, starting with parents, and most of us have experienced some form of love, also beginning with parents. These experiences and forms, after all, differ.

The above caveat aside, some initial clarification is warranted, starting with the concepts of power and leadership.

Power is the capacity to influence others; *leadership* is the exercise of that capacity. In social psychology, a definition of the exercise of power is when Person A is able to get Person B to do something that B might not otherwise have done. Leadership can be defined accordingly, that is, the act of making something happen that would not otherwise occur. The operative phrase here is "making something happen." This chapter is dedicated to that definition.

Before tackling the "making something happen," however, we need some further clarification.

Toward Further Definition

First, leadership is not the same as authority and is different from management. With respect to the latter, Zaleznik (1977) was one of the first to specify differences between leaders and managers. Leaders, for example, are more personal about organizational goals; that is, they see no distinction between one's own goals and the organization's, whereas managers are more impersonal about goals. With respect to relations with others, especially followers, leaders relate more intuitively than managers do, whereas managers relate more according to role, as Zaleznik sees it. He specified other differences as well, and his distinctions were similar to Burns's (1978) transformational (Zaleznik's leader) and transactional (Zaleznik's manager) categories (Burke, 1986). Today, these distinctions are more or less taken for granted; see, for example, Kotter (1990).

Authority concerns the "right to": the right to make decisions that are binding on others, to use and distribute resources, and to perform certain functions (e.g., hire and fire, etc). Obholzer (1994) differentiates three sources of authority—from above, from below, and from within. Authority from above is derived from a particular role in a social system, for example, within an organizational hierarchy in which the "right to" is authority according to the position that one holds. Authority from below, whether formal or informal, is given (authorized) by subordinates (followers) and/or colleagues. One's authority is either sanctioned or withheld from below. Authority from within derives from one's individual capacity to assume his or her own authority (formal, informal, or personal) based on one's personality (e.g., charismatic qualities, personal history, etc.).

Leadership is more associated with authority from below and from within and less with authority from above. Leadership has more to do with the person and less to do with role and position. Leadership is about influence, not command and control. To be successfully influential requires personal skills such as active listening, persuasion, empathy, and being aware of how one as leader is affecting others and in turn how one is being personally affected by others.

Second, leadership requires followership. A person may think that he or she is a leader, but if there is no one to follow, it does not matter what the person's self-concept may be: Without a follower, a person is *not* a leader. Thus, leadership is about influence, but that influence is a reciprocal process. Leadership occurs when a potential follower exists and wants direction.

Third, as noted above and in Chapter 9, Burns's (1978) two categories of leaders, transformational and transactional, also correspond to the two categories of organization change, discontinuous and continuous, respectively. Transformational leadership is therefore more likely to be required for discontinuous change, and transactional for continuous change.

Bass (1998) has developed a measure of these two leadership categories, the Multifactor Leadership Questionnaire (MLQ). From research with this instrument, several components of transformational leadership have emerged: charismatic leadership, inspirational motivation, intellectual stimulation, and individual consideration. Bass points out that charismatic and inspirational motivation usually form a combined single factor that he labels "charismatic-inspirational leadership."

The point is that a significant part of transformational leadership in Bass's MLQ involves charisma. Although Bass does not equate transformational with charisma, one gets the impression nevertheless that the two "go together" more often than not. Moreover, Bass and his colleagues summarize considerable research evidence that transformational as compared with transactional is a superior form of leadership (Avolio, 1999; Bass, 1998). Bass and his colleagues would probably agree that one can be a successful transformational leader without being charismatic (although they might also agree that such a leader is rare). In any case, Colin Marshall was such a person, that is, a highly successful change agent as CEO of British Airways (BA), yet not charismatic, at least not in the classical sense. Marshall led a transformation of BA from a command and control, bureaucratic, insular culture to one that became market oriented, customer focused, and more nimble than bureaucratic in its day-to-day operations; see Chapter 4 in this volume, Chapter 6 in Burke and Trahant (2000), and Goodstein and Burke (1991) for more on the BA story.

An opposite example to Marshall, one that fits more with Bass's contention regarding transformational leaders and charisma, is the case of Roger Goldman, who led a significant organization change at NatWest Bancorp from 1991 to 1996; see Chapter 12 in Burke and Trahant (2000). Goldman led much of the change via the sheer force of his personality. For example, he maintained a special phone line direct to his office (the phone was bright red) labeled *Call Roger* that any employee could use to personally ask him any questions he or she desired. In other words, Goldman answered the phone himself.

Goldman, then, is an interesting contrast to Marshall, yet what the two had in common as they led their respective change efforts was *persistence*. They "stayed the course," kept people focused on the mission and strategy, dealt directly with resistances, and bounced back when mistakes were made. The point is that charismatic leadership, though potentially helpful, is not *required* for successful organization change. What is required include qualities such as persistence, as already noted, having a clear vision about the desired future state, and self-awareness, also noted above. We will focus more on the kind of leader behavior and qualities that are needed for successful organization change as we proceed through this chapter.

Finally, our concern in this chapter is with *executive* leadership, the senior people at the top of the pyramid or at the nexus of a network in organizations. We are less concerned with leadership in the middle or at the first-line supervisory level. Not that leadership is unimportant at these lower levels, quite to the contrary. In fact, as organization change progresses, these middle and lower levels become even more critical to the success of the overall effort. But for purposes of this chapter, our concentration is more at the top of the organizational hierarchy because these executive-level individuals in the early phases of organization change are key to the effort's ultimate success.

With his recent book, Zaccaro (2001) has provided a useful compendium of executive leadership. In a thorough review of the literature, he has identified four primary conceptual perspectives of executive leadership.

Conceptual Complexity. This perspective is based on the premise that organizations operate within highly complex environments and will do so even more in the future (Zaccaro, 2001):

> [This] complexity results in the stratification of organizations, wherein higher levels of leadership are characterized by greater information-processing demands and by the need to solve more ill-defined, novel, and complex organizational problems. To thrive, executive leaders require significant conceptual capacities that allow them to make sense of and navigate successfully within such complex environments. (p. 17)

A prominent example of this perspective is the work of Elliott Jaques (1978, 1986) and his colleagues; see, for example, Jacobs and Jaques (1987) and Jaques and Clement (1991) in what is referred to as *stratified system theory.* Other examples include Mumford, Zaccaro, Harding, Fleishman, and Reiter-Palmon (1993) and Streufert and Swezey (1986).

Behavioral Complexity. This perspective focuses on the leader's behavior in terms of the multiple roles he or she plays and the multiple constituencies to be served. With these many and diverse demands, the leader must be capable of behaving in a variety of ways in a variety of situations. Moreover, the leader, at times, must be capable of balancing competing demands, such as mentoring and developing subordinates, yet at the same time having to deliver difficult feedback regarding, say, poor performance. Examples of this perspective include Mintzburg's (1973) categories of managerial roles, Tsui's (1984) multiple constituency model, and Quinn's (1988) competing values framework.

Strategic Decision Making. This perspective stresses the importance of congruence between the organization and its environment; thus the primary tasks of senior leaders in the organization are to monitor the environment, analyze potential problems, seek opportunities, form policies and strategies, and implement and then evaluate these policies and strategies. With respect to leader qualities, emphasis is given to cognitive abilities, functional expertise, and motives, such as need for achievement and self-efficacy, risk taking, and locus of control. Examples of this perspective include the work of Bourgeois (1985), Lawrence and Lorsch (1967), Thompson (1967), and Wortman (1982).

Visionary and Inspirational. This perspective emphasizes charisma, transformational, and visionary leadership. The primary role of the leader is to develop a vision that will focus and motivate collective action by followers in the organization. Important leader qualities include cognitive abilities, self-confidence, risk taking, and emotional intelligence. Examples of this perspective include Bass (1998), Burns (1978), Bennis and Nanus (1985), Conger (1989), House (1977), and Sashkin (1988).

Summary. As Zaccaro (2001) pointed out, even though there are different emphases, these perspectives about executive leadership overlap in that all emphasize the importance of long-term goals, organizational directions, and boundary management. With respect to our purpose in this chapter, it is important to understand that, although the language of the Burke-Litwin model might lead us to believe that executive leadership is the same as the transformational and visionary perspective, there is more to it than that. As we proceed, let us bear in mind that the senior leader's roles and qualities in leading change are complex and demanding. All four of these executive leadership perspectives are relevant.

Phases of Organization Change and the Leader's Role

The following descriptions of *how* to bring about organization change are derived from theoretical ideas and from experience in consulting with CEOs who were serving as change agents. What follows is written in a prescriptive fashion for the sake of clarity. Caveats are therefore not presented.

An interesting paradox about organization change, as noted in Chapter 1, is that we plan as if the process is linear when in reality, it is anything but linear. It is useful nevertheless to think about the planning process in terms of *phases*. After all, phases are not totally discrete; they overlap. But we must bear in mind that as planned organization change is implemented, (a) more than one phase occurs at the same time; that is, they are not temporally mutually exclusive and (b) contingency plans need to be in place because rarely does anything turn out as planned. Unanticipated consequences occur. It's not possible to think of everything!

The Prelaunch Phase

Leader Self-Examination

Leadership is personal. The process concerns the use of self, how to be persuasive, how to deal with resistance, and how to be political, in the best sense of the phrase: how to embody the vision of where one wants the organization to go. It is important, therefore, for the leader who is about to begin a significant change effort to take some time at the outset to reflect. This reflection can be considered in three categories: self-awareness, motives, and values.

Self-Awareness. There is growing evidence that self-awareness is related to performance; that is, high performers tend to have a greater overlap between how they see themselves and how others see them than do moderate and low performers (Atwater & Yammarino, 1992; Church, 1997). It behooves leaders who want to bring about a successful change effort to be as cognizant as possible of themselves in personal domains such as the following:

- Tolerance for ambiguity: The courses that organization change will take are not exactly predictable; being able to "live with" this kind of ambiguity is important.

- Need for control: It is difficult to be a "control freak" and lead change effectively; organization change is messy, sometimes chaotic and seemingly out of control; thus, being clear about what one can and needs to control and what one is not likely to be able to control is critical.

- Understanding how feelings affect behavior: What is one's typical reaction when others disagree or challenge or when others resist the change that the leader feels strongly about? Knowing oneself in these ways helps the leader manage himself or herself more effectively, especially in trying circumstances.

- Personal dispositions: Most people know whether their preference is extrovert or introvert, but what about other dimensions, such as need for closure and intuition compared with sensing? (These are components of the Myers-Briggs Type Indicator, MBTI, measure, based on Jung's personality theory.) There is some evidence, for example, that intuition (trusting one's hunches, future orientation, and conceptual tendency) is more related to leader behavior than is sensing (being fact-based, concrete, and practical); see, for example, Van Eron and Burke (1992). When the MBTI was used with the top team of a large global corporation a few years ago, 9 of the 11 scored intuitive, including the CEO. For a brief account of this team-building activity, see Burke and Noumair (2002).

- Decision making: It is highly valuable to understand the differences between times when one as a leader needs to take the reins and decide and times when one needs to loosen control and involve others as a part of self-knowledge.

Additional examples could be catalogued here, but the point was to give a flavor of some of the more important aspects of self-awareness for leadership purposes, not to provide an exhaustive list.

Motives. Knowing one's motives is of course a part of self-awareness, but for this section, the emphasis is on which motives are the more important ones for leading change.

Interestingly, according to O'Toole (1999), one of our paramount thinkers and writers in the arena of organization change, *ambition* is the "only inherent character trait [that] is essential for effective leadership" (p. 1). This word, for some, maybe most people, conjures up negative feelings. An ambitious person, especially one with *high* ambition, is to be avoided. But O'Toole argued that a certain amount of ambition is good. O'Toole used the words "appropriately ambitious." As he stated, "Even the saintly Mohandas K. Gandhi had ambition" (p. 2). Gandhi even admitted it himself. So, let us agree with O'Toole that having the *appropriate* amount of ambition is not only a good quality but may also indeed be a necessary motive for effective organization change leadership. Of course, the important issue here is, what is appropriate? O'Toole did not define appropriate, but he stated that the change leader needs to have a "healthy dissatisfaction with the status quo" (p. 2) and then to change it. He also points to the importance of having this ambition in the service of an organization change goal. In a sense, then, he was agreeing with Zaleznik's (1977) idea of a leader being one who experiences no difference between personal goals and those of the organization.

Using McClelland's (1965, 1975) three major motives—need for achievement, power, and affiliation—as discussion points, we can probably agree, first, that having at least a moderate (if not high) need to achieve is critical to success as a leader of change. Second, McClelland's need for power concept is not unlike O'Toole's notion of ambition. In this case, a certain amount of need for power would seem to be necessary for change leadership. If one does not want to influence others, one is not likely to be very effective at it. The McClelland and Burnham (1976) study puts the need for power into context. Using subordinates' ratings of their organization's degree of clarity and amount of team spirit as indices of successful management, McClelland and Burnham found that if a manager was high in power motivation, low in need for affiliation, and high in inhibition (that is, the power need was socialized, mature, and not expressed for self-aggrandizement), the organization's degree of clarity was greater (subordinates knew the goals and what was expected of them) and the team spirit was higher.

There are good reasons for this. Managers who have a high need for affiliation usually want to be liked and to be popular. As a result, their decision making tends to be impulsive, being done to please someone at the moment rather than in rational support of the overall good of the organization. Managers with a high need for power that is personally oriented are not builders of the institution, according to McClelland and Burnham (1976). They tend to demand personal loyalty from their subordinates—loyalty to them as individuals rather than to the organization. The institutional managers are the most successful because they encourage loyalty to the institution rather than to themselves. As a result, the successful manager creates a climate with clarity, team spirit, and opportunities for accomplishment.

The profile of the desirable institutional manager thus has three major elements: high need for power, low need for affiliation, and high inhibition. In addition, successful institutional managers like and are oriented toward organizations. They typically join more organizations and feel greater responsibility for developing them. They enjoy work, they like the discipline of work, and they have a preference for getting things done in an orderly fashion. They place the good of the organization above self-interest. They are judicious; that is, they have a strong sense of fairness. They are generally more mature, less ego-centered and less defensive. They are also more willing to seek advice from experts, and they have longer and broader vision regarding the future.

Finally, McClelland and Burnham (1976) pointed out that successful managers tend to have a style of management characterized by partici- pative and coaching behavior; that is, they are concerned with the needs and development of their subordinates. In summary, according to McClelland and Burnham,

> The general conclusion of these studies is that the top manager of a company must possess a high need for power, that is, a concern for influencing people. However, this need must be disciplined and controlled so that it is directed toward the bene- fit of the institution as a whole and not toward the manager's personal aggrandize- ment. Moreover, the top manager's need for power ought to be greater than his need for being liked by people. (p. 101)

Finally, effective change leaders need to have an above-average level of energy, and be capable of (a) working long hours when needed, (b) interacting with lots of people, and (c) energizing others. Of the thousands of citations in Stodgill's (1974) and later, Bass's (1990) *Handbook on Leadership,* one of the few consistent findings was that effective leaders are typically high-energy people.

Values. As noted with the explanation of the Burke-Litwin model in Chapter 9, the alignment of individual needs and values with the organi- zation's culture (norms and values) is likely to enhance motivation and in turn performance. This alignment is all the more important for the CEO and other change leaders in the organization. But what if we are attempting to change the culture? Then, it is a matter of modifying current values or establishing an entirely new set of values. Establishing these values to undergird and provide direction for the change effort is the responsibility of the CEO-change leader. Not that the values need to come directly from the CEO; the establishing process can involve many people. But in the end, the values must be compatible with the CEO's personal values because he or she must embody them and live them on a daily basis in the organization. In the Dime Bancorp case summarized in Chapter 10, it was a matter of establishing new values (drawn from the mission statement). An internal Dime task force did the work of drafting the new mission statement, but the CEO, Larry Toal, was highly involved. He attended many of the meetings and in the end was com- mitted to the mission statement; and because the new values were elicited from the mission statement, Toal's commitment to these values was easily achieved.

In another merger, that of SmithKline Beecham, values were created to help establish the new culture, as with Dime. In this case, the top team of the global company initiated the work of establishing the values. Bob Bauman, CEO of the newly merged company (SmithKline from the United States and Beecham from the United Kingdom) at the time, 1989, described in his own words the value generation process (Burke & Trahant, 2000):

> So the executive committee and I went away again, this time to define the values that would make up that culture. Obviously, there were certain values that were critical to our company. *Innovation,* for example, was critical. We didn't have much trouble getting people to agree on that. . . . There was no disagreement that *customers* were critical and that our customer base was changing. . . . HMOs were coming in, which brought up the question, "Who's the buyer now, the HMO or the doctor?" and "How do we bridge this gap?" So we knew we had to start thinking more about customers and had to do a better job—not just in providing good drugs but also in how we managed and serviced our customers.
>
> We extended our discussion of customers incidentally to include not just the outside world but also our own organization. Because we thought it important to say that everyone in the company has a customer. I had a customer on the Board. I had customers in dealing with members of the executive committee. We agreed that people on the manufacturing line, in R&D—people everywhere inside the company—had customers. . . . Another value we believed in was winning. We wanted to create a winning attitude inside the company, so we thought *performance* was important. And there was some feeling in our early discussions that we weren't driving as hard in the area of performance as we needed to. . . . We agreed we wanted to be winners and perform better than our competitors. . . . Another value that was clearly agreed to but harder to articulate was *people.* We knew we had to have the best people we could find and that they were key to our competitive advantage. So as part of articulating this value, we emphasized that people needed to contribute to the goals of the organization; we wanted to give everyone a chance to influence and participate in how work was done and how it got measured. And we wanted people to feel ownership for continuously improving the ways they worked on the job.
>
> Finally we agreed to the value of *integrity.* It's something we felt we possessed and that was important to the nature of our industry.
>
> We felt five values was the right number. We believed that if we got too many it would be very hard to drive them all through the organization. (pp. 64-66)

The Dime example was a "bottom-up" process of determining mission and values, whereas the SmithKline Beecham case was more "top-down." Both worked because each organization operationalized its respective sets of values by putting them into behavioral language and then building a multirater feedback program so that all key managers received feedback on behaviors that reflected the values. For more detail on the SmithKline Beecham example, see Bauman, Jackson, and Lawrence (1997), Burke (2000a), Burke and Jackson (1991), and Wendt (1993).

The External Environment

Another critical element of the prelaunch phase is for the CEO and other top leaders in the organization to monitor and gather as much information about their organization's external environment as possible. This would include information such as changing customer needs, changing technology in one's particular industry, changing government regulations, what competitors are up to, and what is occurring in the general economy both domestically and worldwide. And according to strategy guru Michael Porter (1985), it would also include understanding the bargaining power of customers, suppliers and unions, and threats of (a) new entrants into the marketplace and (b) substitute products or services. The CEO and his or her team must then determine how to respond to what the environment is telling them and how to establish a more effective alignment for their organization.

This prelaunch activity conforms, of course, to (a) the reality that for their survival, organizations are *dependent* on their external environment and (b) the theoretical principles of open system theory. Moreover, organization change occurs primarily as a reaction to some change in the environment. Rarely, if ever, do board members, CEOs, and their executive colleagues sit around a boardroom table together and decide to change the organization without regard to the organization's position in or degree of alignment within its external environment. Reading that environment accurately and reacting accordingly is key.

More than 40 years ago, in their classic paper on the "causal texture of organizational environments," Emery and Trist (1965) discussed four different kinds of environments for organizations, ranging from *placid, randomized* to *placid, clustered,* to *disturbed, reactive* to *turbulent fields,* and stated that the world seemed to be moving more toward the turbulent type. They were quite correct, of course; today, most organizational environments are turbulent. Their point further stressed the importance of reading the environment as accurately as possible so that timely and appropriate organizational responses could be made to ensure survival.

The CEO-change leader's responsibility here is to prepare for organization change as thoroughly as possible, by taking the time and expending the effort to gather environmental information carefully and accurately and then to analyze this information, before jumping into the change process too quickly. Impulsive behavior on the part of the CEO at this stage of the change process is to be avoided, if not at all other stages as well.

Establishing the Need for Change

If people in the organization see or feel no need for change, they are not likely to embrace the idea. CEOs and other senior executives are often in a better position to monitor the external environment and therefore are likely to see the need for change sooner and more clearly than the majority of organizational members. They are often in a better position, but not always. Technical people down in the organization may see a technological change coming before senior management does. Often, the sales force and others in the organization who have direct contact with customers see a need to serve them differently before senior management do. Regardless of where the awareness of a need for change originates, it remains the CEO's responsibility to communicate that need to organizational members. And the communication must be convincing. A case example helps to clarify these points.

British Aerospace (BAe), a multibillion-dollar aircraft and defense industry enterprise, was formed in 1977 by putting together six defense and aerospace organizations under one corporate roof. The firm at that time was a government-owned company, but 2 years later, Prime Minister Margaret Thatcher declared that BAe would become a private, stock-owned corporation, as she later did with British Airways and other nationalized industries during the 1980s. BAe was Thatcher's first nationalized company to become privatized. In a sense, BAe was a holding company with six previously autonomous organizations, which had rich histories dating back to World War II and before and possessed quite different corporate cultures. Richard Evans (now Sir Richard), having grown up in one of the six firms of the British aircraft corporation, became CEO on New Year's Day, 1990. He inherited six baronies, each of which viewed itself with considerable pride. After all, "that beautiful bird," as Evans called the Concorde, came from the earlier parts of BAe, as did other highly regarded aircraft (e.g., the Comet, the world's first commercial jet) and sophisticated defense weaponry. Also, by 1990, BAe had a number of joint ventures with French and German companies in the manufacture of the Airbus commercial aircraft. So,

Evans took over a healthy organization from the standpoint of sales, profit, and future customer orders.

One year later, however, things were considerably worse. The stock price had plummeted, orders were down (after all, the Cold War was over), and capital, especially cash, was badly needed. Evans began to cut costs—he laid off thousands of employees, for example—to divest of some of the businesses and to take severe write-offs. But productivity and innovation remained strong, at least in most of the former six companies, and there were many talented people in the ranks. But for some reason, these strengths could not be fully realized.

Monitoring BAe's external environment, Evans saw three large "blips on the radar," as he called them. One came from Boeing, a major competitor. They produced a new version of their 737 that was superior to the Airbus, at least at that time. A second blip was the fact that the capacity of European aerospace and defense firms far exceeded demand. And finally, there was the abysmal performance of BAe's shares on the stock market. These "blips" caused Evans to act yet again; he believed this time that a significant change needed to occur within the company to respond effectively. There were other needs for change as well, for example, correcting the silo effect of the six baronies that comprised BAe. Evans believed that a major culture change was the right action to take. To use Gersick's (1991) language, change in the "deep structure" of BAe was in order. To use Evans's words (Evans & Price, 1999),

> Why did I think that a culture change was the answer? There were of course many operating and strategic fixes that we could do (and did) to improve our competitive standing and our share price. But when you added all these up, and when you looked at the competitive abilities of rivals, there was a shortfall. I couldn't quantify it. I simply had a gut feeling, a conviction that the underlying reason for our deficiencies lay in the culture of the company. (p. 10)

The new culture desired was one that would integrate the various businesses so that, for example, consistent, common approaches could be taken across the corporation. Another change objective was to lessen the rivalries that existed among the former six companies.

So, relying on the wisdom and experience of his new nonexecutive chairman of the board, Bob Bauman, who knew a thing or two about large-scale organization change (recall that he had led the merger of SmithKline Beecham a few years earlier), and the expertise of external consultants, Evans launched the change effort. Working with his top

100 or so executives, Evans's initial work was on crafting a new mission statement with a commensurate list of corporate values. This early work went fairly well, but some of the executives were simply not convinced that all this effort and the occasional angst were worth it. Many of them had been through "culture change" before. Again, to quote Evans (Evans & Price, 1999),

> In the eyes of many of BAe's top managers, the lack of a "burning platform" weakened my argument that change was urgently needed. How could I make them see that the present good times were not symptomatic of the way things would be five years hence? The easier way was to present them with scenarios of likely futures. For this job I turned to one of our top line executives, John Weston, then managing director of Military Aircraft, now my successor as Chief Executive. I seconded him from his regular duties and gave him carte blanche to analyze the company from end to end and then report his findings.
>
> With characteristic thoroughness, John documented "The Case for Change." His report probed every single part of the business, its macroeconomic environment, its competitive structure, the state of technology, and so forth. Time and again he documented a stark conclusion: Our business units' rate of progress and future prospects of performance gains were inadequate, given the emergent threats in the external environment. What's more, even if we took a whip to them to urge them to improve sales and profits and squeeze the cash flow, any conceivable improvement would not change the analysis substantially. At the end of the day, BAe would be trailing and not setting the industry tempo.
>
> Because John Weston was the divisional head of our largest and most profitable business unit, his call to action could not easily be dismissed. If he saw the writing on the wall, so might everyone else. "We wanted to give them the macroeconomic and geopolitical picture right between the eyes. The paradigm for defence and aerospace markets was changing dramatically, and we had to learn superior skills and ways of reacting," says Weston. (p. 17)

The case was indeed made and the culture change at BAe went forth. The rest is history. Today, BAe is successful, its stock price more than triple what it was in 1993. One of its major products, the Airbus, is a formidable competitor with Boeing. Moreover, Evans was knighted in 1996 for his role as CEO in the turnaround of BAe. For the full story of how a CEO may make the case for change and other aspects of successful organization change, see Evans and Price (1999) and Chapter 9 in Trahant and Burke (2000).

Providing Clarity of Vision and Direction

The final point of this prelaunch phase is to craft a vision statement and in so doing, to provide clear direction for the organization change effort. One of the best statements about vision has been articulated by James O'Toole (1999):

> A robust vision mobilizes appropriate behavior. It uses memorable, simple concepts that make clear what needs to be different about tomorrow. It describes the distinctive competencies needed to deliver on the desired end state (for example, "Here's what we have to do differently in order to succeed"). Often, a vision will make choices clear by making the case for change as either an opportunity or a burning platform (for example, "If we don't change in this way, the company won't survive"). That's not asking much, is it?
>
> Leaders don't even have to create visions themselves (although many do). But, at a minimum, they must initiate a process for developing a vision and then engage themselves fully in generating buy-in. Shared commitment to a vision can be built either through wide-scale participation in the act of its creation or through involvement immediately thereafter in its dissemination. . . . We're not talking quantum mechanics here. This is simple stuff—so simple that many leaders gloss over the basics. For example, by definition, vision has to do with "seeing, sight, and sensing with the eyes." Recognizing that simple fact, effective leaders make their visions, well, *visual*. Remember Ronald Reagan's budget message when he explained that a trillion bucks amounts to a stack of dough as high as the Empire State building? By using that visual reference, he got Americans to *see* that federal spending amounts to real money! In doing so, he changed the terms of the national debate and, for the first time, created a majority in support of lower taxes. It was his most effective moment as a leader. (pp. 302-303)

Perhaps the paramount vision statement was delivered by Martin Luther King Jr. in his "I have a dream" speech on the steps of the Lincoln Memorial. He used striking imagery, for example, of children holding hands, that his listeners could "see."

The following are short examples of vision and direction provided by change leaders who have been referenced already:

- At the time of the SmithKline Beecham merger, chairman of the board Henry Wendt's (1993) conceptualization of what a truly global corporation looks like and his and CEO Bob Bauman's crafting of "The Promise" (the merged company's mission statement) provided both the vision and mission for the future. Their clarity of direction was critical to the success of the change that was, at the time, the largest cross-border merger ever. For the full story, see Bauman, Jackson, and Lawrence (1997), Burke (2000a), and Chapter 4 in Burke and Trahant (2000).

- At British Airways, it was Colin Marshall's clear emphasis on what the new culture should be—one that was customer focused and market driven—that provided the necessary vision for what needed to be reached.

- At the BBC, it was John Birt's description of "Extending Choice" (see Chapter 10) that showed the way to the future and the new corporation.

- At British Aerospace, it was Dick Evans's resolve to see that a mission/vision statement was crafted by the top 100 executives that set the stage for organization change. As O'Toole (1999) noted above, the CEO may not write the vision/mission statement himself or herself, but the responsibility for seeing that the job is done is clearly the CEO's. The way Evans did it took time, to be sure, but "at the end of the day," as the British are fond of saying, he had commitment.

By way of a quick summary, recall that in the description of the Burke-Litwin model in Chapter 9, a distinction was made between mission and vision, with vision being associated more with the leadership box or model category. But it is the change leader's or CEO's responsibility to see that both mission and vision are crafted, because both set the tone and the clarity of direction. Without direction, both in terms of who we are and who we want to be in the future, desired organization change will not occur.

The Launch Phase

Communicating the Need

Usually, the CEO is the one who delivers the message about the need for change—but not always. In the BAe example, Dick Evans called on his number two person, John Weston, to deliver the case for change. He made this decision for at least two reasons. First, he had already launched the organization change by involving the 100 executives in the crafting of a new corporate mission statement and in making the choices of values for the corporation as a whole. Although these executives did the work he asked them to, Evans was not convinced that their hearts were in it. And besides, some of them seriously questioned the whole process. In other words, Evans wasn't certain that his credibility as the change leader was as solid as it needed to be. Moreover, some of his executives had been through culture change in their respective businesses and were not exactly sanguine about going through the whole process again.

Second, in making the case for change and communicating the message, Evans believed that Weston would have more credibility because unlike Evans, who came from marketing and sales, he was an engineer and a "numbers guy," as were many of the BAe executives. It would be abundantly clear that Weston had done his homework and knew what he was talking about. This decision by Evans did indeed work, and the buy-in for the organization change began to emerge. The point is that although the CEO does not necessarily have to be the message deliverer, seeing that the delivery occurs, especially by another change leader colleague, is nevertheless his or her responsibility.

In the British Airways case, it was Colin Marshall, the CEO, who delivered the message. In fact, he delivered it again and again, making certain that he came across as consistent with the message each time he gave it and that he was absolutely serious and committed.

Initial Activities

A significant activity to conduct at the outset of organization change is an event that will capture attention, provide focus, and create the reality that the change effort now launched is not merely an exercise. A quote from Marshall, of British Airways, gives first his rationale and then an example of an initial activity (Burke & Trahant, 2000):

> But to get people to work in new ways, we needed a major change in the company's culture. That meant refocusing everyone on the customer, on the marketplace, and away from the exclusively engineering and operations focus we'd had. That had to be done, of course, without sacrificing safety, technical, or maintenance standards. And that proved tricky. People had difficulty understanding why I kept hammering away at the need to focus on customers while also saying, "We've got to fly these aircraft at a very high technical standard, too." The focus before had always been on the technical side alone, but I made the point repeatedly that we had to do both. It was at this point that we saw the explicit need for a culture-change program. . . . The first thing we did was to launch a program called "Putting People First". . . . a two-day seminar. We took roughly 150 employees at a time and drew people from various departments within BA and from various geographical areas. The program focused on how one creates better relationships with people, with one's fellow employees, with customers, even with members of one's own family. (p. 95)

Another example comes from another British organization, the BBC. John Birt, the CEO ("director general" is the proper title), authorized a 1-day workshop on "Extending Choice," the new mission/vision for the corporation. The day was devoted to, first, an overview and explanation of Extending Choice, and second, to small group meetings so that questions could be raised and discussions could be held about how this new "extended" mission affected each of them in their respective roles.

At BAe, the initial activity, as noted above, was the off-site meetings of the top 100 executives to craft the corporate mission statement and to choose the values.

At SmithKline Beecham, for the CEO, Bob Bauman, and his 10 executive direct reports, the initial activity to help shape the newly merged culture was working on the mission and value decisions and team building. The team building at the top had two purposes: to get this top group to work together more effectively and perhaps more importantly, to serve as role models for the rest of the global corporation. Part of the team-building process was (a) use of the MBTI to help the executives learn about their own and their colleagues' communicating, information processing, and decision-making preferences and (b) participation in a multirater feedback process on leadership practices to obtain a clearer understanding of how their self-perceptions regarding leading compared with the perceptions of others, particularly peers and direct reports. Subsequently, both the MBTI and the multirater feedback process permeated the entire managerial population of the company.

Finally, at Dime Bancorp, the initial activities that launched the organization change (a result of a merger; see Chapter 10) consisted of (a) establishing a task force of 15 people who represented all business units and all levels in the hierarchy to draft a new corporate mission statement, (b) determining a new business strategy led by the CEO, and (c) team building for the newly formed top team.

It should be obvious from these examples that the early activity of organization change can take a variety of forms. The point is that a focused symbolic and energizing event (or multiple events occurring at about the same time) is a highly useful way of launching large-scale and planned organization change.

Dealing With Resistance

Recall that in Chapter 5, organization change was considered at three levels: individual, group, and the larger system. As part of the coverage, the nature of resistance to change at each of these levels was included. The prudent change leader will be well aware of the nature of resistance to change and the different forms that this kind of behavior can take at the three organizational levels. Recall further that at the individual level, it is important that the change leader be wary of the imposition of change on people and to find ways whereby organizational members can have choice and be as involved in the process as possible. Also, the change leader needs to differentiate among the various types of resistance—blind, ideological, and political—so that the appropriate responses to and interactions with people in the organization can take place.

At the group level, recall that protecting one's turf, closing ranks, and demanding a new structure and/or leadership can be common forms of resistance. Seeing to it that activities in a group setting to achieve closure regarding the past (for example, having a symbolic funeral) can help in dealing with resistance. Also, recomposing a group with new membership can help and, of course, so can any activity that involves people in key decision making. For example, a highly influential group early in the merger process of SmithKline Beecham was the "merger management committee." Selected by the CEO, this group had the responsibility of selecting who the executives would be for the key positions in the corporation, and unique was the rule instituted by Bauman, the CEO, that no member of the committee could be named for any of these executive jobs. Objectivity was therefore more assured in the decision making regarding who was selected. Even though none of these committee members could have any of the plum positions they were working with, they were highly motivated and strongly committed to the task. After all, they were involved in an activity that would have far-reaching effects on the corporation. A delayed reward for these members was Bauman's making certain that they were eventually placed in important roles and positions for the corporation. The purpose of this brief case was to provide an example of how to involve people in the change process.

At the larger-system level, recall that resistance can take the forms of "This too shall pass"; that is, "We've seen this kind of initiative, or fad, before and it won't last this time, either." Also, there are diversionary tactics, for example, "Other mainstream business needs are far more important than this change thing." It was suggested earlier that coping with these forms of resistance might involve making a strong, compelling case for the change (as in the BAe example) and exerting strong leadership—not in a dictatorial way, but leading with persistence and with clarity of direction, passion, and vision, a point to be emphasized in the next section.

Postlaunch: Further Implementation

Once the organization change has been launched, it becomes quickly apparent to the change leader that so-called change management is an oxymoron. This particular phase of organization change—post-launch—is difficult for many CEOs. After all, they typically have control needs that are considerably above average, and now matters seem "out of control." CEOs can easily experience feelings of (a) anxiety—"What have we unleashed here?" and (b) ambivalence regarding decision making; some organizational members feel the excitement of change unleashed and want to run free, whereas others are asking for the CEO to step in and exercise control, usually taking the form of "a cry for structure" ("What's my new job? Who will be my boss?" etc.). With those control needs being aroused by these latter pleas for structure, many CEOs will want to step in and establish the new order. Because followers are asking for an antidote for all this uncertainty, the advice of Ronald Heifetz (1994) is most appropriate. In essence, he suggests three actions. First, to hold the collective feet to the fire, that is, to be persistent about what it is going to take to make the change successful (e.g., living with ambiguity about exactly how everything is going to work out). Second, draw the system out of its comfort zone but attempt to contain the associated stress so that it does not become dysfunctional (recall the work of Bridges; see Chapter 5). Third, deal with avoidance mechanisms that usually emerge during this time, such as blaming, scapegoating, and appealing to authority figures for answers.

During this postlaunch phase, it may also seem to the change leader that the process has taken on a life of its own. In fact, theory associated with living systems holds that when disturbance occurs (the launch phase), "the components of living systems *self-organize* and new forms and repertoires *emerge* from the turmoil" (Pascale, Millemann, & Gioja, 2000, p. 6) The CEO-change agent must persevere but be patient at the same time so that creativity and innovation "can do their work," or "magic" as some might call it, and allow for new forms to emerge. New forms may mean any number of things, including new ways of doing work, different values, new structures, new products, services, and/or business lines, getting into, if not establishing, new markets, acquiring a business never considered before, and so on.

As the change leader begins to deal with (a) his or her feelings of both excitement and anxiety, (b) follower behaviors of all varieties, and (c) seeming disorder, some more specific actions need to be considered for this postlaunch, change implementation phase. Though not exhaustive, the following five points are some key actions change leaders need to bear in mind.

Multiple Leverage

In large organizations particularly, change is too complicated for one action (intervention) to do the job. Many managers believe, for example, that changing the organizational structure will suffice. In a study of organization change some years ago, failure was most often associated with change of structure when that was essentially all that occurred (Burke, Clark, & Koopman, 1984). Moreover, in recent coverage of seven case studies of successful organization change, two of the summary points that are relevant here were as follows (Burke, 2000b):

- Time and again, these cases illustrate the absolute necessity of strong leadership for change to occur. We see change leaders in living color here. There is no substitute for visionary leadership in times of change. By definition, if there is leadership, there are followers.
- In addition to demonstrating how the phases of organization change work, all these cases show the deployment of multiple interventions. True organization change is too complicated for one intervention. Multiple sources of influence are required. (pp. 9-10)

Examples of levers for change from these case studies included process reengineering, crafting mission statements, developing a new process of supply chain management, training and development, crafting corporate values and leadership behaviors that were manifestations of the values, new pay for performance system, developing a "safety" culture, changing a plant in a chemical company, team building, and establishing self-directed work groups.

Taking the Heat

When organization change is launched, it is safe to say that not everyone will be happy with the idea. In fact, some may be quite upset and angry, looking for a target, a person or a group to blame "for this mess we're about to get ourselves into." The change leader is the most obvious target. Recently, a college president, who had launched an organizational change 5 years earlier, sat through two different meetings with full professors, listening to—and absorbing—their wrath about how poorly the change had been led and why it was such a stupid idea in the first place.

Dick Evans, of BAe, described one of his heat-receiving episodes this way (Burke & Trahant, 2000):

But I got a lot of pushback from people. People asked, "Why do we need to do this? We're operating perfectly well. We all have big change programs to deal with in our own businesses. Why do we need to do all this other stuff?" Many seriously thought and believed that I had some sort of hidden agenda and simply wanted to be told what to do so they could go away and do it. (p. 146)

Pushback, as Evans described it, is to be expected—not from everyone, perhaps only a minority, but heat is generated nevertheless, especially if those who are pushing back are opinion leaders in the organization. These are the times when the change leader must use as much self-control as she or he can muster, working hard (a) to listen, (b) not to be defensive, and (c) to display the patience of Job.

Consistency

During the early days of change, the change leader's behavior is scrutinized by followers. Does the change leader really mean it? Is this for real? Or is this initiative like all the rest, just another fad that will soon pass? In a recent change at a large nonprofit organization, the most frequently asked question by followers in the hallways or at lunch has been "Does he (the change leader) really mean it?" This is, of course, a question about consistency and about perseverance (see the next section). The point here is about trust. Can we (followers) trust the leader? Trusting the leader, of course, means believing that he or she is open, honest, and tells the truth.

Behaviorally, what may be even more important to followers is the extent to which the leader's behavior matches her or his words. This is the essence of consistency in an organization change effort—despite Ralph Waldo Emerson's derogatory comment about consistency, to wit, "A foolish consistency is the hobgoblin of little minds adored by little statesmen and philosophers and divines." The key to this quote, however, is Emerson's adjective *foolish*, and consistency of word and deed by the change leader in the organization's change process is anything but foolish.

Perseverance

"Staying the course" is essentially what is meant by this term. Many potential change leaders falter when the going gets tough. Albeit whimsical, organization change can be likened to losing weight. The first 5 or

10 pounds are easy, but the next 5 or 10 are much, much tougher. The early days of organization change, compared with later, are easy. People are excited and say things like "Finally, things are going to get better around here." But a year later, the change effort may have bogged down, the excitement is gone, and fatigue has set in. This is time for considerable perseverance on the part of the change leader. Perhaps the master of perseverance was Colin Marshall, at British Airways. Here's a perfect example, in his own words (Burke & Trahant, 2000):

> I made a particular point of attending every one of these "Managing People First" sessions. I spent two to three hours with each group. I talked with people about our goals, our thoughts for the future. I got peoples' input about what we needed to do to improve our services and operations. The whole thing proved to be a very useful and productive dialogue. We found it so valuable, in fact, that in cases when I was away, we offered people the opportunity to come back and have a follow-up session with me. So I really did talk to all 110 groups in that five-year period. (p. 99)

A part of leadership in an organization change effort, then, is to stay the course, to continue to encourage people, to exude energy and enthusiasm for continuing down the change path, and to find ways to continue communicating the message.

Repeating the Message

First, what is it that you repeat? The message is the vision and mission, but to be most effective, a *story* needs to be told that incorporates the vision/mission and values. The work of Howard Gardner (1995) is decidedly helpful in this regard. He deliberately uses the term *story* or *narrative* instead of *message* or *theme* because, as he states, he wants to accomplish the following:

> To call attention to the fact that leaders present a *dynamic* perspective to their followers: not just a headline or snapshot, but a drama that unfolds over time, in which they—leaders and followers—are the principal characters or heroes. Together they embarked on a journey in pursuit of certain goals, and along the way and into the future, they can expect to encounter certain obstacles or resistances that must be overcome. . . . the most basic story has to do with issues of *identity*. And so it is the leader who succeeds in conveying a new version of a given group's story who is likely to be effective. Effectiveness here involves fit—the story needs to make sense to audience members at this particular historical moment, in terms of where they have been and where they would like to go. (p. 14)

The change leader tells the story time and again, because people need to be reminded of what it is that we are doing—and why. In addition to the reminding, it is critical that the change leader tell the story to followers in person, face-to-face, not via the Web, a video, a written document, or a CD-Rom. Why? Dialogue with followers is essential. Questions need to be answered or at least responded to, and nuances may need elaboration. In the SmithKline Beecham merger, Henry Wendt, the chairman, and Bob Bauman, the CEO, traveled all over the world meeting with employees face-to-face to tell their story, which was the SmithKline Beecham "Promise": the company's promises to customers, employees, and stockholders.

Another example of a change leader telling the story personally, face-to-face, to 5,000 people, is the case of Roger Goldman, who turned around a retail banking situation that was not only in the red, but overall moribund with respect to performance. In his words (Burke & Trahant, 2000),

> I went on the road for a year to explain my vision of the bank to over 5,000 people in 800 profit centers and support offices. I did this to get people's support and to explain what we needed them to do if we were to be successful. In our case, it was about serving customers, communities, and our fellow employees. "Everyone has to give 110 percent," I told employees. "We're going to reinvent people's jobs and hold everybody more accountable for results." (p. 193)

By way of summary, consider the wonderful children's television show, *Blues Clues*. The same episode is repeated four times after the initial presentation on Monday of each week. The creators of this program have discovered that for the 4- or 5-year-old, repetition is critical for the child's learning. By Friday, the child "gets it." To learn something, adults in organizations may not need four iterations. Actually, they may need more! The point is this: Organization change with all its complexities and nuances needs to have focus, proper emphases on priorities, and explanation, particularly regarding "why we are doing these highly disruptive activities." Repeating this story time and again (message-vision/mission) is one of the most important functions of the change leaders.

Finally, we shall conclude this section on "Further Implementation," the postlaunch phase, with a cautionary note from Dick Evans, CEO of BAe (Evans & Price, 1994):

> One danger that besets change programmes is the curse of superficiality, or too much faith in the power of positive thinking. One day top management says, "Let's have a change programme." And after cranking out mission and vision statements,

backed with a heavy communications programme, hey presto, they've done it. What are omitted from these narratives are the tensions, ambiguities, conflicts, and frustrations that inevitably arise in the implementation phase. These difficulties get swept under the rug, only to return later—most likely in a more virulent form. (p. 16)

To mitigate the danger that Evans emphasizes, change leaders need to use multiple levers for the transformation, take the heat from followers from time to time, provide consistency in terms of words and deeds, persevere even to the point of risking being called stubborn, and repeat the message again and again.

Sustaining the Change

Before considering thoughts about sustaining organization change once things are fully launched and underway (such as unanticipated consequences, momentum, and further new initiatives), let us examine some recent thinking that is highly relevant and applicable. Earlier, in the section on "Further Implementation," a short quote was cited from the book by Pascale et al. (2000). The overall premise of the book is that recent knowledge, particularly in the life sciences, can inform our understanding of organizations in general, and management, leadership, and organization change in particular. Their premise is quite similar to the reasoning underlying the present book. Pascale et al. made the point that so-called chaos theory is not applicable to organizations, for they are not chaotic. But organizations are *complex,* that is, complex adaptive systems, and what they label as "the new science of *complexity*" is the applicable theory. These ideas are congruent with nonlinear complex system theory discussed in Chapter 6, Svyantek and Brown (2000); Gersick's (1991) concept of deep structure; and Capra's (1996) ideas covered in Chapter 3. Pascale and his colleagues have distilled from complexity theory and the life sciences (biology, medicine, and ecology) "four bedrock principles" that they consider to be applicable to organizations especially business enterprises. These principles are as follows:

1. *Equilibrium* is a precursor to *death.* When a living system is in a state of equilibrium, it is less responsive to changes occurring around it. This places it at maximum risk.

2. In the face of threat, or when galvanized by a compelling opportunity, living things move toward the *edge of chaos.* This condition evokes higher

levels of mutation and experimentation and fresh new solutions are more likely to be found.

3. When this excitation takes place, the components of living systems *self-organize*, and new forms and repertoires *emerge* from the turmoil [referred to earlier].

4. Living systems cannot be *directed* along a linear path. Unforeseen consequences are inevitable. The challenge is to *disturb* them in a manner that approximates the desired outcome. (Pascale et al., 2000, p. 6)

These principles are useful to our thinking about the importance of sustaining an organization change effort. This thinking is organized according to four considerations: unanticipated consequences, momentum, choosing successors, and launching yet again new initiatives.

Unanticipated Consequences

Referred to earlier in this chapter and in Chapter 1 was the paradox of planning organization change in a linear, phased way of thinking, yet realizing that the change process itself is *not* linear. This means that when the change is launched, equilibrium is disturbed, and seeming chaos occurs; that is, many and different reactions to the disturbance happen simultaneously, and the system moves to the *edge of chaos*, as Pascale et al. (2000) put it. Some examples of this kind of reaction include the following: (a) different organizational units interpret the change vision and direction to fit their needs, and therefore, the implementing of their part of the change becomes different from all other units (this is not necessarily bad but is often unanticipated), (b) some people who were expected to resist actually embrace and become champions of the change—and vice versa, and (c) desired and expected outcomes regarding a part of the overall change effort simply do not occur. The scary part is going to the edge, but the main point to remember here is that living systems are quite capable of evoking new forms and solutions and of self-organizing with gradual movement (however, not linear) to a new state of equilibrium. Reaching a new state of equilibrium is essentially what Lewin (1947) meant with his third stage of organization change, *refreeze* (see Chapter 7). Also recall Weick and Quinn's (1999) reconceptualizing of Lewin's three-stage model calling for *unfreezing* after a rebalancing to ensure innovation and find new ways of ensuring continuous change, which is applicable to our thinking here (see Chapter 6). The point is that after a disturbance, living systems again seek equilibrium, and Pascale et al. warned that equilibrium "is a precursor to *death*." The important word in their phrase is *precursor*, which means that death is not necessarily immediate. There is some allowable, if not necessary, time for things to resettle after the disturbance. But for the organization change to maintain momentum, resettlement must not be allowed to last.

Momentum

Writing in 1991 about the successful change effort at British Airways, Goodstein and Burke stated,

> It may be that BA's biggest problem now is not so much to manage further change as it is to manage the change that has already occurred. In other words, the people of BA have achieved significant change and success; now they must maintain what has been achieved while concentrating on continuing to be adaptable to changes in their external environment—the further deregulation of Europe, for example. Managing momentum may be more difficult than managing change. (p. 16)

A few years later, BA's performance began to deteriorate in part due to the lack of maintaining sufficient momentum and in part due to Colin Marshall's successor, choosing successors being the subject of the following section.

Maintaining the change momentum is critical because the natural movement toward equilibrium has to be countered. Finding new ways to recognize and reward change champions in the organization and celebrating achievements clearly helps to maintain momentum. The broader principles, however, are as follows: To counter equilibrium, Pascale et al. (2000) state rather provocatively that two forces—the threat of death and the promise of sex—can prevail. The desire to survive is powerful. If you question this, think how difficult it is to end a committee in your organization that was supposed to be ad hoc. Darwinian principles suggest that living systems do not evolve on their own but change as they respond to forces in the external environment. Living systems that survive do so because they mutate; that is, they adapt to the changing forces in their respective environments.

To maintain momentum, then, the change leader must constantly monitor the organization's external environment, being alert to changing forces that require adaptation to ensure survival.

The "promise of sex" leads us to the third ingredient for sustaining the change effort.

Choosing Successors

Another form for countering equilibrium is to prevent homogeneity, according to Pascale et al. (2000):

> Sexual reproduction maximizes diversity. Chromosome combinations are randomly matched in variant pairings, thereby generating more permutations and variety in offspring. [This] benefits a living system [because] harmful [bacteria] find it harder to breach the diverse defenses of a population generated by sexual reproduction than the relatively uniform defenses affected [by a process such as cloning]. (p. 29)

This principle from the science of living systems suggests that change leaders would do well to counter equilibrium and sustain the change effort by infusing "new blood" into their organizations, that is, not cloning themselves. The point is that although a complete overhaul of the people involved in the change would be absurd, having some proportion (20%? 30%?) who are new to the effort (hired from the outside or shifted over from other parts of the organization) counteracts the support equilibrium such as "tired thinking," solidified norms, and "group think."

One of the reasons that Colin Marshall's successor at British Airways, Robert Ayling, did not succeed as CEO was that he had been with the organization for a long time and was peripheral to the change effort that had proceeded under Marshall's leadership. In other words, Ayling was not one of the change leaders and had remained tied to the "old system." Examples of effective succession include the one at BAe from Evans to Weston and the more recent change at GE from Welch to Immelt.

Much has been written about problems of succession and infusing new thinking into an organization. For an overview of some of the central issues, see Levinson (1994).

Launching Yet Again New Initiatives

Finally, it is critical to identify and implement new initiatives that will renew organizational members' energy, spark new ways of thinking, and continue to propel the organization farther down its path of change after some unspecified time into the change effort. These new initiatives, of course, need to be in-line with the original change objectives, provided the external environment is not signaling to the organization that something more drastic needs to happen to ensure survival.

Examples of new initiatives in the service of sustaining the overall change effort might be the following:

- Acquisition of another organization/business.
- Creating a new business line or new product, or both.
- Establishing a strategic alliance or joint venture with another organization (which might even be a competitor or former competitor).
- Starting a new program that will help to improve quality and reduce costs.
- Deploying current products and/or services into markets not yet penetrated; for example, a chemical, metal, or ceramic product that has been sold and marketed only to other businesses can now be considered as a product sold directly to an individual customer.

The important point is for the change leader to be clear and deliberate about "disturbing" the system with new initiatives so that equilibrium does not take over. Incidentally, it is imperative for the change leader to cause these disturbances even if the organizational members plead for the change to come to some end point or conclusion. Conclusion needs to occur only for specific initiatives, *not* for the overall change process.

Summary

To specify what leaders actually do and what they need to do as change leaders, contrasts and comparisons were made between leadership and management, and power and authority. Leadership was considered in terms of transformational (more related to organization change that is discontinuous) and transactional (more associated with continuous change).

An additional refinement of what was being considered as leadership in this chapter addressed the distinction of organizational levels, the point being that the *executive* was our primary focus. For this emphasis, the work of Zaccaro (2001) was particularly helpful. In his survey of the literature, he delineated four different yet overlapping conceptual perspectives about executive leadership: (a) conceptual complexity, having to deal with ever more complex and changing environments; (b) behavioral complexity, the leader's multiple roles in dealing with multiple constituencies; (c) strategic decision making, stressing the importance of congruence between the organization and its environment; and (d) visionary/inspirational, emphasizing the charismatic, transformational, and visionary aspects of leadership. The point was made that what is required to be an effective change leader is highly complex and demanding; therefore, all four of these perspectives are relevant.

Does leadership matter? Some scholars say that leaders, especially at the top of organizations, have little, if any, influence. The bulk of the evidence, however, indicates otherwise, especially with respect to change.

The leader's role and function in organization change was specified according to four primary phases:

- The prelaunch phase:
  - Leader self-examination
  - Gathering information from the external environment
  - Establishing a need for change
  - Providing clarity regarding vision and direction

- The launch phase:
  - Communication of the need for change
  - Initiating key activities
  - Dealing with resistance

- Postlaunch phase or further implementation:
  - Multiple leverage
  - Taking the heat
  - Consistency
  - Perseverance
  - Repeating the message

- Sustaining the change:
  - Dealing with unanticipated consequences
  - Momentum
  - Choosing successors
  - Launching yet again new initiatives

It should be clear by now that we have attempted to address myriad interesting and complex ideas and practices about organization change. Recall the figure in Chapter 1 that was an attempt to represent some of these complexities with the "fall back" loops symbolizing unanticipated consequences that must be addressed and corrected for the overall change effort to keep moving forward.

Perhaps it is also clear that with respect to leading organization change, this chapter has emphasized application and practice more than theory and research. Recall that in introducing the large section on "Phases of Organization Change and the Leader's Role," the point was made that these ideas came from theoretical concepts, for example, Lewin's (1947) three steps of unfreeze, change, and refreeze, which have been expanded by others, from consulting experience, and that caveats would not be presented. Now, to a couple of caveats.

One reason for the greater emphasis on practice was to stay with the earlier promise that the latter half of this book would stress practice more than theory. A second reason for the practice emphasis is the fact that theory and research about leading organization change is rather sparse. This is why, for example, Zaccaro's (2001) recent book was described as helpful. So, if this chapter sparks some ideas for further research and theory development, I will be delighted.

12 Organization Change: Epidemics, Integration, and Future Needs

Early in 2001, I gave a presentation on organization change to a group of graduate students at Pepperdine University that was based in part on the initial draft of this book. One of the faculty members for the Pepperdine program, Chris Worley, a friend and colleague, also attended the presentation. Later, he gave me a book he had recently read because he knew that it related closely to what I had presented. Reading this book was like dealing with an unanticipated consequence to my writing, yet it was clear that I wanted to incorporate it somehow within my manuscript. Summarized in the following section, the book introduces new material here in my final chapter: a different voice and a unique set of ideas that have relevance and applicability to organization change.

A final book chapter is supposed to integrate, pull together disparate content, summarize and draw conclusions, and not introduce new material except for perhaps a discussion about the future. This statement is analogous to planning organization change. The final phase (chapter) is about integration and sustaining the change (learning). But as we now know, organization change does not occur as planned and certainly not in an orderly, predictive, linear manner. So, in true organization-change fashion, disequilibrium is introduced with this new material. Recall that new initiatives can stimulate further change and learning, so it is in that spirit that this new material is introduced. To be fair, I am trying hard to justify my inclusion of this material here at the end because I could not find an obvious way to incorporate it in an earlier chapter. In any case, following this new but highly related material, an integrative summary via six major points will be provided. To conclude the book, I will address the future primarily through a lens of what is needed for research, practice, and for a deeper understanding of organization change.

The Tipping Point

One of the more fascinating accounts of how change occurs has been explained by Malcolm Gladwell (2000) in his compact, well-written, and well-documented book, *The Tipping Point*. The book gets its title from the phenomenon of how, for example, a virus gradually spreads and at a certain point, becomes an epidemic, or how a fashion trend starts small and at once becomes a fad (Gladwell uses the example of the revival of Hush Puppies shoes in the mid-1990s). He also described how the crime rate in New York City during the 90s decade went from one of the worst in the country to one of the best—the rate curve from the mid-1960s to the late 1990s looks like a big arch. A small number of people started behaving very differently in certain situations and that behavior gradually "spread to other would-be criminals in similar situations. . . . [and] somehow a large number of people in New York got 'infected' with an anti-crime virus in a short time" (p. 8).

Gladwell pointed out that these phenomena have three characteristics in common: (a) contagiousness, (b) the fact that small causes can have big effects, and (c) the fact that change occurs at one dramatic moment, not gradually. Contagiousness is easy to understand (the spread of colds or the flu), but there are many "epidemics" that occur from contagiousness that are not health related, such as hearing a song that you love and telling others to listen to it, or singing or whistling to them. Gladwell uses the example of yawning as a contagion that fits as an experience for most, if not all, of us.

The second principle, according to Gladwell—little changes can have large consequences—is perhaps not as easy to grasp. We tend to believe that to have a large impact, we need to do something dramatic and big. In mathematics, however, the principle of geometric progression is more accurate for understanding change, for example, when a virus spreads, it keeps doubling and is *not* proportional. The end result seems out of proportion to the cause. "We need to prepare ourselves for the possibility that sometimes big changes follow from small events, and that sometimes these changes can happen very quickly" (Gladwell, 2000, p. 11).

Gladwell claims that the third characteristic or principle, that of change happening suddenly, may be the most difficult one to accept.

This could be true for the general public, but from what we understand about organizational transformation, it should be fairly easy to accept. The "tipping point" is the moment of critical mass and can occur suddenly and rapidly; for example, the fax machine first sold at 80,000 units in 1984, rose steadily until 1987, when a million machines were sold, and by 1989, sold 2 million. The tipping point was 1987. The same phenomenon occurred for cell phones, pregnancy among teenagers, a syphilis epidemic in Baltimore, and so on.

Various explanations are given for epidemics, such as a technological breakthrough, or crack cocaine use in the Baltimore case. But such explanations do not account for the suddenness of change, the tipping point. Crack cocaine was around before the syphilis epidemic. Gladwell (2000) explained,

> There is more than one way to tip an epidemic, in other words. Epidemics are a function of the people who transmit infectious agents [what Gladwell calls the "Law of the Few"], the infectious agent itself [the "Stickiness Factor"], and the environment in which the infectious agent is operating [the "Power of Context"]. And when an epidemic tips, when it is jolted out of equilibrium, it tips because something has happened, some change has occurred in one (or two or three) of those areas. (pp. 18-19)

The Law of the Few

Change happens in part because of a few people who initiate the spread of the "virus." These people are not ordinary and Gladwell discussed three types: connectors, mavens, and salesmen. Most of us are probably familiar with the notion of "six degrees of separation," the finding that how closely connected a person chosen at random is to another person in some distant part of the country, also chosen at random, is about five or six steps; that is, there are about five people who separately but, when asked, can connect the two randomly chosen individuals (Milgram, 1967). But as Gladwell pointed out, not all of these six degrees are equal; a few people are much more highly connected than most. These connectors have "a special gift for bringing the world together" (p. 38). They are individuals who are curious about people, occupy many different worlds and subcultures, and like people more than most of us do. Connectors do not necessarily start epidemics; they facilitate the process. And, remember, they are few in number.

Mavens are collectors of information. They know the latest prices of any product you might be interested in; they know the best restaurants, how to get tickets for the hottest Broadway show, where the ladies' room is in Macy's, and so on. But the key is that they love to *share* what they know; they are information brokers. This makes them connectors as well. They do not try to sell you on what they know, however. That's the other kind of person who can help with change, according to Gladwell.

To get the message across and have it affect people, one has to be persuasive. To be an effective persuader and salesperson, one understands somehow that little things can make big differences. Small, subtle nonverbal cues (head nod, eye contact, slight smile) are often more important than verbal ones. Good salespeople use themselves effectively by tuning in quickly to the person they are trying to persuade. They pick up on the other person's nonverbal behavior and use this information to relate, to empathize, and to influence. Good salespeople are critical to spreading the "change virus."

The Stickiness Factor

The few connectors, as messengers, do indeed matter, but so does the message content. As examples of getting a message to stick, Gladwell discussed the children's educational television shows *Sesame Street* and *Blues Clues,* as well as other examples from marketing and advertising. Two of his points stand out. One is how important it is to try different forms of communicating the same message and to tinker around the edges with symbols, colors, icons, and so on, to see what will "stick." For example, the warmth and charisma of the Muppets and Big Bird made big differences in what children learned and remembered. Another perhaps more important feature of stickiness is having a story, or narrative, that can be told and told again. This notion underlies the success of *Blues Clues.* As noted in the previous chapter, the importance of the change leader's story cannot be underestimated, and repeating the same message in a variety of ways helps with retention or stickiness. Connectors relay the story, but the story itself needs to have meaning, address the identity of the organization and its members, move people to action, and communicate values in order for change to get launched and to stick.

The Power Context

Again, small matters can have large consequences. It doesn't take much to change the context, the ways that people perceive their immediate environment. Focusing on quality-of-life crimes in New York City, for example, arresting people for (a) jumping turnstiles in subway stations, (b) spraying graffiti, and (c) demanding money when washing car windshields at intersections, changed the context. People, including would-be criminals, began to behave differently. In citing a number of psychological studies such as Zimbardo and his colleagues' (Haney, Banks, & Zimbardo, 1973) mock prison experiment, Darley and Batson's (1973) study of helping behavior, and Hartshorne and May's (1971) research on cheating, Gladwell pointed out that the situation (context) determines in part what people do. We know the importance of the situation, of course, from Lewin's (1947) original "formula" that $B = P/E$, or behavior can be explained only as a function of the combination or interaction of one's *personality* and how one perceives his or her *environment*.

Another aspect of context that Gladwell addressed is the "magic number," 150. This number of people, as it turns out, is a tipping point. We know very well that peer pressure and social norms are huge influences on human behavior. In fact, peer pressure is more powerful than the influence of a boss. So, we understand the power of a group, for either good or bad. What we may not understand as clearly is the importance of group size. For example, a good answer to "What is the ideal size of a work team?" is 7 plus or minus 2. This response is based on "Miller's law." George Miller (1956), a noted psychologist, decades ago found that our mental capacity for keeping up with things all at the same time or remembering sets of independent facts, such as a telephone number, is about 7. Some of us can deal with only about 5 independent activities, tasks, or things we need to remember. Others of us can deal with up to 9 simultaneously, but for most of us it is 7. But what about dealing with 149 other people? To get to this answer, we need to understand two more findings from the behavioral sciences: *social channel capacity* and *transactive memory*.

Gladwell cited the work of British anthropologist Robin Dunbar (1992) to explain our *social channel capacity*. Based on his studies of groups of primates and humans, Dunbar began with the fact that if, for example, you belong to a group of 5 people, you have to keep track of 10 separate relationships: yours and the 4 others in your group and their 6 other two-way relationships. If you belong to a group of 20 people, keeping track becomes more complicated. You now have 190 two-way relationships: 19 for yourself and 171 for the others. So, a small increase significantly multiplies the social and intellectual tasks. Dunbar's research time and again showed that 147.8 (let's round it to 150) is the figure that represents the maximum number of persons "with whom we can have a genuinely social relationship [i.e.,] knowing who they are and how they relate to us" (Gladwell, 2000, p. 179, citing Dunbar).

Quite independently from Dunbar's research, the Hutterites, a religious group referred to by Gladwell, for several hundred years have structured their colonies to be no more than 150 individuals. They claim that when a group is larger than 150, people tend to become strangers to one another and the efficiency of group management dissipates. Taking another example, from the business world, Gladwell discussed the structuring and grouping of employees in Gore Associates, a $1 billion-plus privately held company that manufactures high-tech fabric (Gore-Tex®), dental floss, coatings for computer cables, filter bags, and a variety of tubes for the automobile, semiconductor, pharmaceuticals, and medical industries. Gore Associates sticks with the rule of 150. With thousands of employees across the company, no work unit (e.g., a manufacturing plant) is composed of more than 150 people. They have found from experiences over the years and especially in dealing with growth of the company that "things get clumsy at 150" (Gladwell, 2000, p. 184). Gore Associates is also known, incidentally, for its "free form" of organizing and running its operations—no hierarchy, no titles, and essentially no formal management.

Using the idea of *transactive memory* to further explain the importance of the number 150, Gladwell referred to the work of the psychologist Daniel Wegner (1991). The argument by Wegner is that when "people know each other well, they create an implicit joint memory system—a transactive memory system—which is based on an understanding about who is best suited to remember what kinds of things" (Gladwell, 2000, p. 188). Family members transact all the time: Mom knows where things are in the attic, and Dad knows where everything is in the basement. So, any given family member does not have to keep track of everything. Transactive memory is not just that you know someone or even like the person necessarily; it is more about knowing what the other person is capable of, what his or her skills are, what he or she knows, and whether you can count on the person. As Gladwell (2000) summarized the Gore Associates way of operating,

> [What they have] created, in short, is an organized mechanism that makes it far easier for new ideas and information moving around the organization to tip—to

go from one person or one part of the group to the entire group all at once. That's the advantage of adhering to the Rule of 150. You can exploit the bonds of memory and peer pressure. (p. 191)

With respect to peer pressure, it is a matter of knowing people well enough so that what they think of you makes a difference. So, to expedite your change epidemic, that is, to spread shared ideas and ideals, change leaders need to be aware of this final, important facet of context. Crossing the 150 line will adversely affect both efficiency and effectiveness.

Summarizing an entire book in a few pages does not do justice to the richness of Gladwell's ideas, his primary points, and the thoroughness of his scholarship. Our purpose nevertheless is to apply the tipping point principles to organization change. In other words, what if we took Gladwell's principles seriously and made an effort to use them?

Applying "The Tipping Point" Principles to Planned Organization Change

The ideas in Gladwell's (2000) book suggest ways of understanding (a) organization change more thoroughly, for example, contagiousness and the fact that small events or activities can have large consequences, and (b) ways of planning the process, that is, how to spread a "virus" and cause an epidemic. In short, we must find *the few* that help us (connectors), make certain that our change message (vision, directions, goals) *sticks,* and find ways to change the *context* so that our message becomes a reality and our goals become attainable. At the same time, we need to bear in mind, of course, other principles regarding organization change that we have addressed already, such as open system theory, causing disequilibrium, dealing with resistance and with unanticipated consequences, and ways of sustaining the change process.

Following our phase framework from the previous chapter— prelaunch, launch, postlaunch, and sustaining the change—we will now apply Gladwell's ideas and principles to planned organization change.

Prelaunch

Determining the message, or the virus or epidemic that we want to spread is the first step. This, of course, is our content (see Chapter 7); it's the vision, providing clarity regarding the organization change purpose and direction. We want to make the message stick, so it is cast in the form of a *story* that can easily be remembered. We also want to consider a variety of ways to communicate the story, that is, not rely on a singular form or medium. Remember with the *Sesame Street* experience that teaching points to be remembered are conveyed in a variety of forms.

Also, during the prelaunch phase, we search for our highly *important few:* connectors, mavens, and salesmen, those few who have social power, the ones who will be, according to Gladwell (2000),

> Responsible for starting word-of-mouth epidemics, which means that if you are interested in starting a word-of-mouth epidemic, your resources ought to be solely concentrated on those three groups. (p. 256)

The further point here is that the effort is on selection, or finding the *right* few, not so much on training them. Once they have the story straight and accept it, they will know what to do; that is, they will use their natural motives and abilities.

The Launch

For this phase, our connectors, mavens, and salespeople go forth to spread the message, or the story. Our connectors get people together for common tasks, such as helping to plan an initial event; our mavens facilitate the transactive memories, that is, helping people to learn what, where, and how they can be connected; and our salespeople help to persuade people that this change is indeed the right thing to do; that is, they communicate powerfully the need for change.

The launching of initial, key activities is essentially, in Gladwell's (2000) language, an effort to change the *context*. Recall that in the case of British Airways it was a 1-day event—"Putting People First" (PPF)—stressing that now their primary concerns were customers and the marketplace, with less emphasis on protocol, bureaucracy, and seniority. The BBC's "Extending Choice" workshop was their change launch vehicle, with many of the same themes as British Airway's PPF, for example, focusing more externally, on their audiences and changing technology, and less internally, with the attempt being to avoid insularity. Also, recall that with respect to the size of these launch events, they included 100 people at a time, and the initial stage of the Dime Bank change effort was to focus on the top 125 executives and managers. In other words, the size in all three cases was not more than 150.

Postlaunch

From previous coverage, remember that multiple leverage is critical; that is, one should not rely on a singular change intervention, such as a structural change, to do the job. Moreover, Gladwell's (2000) admonition is to do things that are not all that obvious, such as tinkering with the message to find ways to make it stick by communicating the story in multiple ways and determining which way(s) works best, at least for a particular period of time.

Repeating the message is imperative. Remember the lesson from *Blues Clues:* Repetition, as well as a captivating story, made the message stick.

And in dealing with resistance to the change effort, we rely heavily on our selected few—connectors, mavens, and salesmen—without necessarily telling them that their job is to overcome resistance. As stated earlier, they will know what to do.

Sustaining the Change

It may very well be that the most important ingredient in sustaining organization change is the process of dealing with unanticipated, unforeseen consequences of initiatives and interventions. This is especially true when launching the change process. Gladwell (2000) suggests that we proceed with our intuitions about new initiatives, but he also cautions that when we act on them, we should get data quickly regarding the consequences and change to another approach as needed to keep the change going. A brief case should help illustrate this point.

After approximately 18 months into a major organization change at NatWest Bancorp from 1991 to 1996, the change leader, Roger Goldman, conducted an organization-wide employee opinion survey as one of the ways to monitor progress (for details on the survey, see Chapter 12 in Burke & Trahant, 2000). Using the Burke-Litwin model as the framework for structuring the questions and for analyzing the responses to the survey (see Chapter 10 for examples), the results showed that the transformational factors in the model—perceptions regarding the external environment, mission and strategy, leadership, and culture—were rated highly. Goldman and his executive team members were elated. A few moments later, when the remainder of the survey results were presented, their elation plummeted to depression and then to anger. Some of the transactional factors in the model showed low ratings, for example, a 2 on a 5-point Likert scale, particularly in the systems and motivation boxes. To put it in the vernacular, morale at the bank (as reflected in the motivation ratings) was "in the tank." This outcome was *not* anticipated. Goldman and his team were somewhat distraught and wondered what action to take.

The consultant presenting the survey results suggested that they further examine these outcomes by considering other categories of the model and how they related to the problem. He pointed out that two boxes of the model were pertinent here, one transformational and one transactional: the mission and strategy box and the task requirements and individual skills and abilities (job-person match) box. Recall that in the model, these two boxes are connected by a two-way arrow (see Figure 9.2 in Chapter 9). By referring to this link, the consultant argued that the fact that ratings in both of these categories were high should not be overlooked when further examining the survey results. In other words, it was likely that most employees saw a clear connection between what they were doing in their jobs and the bank's mission and strategy. In fact, statistical analysis of the results supported this argument. This linkage, it was further argued, would eventually influence motivation in a positive way, provided some other actions were taken. A key element contributing to the success of organization performance in general and organization change in particular is when people see how what they do day-to-day relates to and supports the organization's mission and strategy. So, this part of the survey results was strong support for the ultimate success of the organization change effort.

The problem was actually within the *systems* box. Further examination showed that low ratings in this category were associated with information technology—out-of-date computer hardware and software that did not support the needs of the change goals and the new vision and mission of the bank. In other words, most employees did not feel that they had adequate technical support. In a manner of speaking, the employees were saying, "We understand and believe in the vision, mission, and strategy of the bank. We see how our jobs support this direction and these goals. We would very much like to 'get on with it.' But how can we do it with such outmoded technology? We cannot respond to customers in the ways desired, that is, with speed and accurate information. It is extremely frustrating!" Thus, morale was low.

Goldman and his colleagues then proceeded with a new initiative, which would take time and cost money, but updating the information technology aspect of the bank's work was now an imperative. After about another 18 months, a second, Time 2, survey was conducted. Although other problems had emerged, some unanticipated, of course, motivation and systems were rated higher than in Time 1.

Sustaining change means in large measure (a) to understand that many consequences of interventions cannot be anticipated, (b) to *not* allow these unforeseen outcomes to become barriers to the change effort, and (c) to take swift action with different initiatives and tactics to ensure momentum via new paths toward the change goals.

In summary, Gladwell's tipping-point principles do not address all aspects of organization change. That was not his intent. But these principles do help us to understand certain change phenomena more thoroughly. Also, Gladwell's book is explanatory in nature, not a recipe for planned organization change. How to apply his explanations has been our intent, at least in part, and how to think about planning organization change in new and different ways.

Changing the Organization

In an attempt to summarize and integrate, let us consider the key questions to raise and some of the critical tenets about organization change. Six major points are summarized as follows:

First, we must begin with the external environment. Actually, the more astute leaders constantly monitor their organization's environment. But are they asking the right questions, gathering the appropriate information, and seeking opinions and ideas from their primary constituents?

The critical questions are as follows:

- What are the *customers* telling us? How satisfied are they with the quality of our products and services, the timeliness of our delivery, and the degree to which we listen to them? Asking our customers questions and then listening to what they tell us is highly valuable for many reasons, the primary reason being what they may *not* be saying directly, but only hinting at or alluding to. It is not as if our customers are trying to mislead us. It is more a matter of their not quite knowing what they may need, especially for the future. In other words, we must listen to their notions of what is next for them, where they're going, what they may need or want next year and the year after. For more about what customers value and the inherent difficulties obtaining such information, see Goodstein and Butz (1998).

- What are the *capital markets* telling us? Recall from Chapter 1 how critically important this question is. If we are a publicly owned company, how is our stock price doing? Are large investors buying shares? What are analysts saying about us? How easy/difficult is it for us to raise money for activities such as acquisitions, investing in new technology, and expanding certain business lines, particularly on a global basis?

- If we are a nonprofit organization, the fundamental questions are related but somewhat different. The basic question concerns *mission*. How relevant is our mission today? After all, nonprofit organizations have customers, government regulators, and professional audiences. Are we responding appropriately to our constituents? Do we listen sufficiently to those whom we serve?

- What about our *competitors?* Where do we rank in our industry vis-à-vis our competition? Do we have adequate information (in the military it would be called "intelligence") about what our competitors are doing—where they may be expanding, what their R&D objectives are, or where they are investing (new business, new technology, new domains geographically, etc.)? Are they attempting to be low-cost providers, highly differentiated in the marketplace, or niche players?

- What about the people we attract, select, place, and retain in our organization? Do they see us as an attractive organization to join? Do they believe that they will be recognized and rewarded according to merit? Do they believe that they will have challenging work, be able to make a difference, to learn and grow, have good colleagues to work with, and even enjoy what they will be doing?

- And what about *technology?* Are we up to date, on the cutting edge, or falling behind? Do we even have the right technology? It may be that our products and/or services are so dated that we need to change to an entirely new technological base, for example, changing from metals to ceramics or from a physical science base to a bioscience base.

There are additional questions regarding the external environment that need to be raised, such as the possibility of changing government regulations, what is happening in the general economy, demographic shifts, relations with our key supplies and suppliers, social trends, organized labor trends, shifts in educational level of our potential workforce, natural environmental factors, politics, and so on. Depending on the industry and/or how unique our organization might be, some of these additional questions may be more important than the ones listed above as bullet points.

Second, we must take a hard look *inside* our own organizations. Are we still in the right business or set of businesses? This is where an article such as Peter Drucker's (1994) can be very helpful (see Chapter 7 for brief coverage of this paper). Drucker indeed raises the right questions. Other questions regarding an outside and inside look include the following: Do we need to change our industry and technology base? DuPont, for example, has been basically a chemical company for at least a century. Due to the fact that many of their products have reached "maturity" and sales have flattened (for example, nylon), the CEO and other thought leaders in the company are strongly considering shifting from science based on chemistry to a bioscience foundation. This shift would cause a significant change in the kinds of products DuPont might offer in the future.

Do we change some of the business lines and remain with our core or is there a need to change our business altogether? Perhaps not changing overnight, but moving down a different path for the longer term may be the proper course of action.

And again, if we are a nonprofit organization, the priority question would be "What is the level of commitment to or passion about our organization's mission and purpose on the part of our board members, our senior executives, our employees, and our members?"

Third, assuming that some degree of change is needed, how *ready* is our organization for what will be required? The question typically is not whether to change, but "How fast and how deep should the process occur?" Should the change be evolutionary and continuous (transactional in nature) or revolutionary and discontinuous (transformational in nature) or should the change be *both:* that is, slower and continuous for certain areas in the organization and revolutionary in other areas? With respect to readiness on the part of organizational members, it will depend in part on how much change has been occurring already and how many initiatives have been thrust on the organization. With the announcement of yet another change, people in the organization have been known to say, "We've been there, done that—even have a T-shirt to prove it!" Under such circumstances, change leaders will have to stress the difference and uniqueness of the current initiative to help organizational members, especially the jaded ones, to get beyond their fatigue and perhaps cynicism.

Fourth, assuming that the change required is transformational, how *locked into* (to use the language of Foster and Kaplan, 2001; see Chapter 1) are we to our culture, our way of doing things? After all, a transformation means fundamental change of the culture to support the significantly revised mission, if not a new mission altogether, and of course, a new strategy. It will not be business as usual. As we know, culture change, when done correctly, requires new behavior that leads to new attitudes and beliefs and eventually leads to different values. Strong cultures are at best difficult to change, and, depending on the size and complexity of the organization, it can take years. But change they must, should the external environment demand it, that is, the capital markets and other factors being incongruent with the organization's current direction and performance.

Fifth, we must make the case for change: *Why* we need to transform ourselves. The most immediate response can be something like the following: "We've been successful for over 70 years; why do we need to take such drastic, even draconian, steps now?" So, if dramatic change is indeed required, the case must be made. The parlance in today's organization change world is the creation, or establishment, of a "burning platform": the implication being that our very survival is at stake. The section in the previous chapter, "Establishing the Need for Change," provides an actual case example of establishing a "burning platform."

And *finally,* we follow the sequence, spelled out in Chapter 11, of *prelaunch, launch, postlaunch,* and *sustaining the change.* Staying with this sequence and how we "do things," we would be wise to apply our theoretical and research knowledge about the following:

- Open system theory, bearing in mind principles such as the system's survival, is dependent on the external environment; thus, our constant objective is to create negative entropy, and when we change one aspect of the organization, eventually all other aspects will be affected.

- Capra's (1996) ideas about patterns' autopoiesis, structure, and process; the parallels between a cell, a human being, and an organization are not perfect but are sufficient to warrant our understanding so that we are better informed about how organizations change and can be changed.

- The differences between continuous and discontinuous change. These differences have implications for how we plan organization change: If it is discontinuous, we are focusing on transformational factors such as mission, leadership, and culture and we are attempting to affect the deep structure (Gersick, 1991) of the system; if continuous, our focus is on factors such as structure, systems, and climate.

- Understanding level differences in organizations; that is, we plan change and deal with resistance differently depending on whether our focus is the individual, the group, or the system as a whole.

- Understanding of what comes first, that is, behavior before cognition (Chapter 6).

- Measurement, that is, being clear that an alpha change is different from beta and gamma changes; alpha change is a difference along some relatively stable dimension of reality; beta is a recalibration of the intervals along the dimension, and gamma involves a reconceptualization of some domain. Exactly what we are measuring to determine change progress is critical to our understanding (Chapter 6).

- The distinction between content, *what* to change, and process, *how* to change (Chapter 7).

- Organization models; that is, it is useful to have a framework for categorizing as many of the primary dimensions of an organization as possible so that we can plan, implement, and track the change as effectively as possible (Chapters 8, 9, and 10).

- Studies of leadership, with an emphasis on *executive* leadership and the variety of roles and functions, from prelaunch to sustaining the change (Chapter 11).

- The principles explained by the writings of Pascale, Milleman, and Gioja, (2000; see Chapter 11) and Gladwell's (2000) work described in this chapter.

Would that everything about organization change could be summarized in 7 (plus or minus 2) clear and straightforward steps. But surely we have learned one thing clearly: Organization change is entirely too complex and nonlinear to summarize that easily. Thinking about organization change in the sequential terms of prelaunch to sustaining is about the best we can do.

Moreover, if organization change were cast in terms of seven steps or limited to seven principles, we would be fooling ourselves. The complexity of it all is what makes the study and practice of organization change so challenging, so meaningful, so exciting, and so worthwhile.

For the final section of this last chapter, let us turn to the future, not in a predictive sense but in terms of what we need to know more about, or to know in more depth.

Organization Change: What We Need to Know

In a previous article, a few years ago, I wrote about what I thought we knew regarding organization change and what we needed to know (Burke, 1995). With respect to what we needed to know, I chose eight areas to cover. What follows is a synopsis and brief update of these eight areas.

The Process Of Organization Change

Momentum. Recall from the previous chapter that the fourth phase of organization change—sustaining the change—is the most difficult. We must learn more about "organization change momentum," or how to sustain the change once we are underway. Some specific suggestions for what to research and learn more about include keeping people informed, measuring and celebrating achievements, and experimenting with new and different ways of rewarding people for the appropriate changes that they make.

Chaos During Transition. Remember two important phenomena about chaos theory: one is that even though not apparent when in the midst of change, patterns do exist. Figure 1.1 in the first chapter was an attempt to represent this phenomenon. Understanding more about pattern is a fruitful avenue for research. A second phenomenon is the likelihood of innovation and creativity at the "edge of chaos" (Pascale et al., 2000). How long should the change leader allow chaos to continue, hoping for a breakthrough? And how does creativity emerge?

Communication. It is easy to state that during organization change, leaders need to communicate. More important than this simple admonition, however, are the needs to understand more about the *timing* of communication and the *amount* to communicate at any given time.

Organization Change Leadership

Personality and Culture. Because leadership is such a personal matter, understanding more about the proper match between the leader's personality and the desired organizational culture is critical to successful change. Moreover, charismatic leaders can play important roles during times of crisis, but what about afterwards? The classic case of Winston Churchill during and following World War II remains puzzling. Why was he not reelected? More recently and similarly, Rudolph Guiliani, the former mayor of New York, was superb during the aftermath of September 11, 2001, but perhaps not so superb during times of relative normalcy. Successors to charismatic leaders often have a difficult time because the former type of leaders rarely leave adequate infrastructures and systems to maintain what they initiated during their tenure. Understanding more about leadership in terms of personality/circumstances congruence, charisma, crisis, and succession is needed.

Power and Politics. Understanding more about power—the leader's capacity to influence—is needed. Classic works remain informative; for example, see French and Raven's (1959) basic sources of power (reward, coercive, legitimate, expert, and referent), and Kipnis (1976), the question of whether power corrupts (under certain conditions, power does corrupt). But what about the use of power during change? Revolutionary change requires strong, powerful leadership, the transformational type. What is the proper balance between powerful leadership and involving organizational members in decisions that directly affect them? These and related questions are ripe for research.

The Change Leader. Building on the above questions, how does change leadership differ from leadership during times of relative stability? I have made the claim that self-awareness is necessary for effective change leadership, as well as the need for high emotional intelligence. Am I correct?

Organizational Structure

Self-Directed Groups. As a result of organization change, the trend continues toward flatter hierarchies in large systems, with the consequences of greater spans of control for managers. Work units in organizations now operate more on their own, with less supervision. Hackman (1992) has contributed to our understanding of self-directed groups, but we need to know much more.

Centralization/Decentralization. It used to be a question of one versus the other. This is no longer the question; it is rather what functions to centralize (finance?) and what functions to decentralize (human resources?). Learning more about how to do both simultaneously is needed.

Cells. These self-managed groups have been prevalent in manufacturing organizations for quite some time now, but we still do not know enough about how to change to this mode of operating effectively and how to make them work well over time.

Networks. A network is a structural form that has been around for a long time. There are actually many different types of networks. When is one type, a loosely coupled professional association, for example, more effective than another form, a network of, say, computer scientists within the same organization? How do you move effectively from a hierarchy to a network, or vice versa?

Formal and Informal Rewards

Incentives. We know about pay, bonuses, and fringe benefits, but we do not know enough about application: the conditions for when they work well and when they do not. Pay for performance remains an issue. As soon as it becomes expected, any pay-for-performance scheme loses the characteristic of incentive. If pay for performance is an incentive, how long does it last? And how can such schemes be used to support organization change?

Intrinsic Rewards. I believe we need to know much more than we do about intrinsic motivation and reward. We know that "it's the work itself," but what in more depth and with more specificity do we know? Such thinking as Csikszentmihalyi's (1990) work on flow is helpful here, especially his distinction between joy and pleasure. We need to know more about how to make work more satisfying, how to experience flow from time to time, and how to make change more accepted and enjoyable.

Training and Development

Training in the Service of Change. Too often, training in organizations is conducted because competitors are doing it or because some executive believes that conducting a certain program would be a good thing to do, regardless of whether any evidence exists that the program actually works. Training is, indeed, capable of helping organizational members to learn and develop, but training targeted at supporting and enhancing organization change can have considerable payoff. Recall the British Airways case from Chapter 4 and how training was deployed for culture change. Learning more about the use of training at individual and group levels in the service of ultimate organization change is needed.

Action Learning. This form of training and development combines actual problem solving in organizations with learning about how to work together better, how to solve organizational problems more efficiently and effectively, and how to improve the learning process in general—learning about learning. Even though action learning is reasonably well-known, it is not practiced very often. This form of learning can be a powerful vehicle for organization change; see, for example, Tichy and Sherman (1993). We need to know more about the intricacies of this problem-solving and learning process and why it is not used more often.

Teams and Teamwork in Organizations

There are good sources about teams and teamwork. Katzenbach and Smith's (1993) *The Wisdom of Teams* is one of them, as is the more recent *Organizing Genius* by Bennis and Biederman (1997). What surprises me, however, is why this collective wisdom is applied on such a limited basis. Yes, here in the United States, we are an individually focused culture, but we know that teamwork can benefit organization change and performance. I believe now as I did in (Burke) 1995; that is, we need,

To know more about such things as
- why there is so much talk about teamwork, with so little real action;
- what the elements are of a high-performing team;
- what kinds of goals for teams are those that provide "demanding performance challenges"—and I do not mean going over a wall or climbing a mountain together (i.e., "ropes and slopes");
- what it takes to achieve a high degree of personal commitment among team members;
- what synergy is, *really*, and what the conditions are for achieving it;
- the kinds of assumptions that organizational members hold about teamwork; and finally
- how to instill a team culture in an organization and make it last through structural and management changes as well as changes in the reward system. (pp. 167-168)

Organizational Size

Large and Small Simultaneously. The main thesis of Naisbitt's (1994) book, *Global Paradox,* is that in the face of global expansion for nations, there is at the same time a strong emphasis worldwide on ethnic groups, local community, and subparts of countries as the basis for one's primary identify and loyalty. If Naisbitt's thesis holds for large organizations, what does this mean for organization change? Supposedly, the organizational whole should be more than the sum of its parts, but in thinking about organization change in the future, should we consider the opposite, that is, strengthening parts more than the whole? Of course, the answer to this question is "It depends." But what are the pros and cons? These are interesting questions for research.

Silos and Boundary Spanning. This is the newer language for differentiation and integration. Obviously, any large organization needs both. It seems, however, that silos win over cross-functional teams. Is this a phenomenon? If so, don't we need to know more? And how can change toward a greater boundaryless way of working be promoted and realized?

Size of Organizational Units. Remember the discussion earlier in the chapter of Gladwell's (2000) point about the rule of 150? The evidence for an organizational unit's being no larger than 150 people is compelling. Following Wegner's (1991) lead to understand more about how this works and its importance for organization change would be a fascinating stream of research.

Organizational Performance

As part of his review of Jim Collins's (2001) book about how some "good companies become great," Holstein (2001) made the following point:

> Whatever contributions the book offers are called into question by an intellectual assumption that runs throughout: The only way to define a great company is in its return to investors over a continuous and prolonged period. Such a standard doesn't consider how a company could have changed society or the world, how it benefited customers, how it conquered international markets, or how it treated employees. (pp. 3-6)

The point is that defining the degree of greatness of a company according to its stock price, even if measured over time, is a very limited index of performance. The time is overdue for us to consider organizational performance in multiple ways; yes, financial is one measure, but as Kaplan and Norton (1996) have explained (and earlier noted in Chapter 9), there are at least three other ways to measure performance. Moreover, measures of organization change are far too complex to be left only to financial measures. Thus, we need to learn much more about how to define and measure organizational performance than we now know.

Priorities

I like David Whetten's idea: "Imagine a scenario in which the National Science Foundation funds 10 very bright postdoctoral students to work under your supervision to substantially change our scholarly understanding of organization change. What research assignments would you give them?"[1] Another way of asking a similar question was the one I was asked in 1995 in connection with the article referred to above (Burke, 1995):

> In an earlier draft of this article, I was asked which area(s) among the eight that I covered was (were) the most important or critical. This was a fair and difficult question. At the top of the list would be the issue of leadership match with the desired culture. (p. 170)

My second choice at that time was teams and teamwork. Today, my priorities are slightly different, although leadership is still there. September 11, 2001, the date of the World Trade Center tragedy, has affected my priorities. So what would I ask 10 postdoctoral students to study?

Now at the top of my list is *organizational structure*—but not hierarchical factors. Rather, I would like for us to understand more about self-directed groups, cells, and especially *networks,* the web that holds cells together. As executive director of the Organization Development Network for 8 years (1966-1974), I learned about how a network without hierarchy (except perhaps for myself and an advisory board at the center or hub) can accomplish tasks. Key was the fact that our purpose was clear, and therefore, we had clarity of tasks in the service of that purpose. Networks are composed of nodes, where pivotal people serve as connectors (remember Gladwell's, 2000, tipping points) and gatekeepers, those who facilitate or impede entry and participation in the network.

With the help of the Internet, networks today are more sophisticated and complex. Consider the following commentary (Rothstein, 2001):

> But terrorist organizations are generally referred to as networks, which can be quite varied. Instead of being built around a controlling hub surrounded by terrorist cells, a network can be a sprawling, decentralized arrangement. In fact, the declaration

that Americans are engaged in a different sort of war than ever before may have to
do with this structure and not just with terrorism itself. Disabling a network often
requires different strategies from those used to attack a nation or a hierarchical
organization. . . . For better or worse, the world has entered an era of networks.
(p. A13)

Networks that are highly effective are highly focused and have a
structure that is built on trust, that is, political and emotional connections among people who must rely on each other to accomplish tasks.

The initial assignment for my postdoctoral student research team
would be to gain considerable background on networks, to take the
points made above, and dig deeper by reading articles and books such as
the recent one by Arquilla and Ronfeldt (2001) and to interview experts
such as Kathleen Carley, director of the Center for Computational
Analysis and Organizational Systems at Carnegie Mellon University.

Then, we would begin to formulate the questions and hypotheses for
research, such as "The degree of effectiveness (high performance) of a
network is a function of the clarity of purpose—the greater the clarity,
the higher the performance" or "The degree of effectiveness is a function of the extent of trust among members—the greater the trust, the
higher the performance." And we would explore questions such as
"What are the key roles and responsibilities in an effective network?"
"How do decisions get made?" "What is the nature of accountability in
a network?"

My second priority is *organizational leadership.* In addition to
learning more about the leader-culture match, charisma and crisis,
power and politics, self-awareness, and emotional intelligence, I
would suggest two other areas for my postdoctoral student research
team. One is to learn more about the behavioral complexities that
leaders face, interpersonal, informational, and decisional: serving
multiple constituencies, dealing with conflicting values, managing
tensions and paradoxes, for example, serving followers by building a
buffer between them and the higher authorities in the organization
yet keeping them well-informed about what is going on and performing multiple roles (Mintzberg, 1973). This line of research stems from
what is called *behavioral complexity theory;* for more specificity, see
Zaccaro (2001).

The second line of leadership research that I would want to pursue
actually has more to do with followers. As Hogan, Curphy, and Hogan
(1994) have pointed out, leadership research has focused too much on the
leader (for example, trait studies), and not enough on the relationship of

the leader and followers. After all, this relationship is the essence of what defines leadership. Furthermore, research on leadership should concentrate more on what followers accomplish and how these accomplishments can be traced back to the leader's actions and behaviors. And despite my devoting an entire chapter (11) to change leadership, have we become too leader focused? Are there leadership substitutes for organization change that have not been explored sufficiently, such as self-directed groups and networks? Investigating this possibility of leadership substitutes could prove to be a fruitful path to take. And clearly, my two priorities overlap. In any case, there are plenty of studies that could be done regarding the leader's role during each of the four phases of organization change: prelaunch, launch, implementation, and sustaining the change.

Conclusion

How do you end a book about change? After all, as some wise people stated long ago, change is ongoing. Reaching for my trusty *Bartlett's Familiar Quotations,* I found at least three that captured this thought:

> *Nothing endures but change.*
>
> Heraclitus (540-480 B.C.)

> *Nothing in the world lasts save eternal change.*
>
> Honorat de Bueil, Marquis de Racan (1589-1659)

> *There is nothing in this world constant, but inconstancy.*
>
> Jonathan Swift (1667-1745)

Also, I have continued to read things, such as the recent article by Pettigrew, Woodman, and Cameron (2001). They relied on much of the same literature I did, which was nice confirmation. Friends kept telling me about interesting articles and books they had read that needed to be included. And I realized that, like change, this process could go on for the rest of my life. So, we are not ending; it is merely a matter of stopping—for now. Look for a second edition in the future.

Note

1. D. A. Whetten, personal communication, October 10, 2001.

Appendix: Annotated Bibliography

Foster, R. N. & Kaplan, S. (2001). *Creative Destruction: Why Companies That Are Built to Last Underperform the Market—And How to Successfully Transform Them.* New York: Currency and Doubleday.

These two McKinsey consultants argue that with the rapid rate of change that occurs now, unlike in the past, organizations that are successful and "built to last" will not. Nothing breeds failure like success. The better the company, the more efficient its operations and the more "locked in" to their culture, to use their words, they become—and thus, resistant to deep change. Foster and Kaplan are rather blunt about how wrong they believe the message is in *Built to Last,* by Collins and Porras (1994). The message by Foster and Kaplan, incidentally, is much like the that in Drucker's (1994) *Harvard Business Review* article, "The Theory of the Business"; that is, frequent examination of and questioning what business you are in is imperative for long-term survival.

Creative Destruction is based on a straightforward theory of how capital markets work and how they are more amorphous and change more rapidly than do corporations. The mission of the corporation is to adapt as rapidly as possible to these forces and to fight against the rigidities of thinking by executives. Interestingly, the authors draw on research from cognitive psychology to explain how executives make decisions when they are faced with the "enigmas, dilemmas, paradoxes, puzzles, riddles, and mysteries" (p. 62) from the marketplace. Changing mental sets of these executives is the challenge.

Duck, J. D. (2001). *The Change Monster: The Human Forces That Fuel or Foil Corporate Transformation and Change.* New York: Crown Business.

Jeanie Daniel Duck is a senior vice president at the Boston Consulting Group and has years of experience as an organization change consultant. The premise of her book is the notion that during and especially early in the process of organization change, human emotions and social dynamics "emerge like a dragon surfacing from the ocean depths" (p. xi). This emerging dragon is the "change monster." All organization transformations, of course, involve people, and that means emotions are rampant and egos are on the loose. This notion is another way of explaining what Pascale, Milleman, and Gioja (2000) referred to as "being on the edge of chaos." These emotional aspects are scary for change leaders and they tend to avoid them. The purpose of Duck's book, therefore, is to help executives deal with seemingly uncontrollable and irrational responses to organization change.

Duck provided a sequenced set of actions to deal with the change monster. The first is to confront *stagnation,* that is, to deal with denial that change is needed. The second is *preparation,* in which change leaders engage in planning and communication. Duck advised going slow at first and then going faster later. Third is *implementation,* which means to form new habits, and fourth is *determination,* or staying the course. The final set in the sequence is what Duck called "fruition," when emotions are the most intense. The payoff comes with new behavior and deep change. Duck provided many examples along the way.

Capra, F. (1996). *The Web of Life.* New York: Anchor Books (paperback by Doubleday).

Fritjof Capra was originally trained in theoretical physics, and as a writer, he has significantly contributed to our understanding of modern science. With his expansive mind, he has drawn from the variety of research and theory in biochemistry, biology, and other related life sciences, by luminaries such as Prigogine, Maturana, Varela, Margulis, and Kauffman, to provide a new scientific understanding of life at all levels, from organisms to social systems to ecosystems. He explained how we are shifting paradigmatically from a mechanistic world based on physics to an ecological world based on the life sciences and systems theory. Capra helps us to see the world as an integrated whole rather than an aggregation of dissociated parts and to realize that all phenomena are fundamentally interdependent. Moreover, he showed how all of us—organisms, individuals, organizations, societies—are embedded in and are ultimately dependent on the cyclical processes of nature.

Capra, then, is an integrator, his book being a synthesis of recent theories, complexity, Gaia, and chaos theories. It is useful to consider how organizations fit within the larger ecosystem and at the other end of the spectrum, how organizations are like and imitate organisms but also differ, that is, being a creation of humans, not of nature per se.

Pascale, R. T., Milleman, M., & Gioja, L. (2000). *Surfing the Edge of Chaos: The Laws of Nature and the New Laws of Business.* New York: Crown Business.

These authors also chose an organism as the best metaphor for an organization. In fact, they argue that because an organization is a living system, the organism notion is more a reality than a metaphor. They drew from the life sciences what they referred to as "four cornerstone principles," which are just as valid for organizations as they are for species. These cornerstone principles are (a) equilibrium leads to death, (b) innovation often occurs "on the edge of chaos," (c) self-organization and emergence happen quite naturally, and (d) organizations can only be disturbed ("perturbed"), not directed. Using examples from well-known organizations, including Sears, Hewlett Packard, and the U.S. Army, Pascale and his colleagues demonstrated that organizations act like species: They either respond to change and evolve—or die.

These authors claimed via their parallels with the life sciences that change for organizations is a constant and those that survive learn how to adapt themselves to the perpetually changing external environment.

Burke, W. W., & Trahant, W. (2000). *Business Climate Shifts: Profiles of Change Makers.* Boston: Butterworth-Heinemann.

This book is about examples of organization change and more particularly, about change leaders. The first two chapters (a) set the stage regarding the external environment for organizations, especially corporations, in this early part of the 21st century, and (b) provide a framework—the Burke-Litwin model—for how each chapter is positioned, in other words, which dimensions (boxes) of the model are emphasized as the primary levers for change. Each remaining chapter is then devoted to an interview, including summary comments at the end, with a senior executive who is in most cases, the CEO of a large, complex organization and had the primary responsibility for leading a significant transformation of his or her enterprise. These executives included Mac McDonald, head of Royal Dutch Shell, South Africa; Bob Bauman, of SmithKline Beecham; Lee Griffin, of Bank One, Louisiana; Lord Colin Marshall, British Airways; Bill Henderson, Postmaster General, U.S. Postal System; Sir Richard Evans, British Aerospace; Jane Garvey, Federal Aviation Administration; and Roger Goldman, NatWest Bank.

Gladwell, M. (2000). *The Tipping Point: How Little Things Can Make a Big Difference.* Boston: Little, Brown.

A writer for the *New Yorker,* Malcolm Gladwell was intrigued with the phenomenon of how and why major changes in society frequently happen suddenly and unexpectedly. Why did crime in New York City decline as suddenly as it did during the mid-1990s? Why did Hush Puppies shoes all of a sudden make a comeback? Why was Paul Revere's ride so successful when William Dawes's ride in another direction—but with the same warning about the British—was so unsuccessful? Gladwell compares these social epidemics to viral epidemics and points to the parallels; that is, when they reach a critical mass, they take off. They have reached the *tipping point.*

Parallels can also be drawn between the ideas and facts that Gladwell presented and organization change. The perspective that needs to be maintained is the difference between change that simply occurs and *planned* change. Gladwell's notions can indeed be applied to planned organization change.

Note: The following five books and a video served as general background sources for this book.

Gleick, J. (1987). *Chaos: Making a New Science.* New York: Penguin Books.

The introduction to chaos theory, at least for us neophytes, is this book by James Gleick. He provided for us the fundamentals of chaos theory as well as the histories of how it all evolved. Moreover, Gleick's manner of writing is most helpful in two primary ways. One, he simply is an excellent writer. He takes incredibly complex ideas and explains them in such a way that nearly anyone can understand. Two, Gleick tells stories about the scientists involved, which, of course, makes the reading all the more interesting. Also, there are pictures—some in beautiful colors!

As Gleick stated, "Where chaos begins, classical science stops" (p. 3). The implication is that classical science is about order, predictability, and regularity. Chaos theory is the opposite. By the 1970s, a handful of scientists in the United States and abroad began to see "things" within disorder and irregularity that had not been seen before. These things, to name a few, became known as the *butterfly effect, nonlinearity, fractal, attractors, bifurcation, arrhythmia, the Mandelbrot set,* and the phenomenon we have all experienced, especially in airplanes, *turbulence.* And the beauty of it all, and certainly for those of us who need some closure, is that underlying apparent chaos is often order, pattern, and even at times, symmetry.

Kauffman, S. (1995). *At Home in the Universe: The Search for Laws of Self-Organization and Complexity.* New York: Oxford University Press.

Kauffman, a biologist, is clear that although Darwin's theory of evolution has been "spectacularly successful," it is not sufficient to explain much of life. Evolutionary theory, after all, is steeped in scientific reductionism, that is, breaking complex systems into their respective parts. But the whole often, if not always, has properties that cannot be explained by understanding the parts. This kind of complexity and whole-system way of thinking is not new. Yet Kauffman, using as his base biology and mathematics, provided compelling evidence with examples that show dramatically that we can understand systems without knowing all the details. He pointed out that one needs to know which properties of a system are important and which properties of a system are less so. Then, one is in a position to independently explain the details of what the nature of a system is. An effective organizational model can have these characteristics. In chapter after chapter, Kauffman validated this point. Implicitly, we have believed for quite some time that a group and an organization are more than the sums of their parts. Now there is hard evidence. Kauffman also helps us understand more about principles such as self-organization, the edge of chaos, and complexity. Recall that Capra (1996) in his book, *The Web of Life,* drew on the work of Stuart Kauffman.

Buchanan, M. (2000). *Ubiquity: The Science of History . . . Or Why the World Is Simpler Than We Think.* London: Weidenfeld & Nicolson.

This book is in the genre of books like the ones cited already by Capra, Gladwell, and Gleick, that is, writings about science for the broader public. In this case, Buchanan, a science writer with a PhD in theoretical physics, began similarly to Gladwell in his *Tipping Point* by pointing out that sudden upheavals, such as world wars, earthquakes, gigantic forest fires, and stock market crashes, all erupt from very different roots but have at the same time "an intriguing similarity." In each instance, the "organization of the system" made it possible for a small triggering event to cause reactions far out of proportion to the event itself. This small triggering event is called by physicists the *critical state,* an "unstable and unusual condition that arises only under the most exceptional circumstances" (p. 13)—a slight grain of sand falling into a pile of sand that causes an avalanche, a slight shift in the earth's surface that causes an earthquake, one stockowner's decision to sell that causes a market crash, the butterfly effect, and so on. Buchanan's book is loaded with these kinds of examples, and these examples indeed make his conclusions persuasive. It is interesting to speculate about the applicability of these ideas for organization change. A small lever in the direction of the desired change, for example, a brief exchange between the CEO and a few key people, could cause a revolution.

McClure, B. A. (1998). *Putting a New Spin on Groups: The Science of Chaos.* Mahwah, NJ: Lawrence Erlbaum Associates.

The initial premise of this book is that the models and theories of small group development from the 1950s and 60s, when put to use, are really not very valid. They tend to be overly linear and too static, for example, groups go through stages such as "forming, storming, and norming" (p. 34). McClure did not argue that these ideas should be discarded; he preferred to add new concepts from chaos theory and from the evolution theory work of Arthur Young (1976) to build a new model of group development. McClure's model is neither linear nor unidimensional, and he emphasizes the central function of conflict. Although there is a progressive quality to his model, the focus is more on how groups change, evolve, and mature. McClure is not as comprehensive as Gleick in his coverage of chaos theory, but he did introduce us to the terminology and to some of the primary ideas and concepts, particularly those that he finds most applicable to group development, such as self-organization and behavior in systems far from equilibrium. Based on Young's ideas of how evolution occurs, that is, nonlinearly, McClure has derived an "arc" of group development having seven stages and beginning and ending with *performing*. After the initial performing stage comes *unity*, then *disunity*, followed by the central focus or nadir of his arc, *conflict/confrontation*, followed by *disharmony, harmony*, and ending with a new version of *performing*. His model is more complex than the above may sound and does indeed reflect thinking from chaos theory and Young's work.

Stickland, F. (1998). *The Dynamics of Change: Insights Into Organisational Transition From the Natural World.* London and New York: Routledge.

As Stickland pointed out, many books have been written about *how* to manage change, but few about the nature of change itself, the *what*. His book, therefore, addresses the content; that is, he explored what organization change is as a phenomenon. Stickland's fundamental question is this: How can we really understand the process of leading and managing organization change if we are not sufficiently clear about what it is in the first place? He then proceeded to explain systems thinking, that is, general systems theory, or metaphorical ways of understanding organization change. Then, he moved on to summarize much of the relevant literature, referring to familiar names such as Kurt Lewin, William Bridges, and Andrew Pettigrew. Seeking a definition of organization change, Stickland then explored different perspectives, particularly from the social sciences and the physical sciences. For the remainder of his book, Stickland used the perspective of the natural and physical sciences to examine the nature of change and how to apply this kind of understanding to organizations. In his final chapter, he explored two interesting questions: "What constitutes successful change, and when does a change metaphor become reality?" (p. 155). In the scholarly tradition, at the end, Stickland suggested areas for further research in the quest for a deeper understanding of the nature of organization change itself.

Capra, B. (1990). *Mindwalk: A Film for Passionate Thinkers,* with Liv Ullmann, Sam Waterston, and John Heard. Hollywood, CA: Paramount Pictures

Based on Fritjof Capra's (1982) book, *The Turning Point,* this movie is an extensive conversation among three people—an academic (Ullmann), a politician (Waterston), and a poet (Heard)—who happen to be on a respite of sorts at the same location, the beautiful island abbey of Mont St. Michel. The academic waxes eloquently and philosophically about organisms, patterns, ecosystems, the whole earth, and the universe, while the politician scoffs at the impracticality of it all and the poet provides some levity on occasion, but mostly perspective—and a bit of poetry. Not quite 2 hours in length, the movie is a useful medium for introducing ideas from the "new science": chaos and complexity theories, self-organization, patterns, autopoesis, and open system theory. This movie is not for your average 10-year-old, but for "passionate thinkers" who are somewhat older. It can be a worthy alternative to heavy tomes on the same subject matter.

References

Adizes, I. (1979). Organizational passages: Diagnosing and treating life cycle problems of organizations. *Organizational Dynamics, 8*(1), 3-25.

Alderfer, C. P. (1977a). Group and intergroup relations. In J. R. Hackman and J. L. Suttle (Eds.), *Improving life at work: Behavioral science approaches to organizational change* (pp. 227-296). Santa Monica, CA: Goodyear.

Alderfer, C. P. (1977b). Organization development. *Annual Review of Psychology, 28,* 197-223.

Aldrich, H. E. (1979). *Organizations and environments.* Englewood Cliffs, NJ: Prentice-Hall.

Alexander, Y. (2002). *The impact of cross-cultural differences on the relationship of management practices, organizational climate, and employee satisfaction.* Unpublished doctoral dissertation, Columbia University, New York, NY.

Alinsky, S. (1946). *Reveille for radicals.* Chicago: University of Chicago Press.

Allport, F. H. (1962). A structural conception of behavior: Individual and collective. I. Structural theory and the master problem of social psychology. *Journal of Abnormal and Social Psychology, 64,* 3-30.

Allport, G. W. (1945). *The nature of prejudice.* Cambridge, MA: Addison-Wesley.

Amburgey, T. L., & Dacin, T. (1994). As the left foot follows the right? The dynamics of strategic and structural change. *Academy of Management Journal, 37,* 1427-1452.

Anderson-Rudolf, M. K. (1996). *A longitudinal study of organizational change: How change in individual perceptions of transformational and transactional constructs predicts change in organizational performance.* Unpublished doctoral dissertation, Columbia University, New York, NY.

Argyris, C. (1964). T-groups for organizational effectiveness. *Harvard Business Review, 42*(2), 60-74.

Argyris, C. (1970). *Intervention theory and method.* Reading, MA: Addison-Wesley.

Argyris, C. (1971). *Management and organizational development.* New York: McGraw-Hill.

Argyris, C., Putnam, R., & Smith, D. M. (1985).*Action science.* San Francisco/London: Jossey-Bass.

Argyris, C., & Schön, D. (1978).*Organizational learning: A theory of action perspective.* Reading. MA: Addison-Wesley.

Argyris, C., & Schön, D. (1982). *Theory in practice.* San Francisco: Jossey-Bass.

Arquilla, J., & Ronfeldt, D. F. (2001). *Networks and netwars: The future of terror, crime and militancy.* Santa Monica, CA: RAND Corporation.

Ashkanasy, N. M., Wilderom, C. P. M., & Peterson, M. F. (Eds.). (2000). *Handbook of organizational culture and climate.* Thousand Oaks, CA: Sage.

At Emery Air Freight: Positive reinforcement boosts performance. (1973). *Organizational Dynamics, 1*(3), 41-67.

Atkinson, J. W. (1958). *Motives in fantasy, action, and society.* Princeton, NJ: Van Nostrand.

Atwater, L., & Yammarino, F. (1992). Does self-other agreement on leadership perceptions moderate the validity of leadership predictions? *Personnel Psychology, 45,* 141-164.

Audia, P. G., Locke, E. A., & Smith, K. G. (2000).The paradox of success: An archival and a laboratory study of strategic persistence following radical environmental change. *Academy of Management Journal, 43,* 837-853.

Avolio, B. J. (1999). *Full leadership development: Building the vital forces in organizations.* Thousand Oaks, CA: Sage.

Bachman, J., Smith, C., & Slesinger, J. (1966). Control, performance, and satisfaction: An analysis of structural and individual effects. *Journal of Personality and Social Psychology, 4,* 127-136.

Bargh, J. A., & Chartrand, T. L. (1999). The unbearable automaticity of being. *American Psychologist, 54,* 462-479.

Barrick, M. R., Day, D. V., Lord, R. G., & Alexander, R. A. (1991). Assessing the utility of executive leadership. *Leadership Quarterly, 2,* 9-22.

Bass, B. M. (1998). *Transformational leadership: Industrial, military, and educational impact.* Mahwah, NJ: Lawrence Erlbaum.

Bass, B. M. (1990). *Bass and Stodgill's handbook of leadership* (3rd ed.). New York: Free Press.

Bateson, G. (1979). *Mind and nature: A necessary unity.* New York: Dutton.

Bauman, R. P., Jackson, P., & Lawrence, J. T. (1997). *From promise to performance: A journey of transformation at SmithKline Beecham.* Boston: Harvard Business School Press.

Beckhard, R. (1967). The confrontation meeting. *Harvard Business Review, 45*(2), 149-155.

Beckhard, R. (1972). Optimizing team-building efforts. *Journal of Contemporary Business, 1*(3), 23-32.

Beckhard, R. (1997). *Agent of change: My life, my practice.* San Francisco: Jossey-Bass.

Beckhard, R., & Harris, R. T. (1977). *Organizational transitions: Managing complex change.* Reading, MA: Addison-Wesley.

Beckhard, R., & Harris, R. T. (1987). *Organizational transitions: Managing complex change* (2nd ed.). Reading, MA: Addison-Wesley.

Beer, M. (1980). *Organization change and development.* Santa Monica, CA: Goodyear.

Beer, M., Eisenstat, R. A., & Spector, B. (1990). *The critical path to corporate renewal.* Boston: Harvard Business School Press.

Beer, M., Spector, B., Lawrence, P. R., Mills, D. Q., & Walton, R. E. (1984). *Managing human assets.* New York: Free Press.

Beer, M., & Walton, A. E. (1987). Organization change and development. *Annual Review of Psychology, 38,* 339-367.

Bennis, W., & Biederman, P. W. (1997). *Organizing genius: The secrets of creative collaboration.* Reading, MA: Addison-Wesley.

Bennis, W. G., & Nanus, B. (1985). *Leaders: The strategies for taking charge.* New York: Harper & Row.

Bernstein, W. M., & Burke, W. W. (1989). Modeling organizational meaning systems. In R. W. Woodman & W. A. Pasmore (Eds.), *Research in organizational change and development* (Vol. 3, pp. 117-159). Greenwich, CT: JAI.

Bion, W. R. (1961). *Experience in groups.* New York: Basic Books.

Blake, R. R., & Mouton, J. S. (1964). *The managerial grid.* Houston: Gulf.

Blake, R. R., & Mouton, J. S. (1968). *Corporate excellence through grid organization development.* Houston: Gulf.

Blake, R. R., & Mouton, J. S. (1978). *The new managerial grid.* Houston: Gulf.

Blake, R. R., Shepard, H. A., & Mouton, J. S. (1964). *Managing intergroup conflict in industry.* Houston: Gulf.

Blumburg, M., & Pringle, C. D. (1983). How control groups can cause loss of control in action research: The case of Rushton Coal Mine. *Journal of Applied Behavioral Science, 19,* 409-425.

Bonabeau, E., & Meyer, C. (2001). Swarm intelligence: A whole new way to think about business. *Harvard Business Review, 79*(5), 106-114.

Bourgeois, L. J. III. (1985). Strategic goals, perceived uncertainty, and economic performance in volatile environments. *Academy of Management Journal, 28,* 548-573.

Bower, M. (1979). *Perspective on McKinsey.* New York: McKinsey & Co.

Bowers, D. G. (1964). Organizational control in an insurance company. *Sociometry, 27,* 230-244.

Boyatzis, R. (1982). *The competent manager.* New York: Wiley & Sons.

Bracken, D. W. (1996). Multisource (360-degree) feedback: Surveys for individual and organizational development. In A. I. Kraut (Ed.), *Organizational surveys: Tools for assessment and change* (pp. 117-143). San Francisco: Jossey-Bass.

Brehm, J. W. (1966). *A theory of psychological reactance.* New York: Academic Press.

Bridges, W. (1980). *Transitions: Making sense of life's changes.* Reading, MA: Addison-Wesley.

Bridges, W. (1986). Managing organizational transitions. *Organizational Dynamics, 15*(1), 24-33.

Briggs, K. C., & Myers, I. B. (1943). *Myers-Briggs Type Indicator.* Palo Alto, CA: Consulting Psychologists Press.

Brooker, K. (2001). The chairman of the board looks back. *Fortune, 143*(11), 62-76.

Bullock, R. J., & Lawler, E. E. III. (1984). Gainsharing: A few questions and fewer answers. *Human Resource Management, 23,* 23-40.

Bunker, B. B., & Alban, B. T. (1997). *Large group interventions: Engaging the whole system for rapid change.* San Francisco: Jossey-Bass.

Bunker, D. R., & Knowles, E. S. (1967). Comparison of behavioral changes resulting from human relations training laboratories of different lengths. *Journal of Applied Behavioral Science, 3,* 505-524.

Burck, G. (1965, December). Union Carbide's patient schemers. *Fortune,* pp. 147-149.

Burke, M. J., & Pearlman, K. (1988). Recruiting, selecting, and matching people with jobs. In J. P. Campbell, R. S. Campbell, and Associates, *Productivity in organizations* (pp. 97-142). San Francisco: Jossey-Bass.

Burke, W. W. (1974). Managing conflict between groups. In J. D. Adams (Ed.), *New technologies in organization development* (Vol. 2, pp. 255-268). San Diego: University Associates.

Burke, W. W. (1980). System theory, gestalt therapy, and organization development. In T. G. Cummings (Ed.), *Systems theory for organization development* (pp. 209-222). Sussex, England: Wiley.

Burke, W. W. (1982). *Organization development: Principles and practices.* Boston: Little, Brown.

Burke, W. W. (1994). *Organization development: A process of learning and changing* (2nd ed.). Reading, MA: Addison-Wesley.

Burke, W. W. (1986). Leadership as empowering others. In S. Srivastva and Associates (Eds.), *Executive power: How executives influence people and organizations* (pp. 51-77). San Francisco: Jossey-Bass.

Burke, W. W. (1995). Organization change: What we know, what we need to know. *Journal of Management Inquiry, 4,* 158-171.

Burke, W. W. (1997). Leadership development. In L. J. Bassi & D. Russ-Eft (Eds.), *What works: Training and development practices* (pp. 1-25). Alexandria, VA: American Society for Training and Development.

Burke, W. W. (2000a). SmithKline Beecham. In D. Giver, L. Carter, & M. Goldsmith (Eds.), *Best practices in organization and human resources development handbook* (pp. 103-118). Lexington, MA: Linkage.

Burke, W. W. (2000b). The broad band of organization development and change: An introduction. In D. Giver, L. Carter, & M. Goldsmith (Eds.), *Best practices in organization and human resources development handbook* (pp. 5-10). Lexington, MA: Linkage.

Burke, W. W., & Biggart, N. W. (1997). Interorganizational relations. In D. Druckman, J. E. Singer, & H. Van Cott (Eds.), *Enhancing organizational performance* (pp. 120-149). Washington, DC: National Academy Press.

Burke, W. W., Clark, L. P., & Koopman, C. (1984). Improve your OD project's chances for success. *Training and Development Journal, 38*(8), 62-68.

Burke, W. W., & Coruzzi, C. A. (1987). Competence in managing lateral relations. In J. W. Pfeiffer (Ed.), *The 1987 annual: Developing human resources* (pp. 151-156). San Diego: University Associates.

Burke, W. W., & Jackson, P. (1991). Making the SmithKline Beecham merger work. *Human Resource Management, 30,* 69-87.

Burke, W. W., Javitch, M., Waclawski, J., & Church, A. (1997). The dynamics of midstream consulting. *Consulting Psychology Journal: Practice and Research, 49,* 83-95.

Burke, W. W., & Litwin, G. H. (1992). A causal model of organizational performance and change. *Journal of Management, 18*(3), 532-545.

Burke, W. W., & Noumair, D. A. (2002). The role and function of personality assessment in organization development. In J. Waclawski & A. H. Church (Eds.), *Organization development: Data-driven methods for change* (pp. 55–77). San Francisco: Jossey-Bass.

Burke, W. W., Richley, E. A., & DeAngelis, L. (1985). Changing leadership and planning processes at the Lewis Research Center, National Aeronautics and Space Administration. *Human Resource Management, 24,* 81-90.

Burke, W. W., & Schmidt, W. H. (1971). Primary target for change: The manager or the organization? In H. A. Hornstein, B. B. Bunker, W. W. Burke, M. Gindes, & R. J. Lewicki (Eds.), *Social intervention: A behavioral science approach* (pp. 373-385). New York: Free Press.

Burke, W. W., & Trahant, B. (2000). *Business climate shifts: Profiles of change makers.* Boston: Butterworth Heineman.

Burns, J. M. (1978). *Leadership.* New York: Harper & Row.

Burns, T., & Stalker, G. (1961). *The management of innovation.* London: Tavistock.

Cameron, K. S. (1980). Critical questions in assessing organizational effectiveness. *Organizational Dynamics, 9*(2), 66-80.

Cameron, K. S., & Whetten, D. A. (1981). Perceptions of organizational effectiveness over organizational life cycles. *Administrative Science Quarterly, 26,* 525-544.

Cameron, K. S., & Whetten, D. A. (Eds.). (1982). *Organizational effectiveness: A comparison of multiple models.* New York: Academic Press.

Campbell, J. P., & Dunnette, M. D. (1968). Effectiveness of T-group experiences in managerial training and development. *Psychological Bulletin, 70,* 73-104.

Capra, F. (1975). *The Tao of physics.* (3rd ed., 1991). Boston: Shambhala.

Capra, F. (1982). *The turning point.* New York: Simon & Schuster.

Capra, F. (1996). *The web of life.* New York: Anchor.

Carlzon, J. (1987). *Moments of truth: New strategies for today's customer-driven economy.* Cambridge, MA: Ballinger.

Carnall, C. A. (1982). *The evaluation of organizational change.* Brookfield, VT: Gower.

Chandler, A. (1962). *Strategy and structure.* Cambridge, MA: MIT Press.

Chin, R., & Benne, K. D. (1985). General strategies for effecting changes in human systems. In W. G. Bennis, K. D. Benne, & R. Chin (Eds.), *The planning of change* (4th ed., pp. 22-43). New York: Holt, Rinehart & Winston.

Church, A. H. (1997). Managerial self-awareness in high-performing individuals in organizations. *Journal of Applied Psychology, 82,* 281-292.

Church, A. H., Waclawski, J., & Burke, W. W. (2001). Multisource feedback for organization development and change. In D. W. Bracken, C. W. Timmreck, & A. H. Church (Eds.), *The handbook of multisource feedback* (pp. 301-317). San Francisco: Jossey-Bass.

Coch, L., & French, J. R. P. (1948). Overcoming resistance to change. *Human Relations, 1,* 512-532.

Collins, J. (2001). *Good to great: Why some companies make the leap and others don't.* New York: HarperCollins.

Collins, J. C., & Porras, J. I. (1994). *Built to last: Successful habits of visionary companies.* New York: Harper Business.

Conger, J. A. (1989). *The charismatic leader: Behind the mystique of exceptional leadership.* San Francisco: Jossey-Bass.

Coser, L. (1967). *Continuities in the study of social conflict.* New York: Free Press.

Costa, P. T., & McCrae, R. R. (1985). *NEO Personality Inventory.* Odessa, FL: PAR Psychological Assessment Resources.

Crockett, W. J. (1970). Team building—one approach to organizational development. *Journal of Applied Behavioral Science, 6,* 291-306.

Csikszentmihalyi, M. (1990). *Flow: The psychology of optimal experience.* New York: Harper & Row.

Darley, J., & Batson, D. (1973). From Jerusalem to Jericho: A study of situational and dispositional variables in helping behavior. *Journal of Personality and Social Psychology, 27,* 100-119.

Davis, S. A. (1967). An organic problem-solving method of organizational change. *Journal of Applied Behavioral Science, 3,* 3-21.

Deal, T. E., & Kennedy, A. A. (1982). *Corporate cultures: The rites and rituals of corporate life.* Reading, MA: Addison-Wesley.

Deutsch, M. (1969). Conflicts: Productive and destructive. *Journal of Social Issues, 25,* 7-40.

Deutsch, M. (1985). *Distributive justice: A social psychological perspective.* New Haven, CT: Yale University Press.

Dickson, W. J., & Roethlisberger, F. J. (1966). *Counseling in an organization: A sequel to the Hawthorne researchers.* Boston: Harvard Business School, Division of Research.

Dime Savings Bank. (1997). *Our vision; our mission.* New York: Dime Bancorp.

Dixon, N. F. (1976). *On the psychology of military incompetence.* London: Futura.

Drucker, P. F. (1969). *The age of discontinuity: Guidelines to our changing society.* New Brunswick, NJ: Transaction Publishing.

Drucker, P. F. (1974). *Management: Tasks, responsibilities, practices.* New York: Harper & Row.

Drucker, P. F. (1994). The theory of the business. *Harvard Business Review, 72*(5), 95-104.

Druckman, D., Singer, J. E., & Van Cott, H. (1997). (Eds.). *Enhancing organizational performance.* Washington, DC: National Academy Press.

Duck, J. D. (2001). *The change monster: The human forces that fuel or foil corporate transformation and change.* New York: Crown Business.

Dunbar, R. I. M. (1992). Neocortex size as a constraint on group size in primates. *Journal of Human Evolution, 20,* 469-493.

Duncan, J. R. (1979). What is the right organization structure? *Organizational Dynamics (7)*3, 59-80.

Dunnette, M. D. (1969). People feeling: Joy, more joy, and the slough of despond. *Journal of Applied Behavioral Science, 5,* 25-44.

Dyer, W. G. (1987). *Team building: Issues and alternatives* (2nd ed.). Reading, MA: Addison-Wesley.

Easterby-Smith, M. (1997). Disciplines of organizational learning: Contributions and critiques. *Human Relations, 50,* 1085-1103.

Emery, F. E., & Trist, E. L. (1965). The causal texture of organizational environments. *Human Relations, 18,* 21-32.

Evans, R., & Price, C. (1999). *Vertical take-off: The inside story of British Aerospace's comeback from crisis to world class.* London: Nicholas Brealey.

Faucheux, C., Amado, G., & Laurent, A. (1982). Organizational development and change. *Annual Review of Psychology, 33,* 343-370.

Flamholtz, E. (1979). Organizational control systems as a managerial tool. *California Management Review, 22*(2), 50-59.

Fleishman, E. A. (1953). Leadership climate, human relations training, and supervisory behavior. *Personnel Psychology, 6,* 205-222.

Fordyce, J. K., & Weil, R. (1979). *Managing with people.* (2nd ed.). Reading, MA: Addison-Wesley.

Foster, R. N., & Kaplan, S. (2001). *Creative destruction: Why companies that are built to last underperform the market—and how to successfully transform them.* New York: Currency.

Fox, M. M. (1990). *The role of individual perceptions of organization culture in predicting perceptions of work unit climate and organizational performance.* Unpublished doctoral dissertation, Columbia University, New York, NY.

French, J. R. P., & Raven, B. H. (1959). The bases of social power. In D. Cartwright (Ed.), *Studies in social power* (pp. 150-167). Ann Arbor: University of Michigan, Institute for Social Research.

French, W. L., & Bell, C. H. Jr. (1995). *Organization development: Behavioral science interventions for organization improvement* (5th ed.). Englewood Cliffs, NJ: Prentice-Hall.

Friedlander, F. (1970). The primacy of trust as a facilitator of further group accomplishment. *Journal of Applied Behavioral Science, 6,* 387-400.

Friedlander, F., & Brown, L. D. (1974). Organization development. *Annual Review of Psychology, 25,* 313-341.

Galbraith, J. R. (1973). *Designing complex organizations.* Reading, MA: Addison-Wesley.

Galbraith, J. R. (1977). *Organization design.* Reading, MA: Addison-Wesley.

Galbraith, J. R. (1995). *Designing organizations: An executive briefing on strategy, structure, and process.* San Francisco: Jossey-Bass.

Gardner, H. (1995). *Leading minds: An anatomy of leadership.* New York: Basic Books.

Georgiades, N., & Macdonell, R. (1998). *Leadership for competitive advantage.* Chichester, England: Wiley.

Gersick, C. J. G. (1988). Time and transition in work teams: Toward a new model of group development. *Academy of Management Journal, 31,* 9-41.

Gersick, C. J. G. (1991). Revolutionary change theories: A multilevel exploration of the punctuated equilibrium paradigm. *Academy of Management Review, 16,* 10-36.

Gladwell, M. (2000). *The tipping point: How little things can make a big difference.* Boston: Little, Brown.

Goleman, D. (1995). *Emotional intelligence.* New York: Bantam.

Golembiewski, R. T., Billingsley, K., & Yeager, S. (1976). Measuring change and persistence in human affairs: Types of change generated by OD designs. *Journal of Applied Behavioral Science, 12,* 133-157.

Goodman, P. S., Devadas, R., & Griffith Hughson, T. L. (1988). Groups and productivity: Analyzing the effectiveness of self-managing teams. In J. P. Campbell, R. J. Campbell, & Associates (Eds.), *Productivity in organizations* (pp. 295-327). San Francisco: Jossey-Bass.

Goodstein, L. D., & Burke, W. W. (1991). Creating successful organizational change. *Organizational Dynamics, 19*(4), 5-17.

Goodstein, L. D., & Butz, H. E. (1998). Customer value: The linchpin of organizational change. *Organizational Dynamics, 27*(1), 21-34.

Gordon, G. G. (1985). The relationship of corporate culture to industry sector and corporate performance. In R. H. Kilmann, M. J. Saxton, R. Serpa, & Associates (Eds.), *Gaining control of the corporate culture* (pp. 103-125). San Francisco: Jossey-Bass.

Gould, S. J. (1977). *Ever since Darwin.* New York: Norton.

Gould, S. J. (1980). *The panda's thumb.* New York: Norton.

Greiner, L. (1972). Evolution and revolution as organizations grow. *Harvard Business Review, 50*(4), 37-46.

Guzzo, R. A., Jette, R. D., & Katzell, R. A. (1985). The effects of psychologically based intervention programs on worker productivity. *Personnel Psychology, 38,* 275-291.

Gyllenhammar, P. G. (1977). *People at work.* Reading, MA: Addison-Wesley.

Hackman, J. R. (1992). The psychology of self-management in organizations. In R. Glaser (Ed.), *Classic readings in self-managing teamwork* (pp. 143-193). King of Prussia, PA: Organization Design and Development.

Hackman, J. R., & Oldham, G. R. (1980). *Work redesign.* Reading, MA: Addison-Wesley.

Haken, H. (1981). Synergetics: Is self-organization governed by universal principles? In E. Jantsch (Ed.), *Toward a unifying paradigm of physical, biological, and sociocultural evolution* (pp. 15-23). Boulder, CO: Westview.

Hall, J., & Williams, M. S. (1966). A comparison of decision-making performances in established and ad hoc groups. *Journal of Personality and Social Psychology, 3,* 214-222.

Hall, J., & Williams, M. S. (1970). Group dynamics training and improved decision making. *Journal of Applied Behavioral Science, 6,* 39-68.

Hambrick, D. C. (1989). Guest editor's introduction: Putting top managers back in the strategy picture. *Strategic Management Journal, 10,* 5-15.

Hambrick, D. C., & Cannella, A. A. Jr. (1989). Strategy implementation as substance and selling. *Academy of Management Executive, 3*(4), 278-285.

Haney, C., Banks, C., & Zimbardo, P. (1973). Interpersonal dynamics in a simulated prison. *International Journal of Criminology and Penology, 1,* 69-97.

Hartshorne, H., & May, M. (1971). Studies in the organization of character. In H. Munsinger (Ed.), *Readings in child development* (pp. 190-197). New York: Holt, Rinehart & Winston.

Harvey, J. B. (1974). The Abilene paradox: The management of agreement. *Organizational Dynamics, 3*(1), 63-80.

Harvey, J. B. (1977). Consulting during crises of agreement. In W. W. Burke (Ed.), *Current issues and strategies in organization development* (pp. 160-186). New York: Human Sciences Press.

Hayakawa, S. I. (1941). *Language in thought and action.* New York: Harcourt, Brace, & World.

Heifetz, R. A. (1994). *Leadership without easy answers.* Cambridge, MA: Belknap Press of Harvard University Press.

Herzberg, F. (1966). *Work and the nature of man.* Cleveland, OH: World.

Herzberg, F., Mausner, B., & Snyderman, B. (1959). *The motivation to work.* New York: Wiley.

Hitt, M. A., & Tyler, B. B. (1991). Strategic decision models: Integrating different perspectives. *Strategic Management Journal, 12,* 327-351.

Hofstede, G. (1991). *Cultures and organisations: Intercultural cooperation and its importance to survival.* Glasgow, Scotland: Harper & Collins.

Hogan, R., Curphy, G. J., & Hogan, J. (1994). What we know about leadership. *American Psychologist, 52*(2), 130-139.

Hogan, R., Raskin, R., & Fazzini, D. (1990). The dark side of charisma. In K. E. Clark & M. B. Clark (Eds.), *Measures of leadership* (pp. 343-354). West Orange, NJ: Leadership Library of America.

Holstein, W. J. (2001, November 25). Three user's manuals for modern management. *The New York Times,* sec. 3, p. 6.

Homans, G. C. (1950). *The human group.* New York: Harcourt Brace.

Hornstein, H. A. (1996). *Brutal bosses and their prey.* New York: Riverhead Books.

Hornstein, H. A., Bunker, B. B., Burke, W. W., Gindes, M., & Lewicki, R. J. (1971). *Social interventions: A behavioral science approach.* New York: Free Press.

Hornstein, H. A., Callahan, D. M., Fisch, E., & Benedict, B. A. (1968). Influence and satisfaction in organizations: A replication. *Sociology of Education, 41,* 380-389.

House, R. J. (1977). A 1976 theory of charismatic leadership. In J. G. Hunt & L. Larson (Eds.), *Leadership: The cutting edge.* Carbondale: Southern Illinois University Press.

How mergers go wrong. (2000, July 22). *The Economist,* p. 19.

Huber, G. P. (1991). Organizational learning: An examination of the contributing processes and a review of the literature. *Organization Science, 2,* 88-115.

Hughes, R. L., Ginnett, R. A., & Curphy, G. S. (1993). *Leadership: Enhancing the lessons of experience.* Homewood, IL: Irwin.

Hunter, J. E., & Schmidt, F. L. (1982). Fitting people to jobs: Implications of personnel selection on national productivity. In E. A. Fleischman & M. D. Dunnette (Eds.), *Human performance and productivity: Human capability assessment, 1,* 233-284. Hillsdale, NJ: Erlbaum.

Huselid, M. A., Jackson, S. E., & Schuler, R. S. (1997). Technical and strategic human resource management effectiveness as determinants of firm performance. *Academy of Management Journal, 40,* 171-188.

Jacobs, T. O., & Jaques, E. (1987). Leadership in complex systems. In J. Zeidner (Ed.), *Human productivity enhancement.* New York: Praeger.

James, W. (1890). *Principles of psychology* (Vols. 1 and 2). New York: Holt.

Jaques, E. (1978). *A general theory of bureaucracy.* Exeter, NH: Heinemann.

Jaques, E. (1986). The development of intellectual capability: A discussion of stratified systems theory. *Journal of Applied Behavioral Science, 22,* 361-384.

Jaques, E., & Clement, S. D. (1991). *Executive leadership.* Arlington, VA: Cason Hall.

Jick, T. D. (1990). *The recipients of change.* (Teaching materials). Boston: Harvard Business School.

Johnson, S. (1998). *Who moved my cheese?* New York: Putnam.

Jordan, P. C. (1986). Effects of an extrinsic reward on intrinsic motivation. A field experiment. *Academy of Management Journal, 29,* 405-412.

Joyce, W. F., & Slocum, J. W. (1984). Collective climate: Agreement as a basis for defining aggregate climates in organizations. *Academy of Management Journal, 27,* 721-742.

Kanter, R. M. (1982). Dilemmas of managing participation. *Organizational Dynamics, 11*(1), 5-27.

Kaplan, R. S., & Norton, D. P. (1996). *The balanced scorecard: Translating strategy into action.* Boston: Harvard Business School Press.

Katz, D., & Kahn, R. L. (1978). *The social psychology of organizations* (2nd ed). New York: Wiley.

Katzell, R. A., & Thompson, D. E. (1990). Work motivation, theory and practice. *American Psychologist, 45*(2), 144-153.

Katzenbach, J. R., & Smith, D. K. (1993*). The wisdom of teams: Creating the high-performance organization.* Boston: Harvard Business School Press.

Kerr, J., & Slocum, J. W. (1987). Managing corporate culture through reward systems. *Academy of Management Executive, 1,* 99-108.

Kimberly, J., Miles, R., & Associates. (1980). *The organizational life cycle.* San Francisco, CA: Jossey-Bass.

Kimberly, J. R., & Nielsen, W. R. (1975). Organization development and change in organizational performance. *Administrative Science Quarterly, 20,* 191-206.

King, D. (1972). Selecting personnel for a System 4 organization. In W. W. Burke (Ed.), *Contemporary organization development: Conceptual orientations and interventions* (pp. 201-211). Washington, DC: NTL Institute for Applied Behavioral Science.

Kipnis, D. (1976). *The powerholders.* Chicago: University of Chicago Press.

Koch, C., & Laurent, G. (1999). Complexity and the nervous system. *Science, 284,* 96-98.

Kotter, J. P. (1990). *A force for change: How leadership differs from management.* New York: Free Press.

Kraemer, K. L., King, J. L., Dunkle, D. E., & Lane, J. P. (1989). *Managing information systems: Change and control in organizational computing.* San Francisco: Jossey-Bass.

Kraut, A. I. (Ed.). (1996). *Organizational surveys: Tools for assessment and change.* San Francisco: Jossey-Bass.

Kubler-Ross, E. (1969). On death and dying. New York: MacMillan,

Kuhn, T. S. (1970). *The structure of scientific revolution* (2nd ed.). Chicago: University of Chicago Press.

Laird, J. D., & Bresler, C. (1990). William James and the mechanisms of emotional experience. *Personality and Social Psychology Bulletin, 16,* 636-651.

Lange, C. G. (1922). *The emotions* (I. A. Haupt, Trans., pp. 33-90). Baltimore, MD: Williams & Wilkens. (Original work published in 1885).

Lawler, E. E. III. (1973). *Motivation in work organizations.* Monterey, CA: Brooks/Cole.

Lawler, E. E. III. (1977). Reward systems. In J. R. Hackman & J. L. Suttle (Eds.), *Improving life at work* (pp. 163-226). Santa Monica, CA: Goodyear.

Lawler, E. E. III. (1990). *Strategic pay: Aligning organizational strategies and pay systems.* San Francisco: Jossey-Bass.

Lawrence, P. R. & Lorsch, J. W. (1967). *Organization and environment.* Boston: Harvard University Business School, Division of Research.

Lawrence, P. R., & Lorsch, J. W. (1969*). Developing organizations: Diagnosis and action.* Reading, MA: Addison-Wesley.

Leavitt, H. J. (1965). Applied organizational change in industry. In J. G. March (Ed.), *Handbook of organizations* (pp. 1144-1170). New York: Rand McNally.

Legge, K. (1984). *Evaluating planned organizational change.* Orlando, FL: Academic.

Levine, A. (1980). *Why innovation fails: The institutionalization and termination of innovation in higher education.* Albany: State University of New York Press.

Levinson, D. J. (1978). *The seasons of a man's life*. New York: Knopf.

Levinson, D. J. (1986). A conception of adult development. *American Psychologist, 41,* 3-13.

Levinson, H. (1972). *Organizational diagnosis.* Cambridge, MA: Harvard University Press.

Levinson, H. (1974). Don't choose your own successor. *Harvard Business Review, 52,* 53-62.

Levinson, H. (1975). *Executive stress.* New York: Harper.

Levinson, H. (1976). *Psychological man.* Cambridge, MA: The Levinson Institute.

Levinson, H. (1994). Beyond the selection failure. *Consulting Psychology Journal: Practice and Research, 46,* 3-8.

Lewin, K. (1947). Group decision and social change. In T. M. Newcomb, E. L. Hartley, & Others, *Readings in social psychology* (pp. 330-344). New York: Henry Holt.

Lewin, K. (1951). *Field theory in social science.* New York: Harper.

Lewin, K. (1958). Group decision and social change. In E. E. Maccoby, T. M. Newcomb, & E. L. Hartley (Eds.), *Readings in social psychology* (pp. 197-211). New York: Holt, Rinehart & Winston.

Liebovitch, L. S. (1998). *Fractals and chaos simplified for the life sciences.* New York: Oxford University Press.

Likert, R. (1961). *New patterns of management.* New York: McGraw-Hill.

Likert, R. (1967). *The human organization.* New York: McGraw-Hill.

Lippitt, R., Watson, J., & Westley, B. (1958). *Dynamics of planned change.* New York: Harcourt Brace.

Litwin, G. H., Bray, J., & Brooke, K. L. (1996). *Mobilizing the organization: Bringing strategy to life.* London: Prentice-Hall.

Litwin, G. H., Humphrey, J. W., & Wilson, T. B. (1978). Organizational climate: A proven tool for improving performance. In W. W. Burke (Ed.), *The cutting edge: Current theory and practice in organization development* (pp. 187-205). La Jolla, CA: University Associates.

Litwin, G. H., & Stringer, R. A. (1968). *Motivation and organizational climate.* Boston: Harvard Business School Press.

London, M. (2001). The great debate: Should multisource feedback be used for administration or development only? In D. W. Bracken, C. W. Timmereck, & A. H. Church (Eds.), *The handbook of multisource feedback* (pp. 368-385). San Francisco: Jossey-Bass.

Lundberg, G. C. (1989). On organizational learning: Implications and opportunities for expanding organizational development. *Research in Organization Change and Development, 3,* 61-82.

Luthans, F. (1988). Successful vs. effective real managers. *Academy of Management Executive, 2,* 127-132.

Mann, F. C. (1957). Studying and creating change: A means to understanding social organization. *Research in Industrial Human Relations.* (Industrial Relations Research Association, Publication No. 17).

Marrow, A. J., Bowers, D. G., & Seashore, S. E. (1967). *Management by participation.* New York: Harper & Row.

Maslow, A. H. (1954). *Motivation and personality.* New York: Harper.

Maturana, H., & Varela, F. (1987). *The tree of knowledge.* Boston: Shambhala.

McClelland, D. C. (1961). *The achieving society.* Princeton, NJ: Van Nostrand.

McClelland, D. C. (1965). Achievement and entrepreneurship: A longitudinal study. *Journal of Personality and Social Psychology, 1,* 389-392.

McClelland, D. C. (1975). *Power: The inner experience.* New York: Irvington.

McClelland, D. C., & Burnham, D. H. (1976). Power is the great motivator. *Harvard Business Review, 54*(2), 100-110.

McGregor, D. (1960). *The human side of enterprise.* New York: McGraw-Hill.

McGregor, D. (1967). *The professional manager.* New York: McGraw-Hill.

Meglino, B. M., & Ravlin, E. C. (1998). Individual values in organizations: Concepts, controversies, and research. *Journal of Management, 24,* 351-389.

Miles, R. E., & Snow, C. C. (1978). *Organizational strategy, structure, and process.* New York: McGraw-Hill.

Milgram, S. (1967). The small world problem. *Psychology Today, 1,* 60-67.

Miller, C. C., & Cardinal, L. B. (1994). Strategic planning and firm performance: A synthesis of more than two decades of research. *Academy of Management Journal, 37,* 1649-1665.

Miller, D. (1996). A preliminary typology of organizational learning: Synthesizing the literature. *Journal of Management, 22,* 485-505.

Miller, E. C. (1978). The parallel organization structure at General Motors: An interview with Howard C. Carlson. *Personnel, 55*(4), 64-69.

Miller, G. A. (1956). The magical number seven, plus or minus two: Some limits on our capacity for processing information. *Psychological Review, 63,* 81-97.

Mintzberg, H. (1973). *The nature of managerial work.* New York: Harper & Row.

Mintzberg, H. (1989). *Mintzberg on management: Inside our strange world of organizations.* New York: Free Press.

Mirvis, P. H. (1996). Historical foundations of organizational learning. *Journal of Organization Change Management, 9,* 13-31.

Morgan, G. (Ed.). (1983). *Beyond method: Strategies for social research.* Beverly Hills, CA: Sage.

Morgan, G. (1997). *Images of organizations* (2nd ed.). Thousand Oaks, CA: Sage.

Mumford, M. D., Zaccaro, S. J., Harding, F. D., Fleishman, E. A., & Reiter-Palmon, R. (1993). *Cognitive and temperament predictors of executive ability: Principles for developing leadership capacity.* Alexandria, VA: U.S. Army Research Institute for the Behavioral and Social Sciences.

Nadler, D. A., & Tushman, M. L. (1977). A diagnostic model for organization behavior. In J. R. Hackman, E. E. Lawler III, & L. W. Porter (Eds.), *Perspectives in behavior in organizations* (pp. 85-100). New York: McGraw-Hill.

Nadler, D. A., & Tushman, M. L. (1989). Organizational frame bending: Principles for managing reorientation. *Academy of Management Executive, 3,* 194-204.

Naisbitt, J. (1994). *Global paradox.* New York: William Morrow.

Naples Daily News (2001, June 1), p. 6A

Obholzer, A. (1994). Authority, power and leadership: Contributions from group relations training. In A. Obholzer & V. Z. Roberts (Eds.), *The unconscious at work: Individual and organizational stress in the human services* (pp. 39-47). New York and London: Routledge.

Orlikowski, W. S. (1996). Improvising organizational transformation overtime: A situated change perspective. *Information Systems Research, 7*(1), 63–92.

O'Toole, J. (1995). *Leading change: Overcoming the ideology of comfort and the tyranny of custom.* San Francisco: Jossey-Bass.

O'Toole, J. (1999). *Leadership A to Z: A guide for the appropriately ambitious.* San Francisco: Jossey-Bass.

Pascale, R. T., Milleman, M., & Gioja, L. (2000). *Surfing the edge of chaos: The laws of nature and the new laws of business.* New York: Crown Business.

Pasmore, W. A. (1988). *Designing effective organizations: The sociotechnical systems perspective.* New York: Wiley.

Peabody, G. L. (1971). Power, Alinsky and other thoughts. In H. A. Hornstein, B. B. Bunker, W. W. Burke, M. Gindes, & R. J. Lewicki (Eds.), *Social intervention: A behavioral science approach* (pp. 521-532). New York: Free Press.

Pearce, J. A., & David, F. (1987). Corporate mission statements: The bottom line: *Academy of Management Executive, 1,* 109-116.

Pearson, C. A. L. (1992). Autonomous work groups: An evaluation at an industrial site. *Human Relations, 45,* 905-936.

Peters, T. (2001, December). Tom Peters's true confessions. *Fast Company, 53,* 78-92.

Peters, T. J., & Waterman, R. H. Jr. (1982). *In search of excellence: Lessons from America's best-run companies.* New York: Harper & Row.

Pettigrew, A. M., Woodman, R. W., & Cameron, K. S. (2001). Studying organization change and development: Challenges for future research. *Academy of Management Journal, 44,* 697-713.

Pfeiffer, J., & Salancik, G. R. (1978). *The external control of organizations: A resource dependent perspective.* New York: Harper & Row.

Porras, J. I. (1987). *Stream analysis: A powerful way to diagnose and manage organizational change.* Reading, MA: Addison-Wesley.

Porras, J. I., & Robertson, P. J. (1987). Organization development theory: A typology and evaluation. In R. W. Woodman & W. A. Pasmore (Eds.), *Research in organization change and development* (Vol. 1). Greenwich, CT: JAI.

Porras, J. I., & Robertson, P. J. (1992). Organizational development: Theory, practice and research. In M. D. Dunnette & L. M. Hough (Eds.), *Handbook of industrial and organizational psychology* (Vol. 3, 2nd ed., pp. 719-822). Palo Alto, CA: Consulting Psychologists Press.

Porras, J. I., & Silvers, R. C. (1991). Organization development and transformation. *Annual Review of Psychology, 42,* 51-78.

Porter, M. (1985). *Competitive advantage: Creating and sustaining superior performance.* New York: Free Press.

Power, C. (1989, October 9). From "bloody awful" to bloody awesome. *Business Week,* p. 97.

Prescott, J. E. (1986). Environments as moderators of the relationship between strategy and performance. *Academy of Management Journal, 29,* 329-346.

Prigogine, I., & Stengers, I. (1984). *Order out of chaos: Man's new dialogue with nature.* New York: Bantam.

Quinn, R. E. (1988). *Beyond rational management: Mastering paradoxes and competing demands of high performance.* San Francisco: Jossey-Bass.

Rajagopalan, N., & Spreitzer, G. M. (1997). Toward a theory of strategic change: A multi-lens perspective and integrative framework. *Academy of Management Review, 22,* 48-79.

Rasiel, E. M. (1999). *The McKinsey way.* New York: McGraw-Hill.

Richter, F. M. (1986). Non-linear behavior. In D. W. Fiske & R. A. Shweder (Eds.), *Meta-theory in social science: Pluralisms and subjectivities* (pp. 284-292). Chicago: University of Chicago Press.

Riegel, K. F. (1976). The dialectics of human development. *American Psychologist, 31,* 689-700.

Roethlisberger, F. J., & Dickson, W. J. (1939). *Management and the worker: An account of a research program conducted by the Western Electric Company.* Cambridge, MA: Harvard University Press.

Roethlisberger, F. J. (1980). The Hawthorne experiments. In D. Mankin, R. E. Ames Jr., & M. A. Grodsky (Eds.). *Classics of industrial and organizational psychology* (pp. 29-39). Oak Park, IL: Moore.

Rogers, C. R. (1968). Interpersonal relations: W.S.A. 2000. *Journal of Applied Behavioral Science, 4,* 265-280.

Romanelli, E., & Tushman, M. L. (1986). Inertia, environments, and strategic choice: A quasi-experimental design for comparative longitudinal research. *Management Science, 32,* 608-621.

Rosenberg, R. D., & Rosenstein, E. (1980). Participation and productivity: An empirical study. *Industrial and Labor Relations Review, 33,* 355-367.

Rosenthal, R. (1976). *Experimenter effects in behavioral science* (enlarged ed.). New York: Halsted.

Rost, J. C. (1991). *Leadership for the twenty-first century.* Westport, CT: Praeger.

Rothstein, E. (2001, October 20). A lethal weapon with no spider. *The New York Times,* pp. A13, A15.

Rubin, I. (1967). Increasing self-acceptance: A means of reducing prejudice. *Journal of Personality and Social Psychology, 5,* 233-238.

Sagie, A., & Elizur, D. (1996). Work values: A theoretical overview and a model of their effects. *Journal of Organizational Behavior, 17,* 503-514.

Sashkin, M. (1988). The visionary leader. In J. A. Conger & R. N. Kanungo (Eds.), *Charismatic leadership: The elusive factor in organizational effectiveness.* San Francisco: Jossey-Bass.

Sashkin, M., & Burke, W. W. (1990). Understanding and assessing organizational leadership. In K. E. Clark & M. B. Clark (Eds.), *Measures of leadership* (pp. 297-325). West Orange, NJ: Leadership Library of America.

Schacter, S. (1959). *The psychology of affiliation.* Stanford, CA: Stanford University Press.

Schein, E. H. (1972). *Organizational psychology* (2nd ed.). Englewood Cliffs, NJ: Prentice-Hall.

Schein, E. H. (1980). *Organizational psychology* (3rd ed). Englewood Cliffs, NJ: Prentice-Hall.

Schein, E. H. (1983). The role of the founder in creating organizational cultures. *Organizational Dynamics, 12*(1), 13-28.

Schein, E. H. (1985). *Organizational culture and leadership.* San Francisco: Jossey-Bass.

Schein, E. H. (1987). *Process consultation: Vol. 2. Its role in organization development* (2nd ed.). Reading, MA: Addison-Wesley.

Schein, E. H. (1992). *Organizational culture and leadership* (2nd ed.). San Francisco: Jossey-Bass.

Schneider, B. (1980). The service organization: Climate is crucial. *Organizational Dynamics, 9*(2), 52-65.

Schneider, B. (1985). Organizational behavior. *Annual Review of Psychology, 36,* 573-611.

Schneider, B. (1990a). The climate for service: Application of the construct. In B. Schneider (Ed.), *Organizational climate and culture* (pp. 383-412). San Francisco: Jossey-Bass.

Schneider, B. (Ed.). (1990b). *Organizational climate and culture.* San Francisco: Jossey-Bass.

Schneider, B., & Bowen, D. E. (1985). Employee and customer perceptions of service in banks: Replication and extension. *Journal of Applied Psychology, 70,* 423-433.

Schneider, B., & Bowen, D. E. (1995). *Winning the service game.* Boston: Harvard Business School Press.

Schneider, B., & Snyder, R. A. (1975). Some relationships between job satisfaction and organizational climate. *Journal of Applied Psychology, 60,* 318-328.

Senge, P. (1990). *The fifth discipline: The art and practice of the learning organization.* New York: Doubleday Currency.

Sherif, M. (1966). *In common predicament.* Boston: Houghton Mifflin.

Sherif, M., Harvey, O. J., White, B. J., Hood, W. R., & Sherif, C. W. (1961). *Intergroup conflict and cooperation: The robbers cave experiment.* Norman: University of Oklahoma, Institute of Group Relations.

Sherif, M., & Sherif, C. W. (1953). *Groups in harmony and tension.* New York: Harper & Row.

Sherif, M., & Sherif, C. W. (1969). *Social psychology.* New York: Harper & Row.

Skinner, B. F. (1948). *Walden two.* New York: Macmillan.

Smith, J. E., Carson, K. P., & Alexander, R. A. (1984). Leadership: It can make a difference. *Academy of Management Journal, 27,* 765-776.

Starbuck, W. H. (1983). Organizations as action generators. *American Sociological Review, 48,* 91-102.

Stodgill, R. M. (1974). *Handbook of leadership: A survey of theory and research.* New York: Free Press.

Streufert, S., & Swezey, R. W. (1986). *Complexity, managers, and organizations.* Orlando, FL: Academic Press.

Svyantek, D. J. (1997). Order out of chaos: Nonlinear systems and organizational change. *Current Topics in Management, 2,* 167-188.

Svyantek, D. J., & Brown, L. L. (2000). A complex-systems approach to organizations. *Current Directions in Psychological Science, 9,* 69-74.

Svyantek, D. J., & DeShon, R. P. (1993). Organizational attractors: A chaos theory explanation of why cultural change efforts often don't. *Public Administration Quarterly, 17,* 339-355.

Tagiuri, R., & Litwin, G. H. (Eds.). (1968). *Organizational climate: Explorations of a concept.* Cambridge, MA: Harvard University Press.

Tannenbaum, A. S., & Kahn, R. L. (1957). Organizational control structure: A general descriptive technique as applied to four local unions. *Human Relations, 10,* 127-40.

Tannenbaum, A. S., & Kahn, R. L. (1958). *Participation in union locals.* Evanston, IL: Row Peterson.

Taylor, F. W. (1980). The principles of scientific management. In D. Mankin, R. E. Arnes Jr., & M. A. Grodsky (Eds.), *Classics of industrial and organizational psychology* (pp. 15-28). Oak Park, IL: Moore.

Thompson, J. D. (1967). *Organization in action.* New York: McGraw-Hill.

Tichy, N. M. (1983). *Managing strategic change: Technical, political, and cultural dynamics.* New York: Wiley.

Tichy, N. M., Hornstein, H. A., & Nisberg, J. N. (1977). Organization diagnosis and intervention strategies: Developing emergent pragmatic theories of change. In W. W. Burke (Ed.), *Current issues and strategies in organization development* (pp. 361-383). New York: Human Sciences.

Tichy, N. M., & Sherman, S. (1993). *Control your destiny or someone else will: How Jack Welch is making General Electric the world's most competitive corporation.* New York: Doubleday.

Trist, E. (1993). Introduction to volume II. In E. Trist & H. Murray (Eds.), *The social engagement of social science: A Tavistock anthology: Vol. 2. The socio-technical perspective* (pp. 36-60). Philadelphia: University of Pennsylvania Press.

Tsui, A. S. (1984). A multiple constituency framework of managerial reputational effectiveness. In J. G. Hunt, D. Hosking, C. Schriesheim, & R. Stewart (Eds.), *Leaders and managers: International perspectives on managerial behavior and leadership* (pp. 28-44). New York: Pergamon.

Tushman, M. L., & Romanelli, E. (1985). Organizational evolution: A metamorphosis model of convergence and reorientation. In L. L. Cummings & B. M. Staw (Eds.), *Research in organizational behavior, 7,* 171-122. Greenwich, CT: JAI.

Van Eron, A. M., & Burke, W. W. (1992). The transformational/transactional leadership model: A study of critical components. In K. E. Clark, M. B. Clark, & D. P. Campbell (Eds.), *Impact of leadership* (pp. 149-167). Greensboro, NC: Center for Creative Leadership.

Van de Ven, A. H., & Poole, M. S. (1995). Explaining development and change in organizations. *Academy of Management Review, 20,* 510-540.

Von Bertalanffy, L. (1950). An outline of general systems theory. *British Journal of the Philosophy of Science, 1,* 134-165.

Vroom, V. (1964). *Work and motivation.* New York: Wiley.

Wake, D. B., Roth, G., & Wake, M. H. (1983). On the problem of stasis in organismal evolution. *Journal of Theoretical Biology, 101,* 211-224.

Walton, R. E. (1975). The diffusion of new work structures: Explaining why success didn't take. *Organizational Dynamics, 3*(3), 2-22.

Watkins, K. E., & Marsick, V. S. (1993). *Sculpting the learning organization: Lessons in the art and science of systemic change.* San Francisco: Jossey-Bass.

Wegner, D. (1991). Transactive memory in close relationships. *Journal of Personality and Social Psychology, 61,* 923-929.

Wegner, D. M., & Wheatley, T. (1999). Apparent mental causation. *American Psychologist, 54,* 480-492.

Weick, K. E. (1979). *The social psychology of organizing* (2nd ed.). Reading, MA: Addison-Wesley.

Weick, K. E. (1995). *Sensemaking in organizations.* Thousand Oaks, CA: Sage.

Weick, K. E., & Quinn, R. E. (1999). Organizational change and development, *Annual Review of Psychology, 50,* 361-386.

Weiner, N., & Mahoney, T. A. (1981). A model of corporate performance as a function of environmental, organizational, and leadership influences. *Academy of Management Journal, 24,* 453-470.

Weisbord, M. R. (1976). Organizational diagnosis: Six places to look for trouble with or without a theory. *Group and Organization Studies, 1,* 430-447.

Weisbord, M. R. (1987). *Productive workplaces: Organizing and managing for dignity, meaning, and community.* San Francisco: Jossey-Bass.

Wendt, H. (1993). *Global embrace: Corporate challenges in a transnational world.* New York: Harper Business.

Whetten, D. A. (1989). What constitutes a theoretical contribution? *Academy of Management Review, 14,* 490-495.

Whetten, D. A. (in press). Modeling-as-theorizing: A methodology for theory development. In D. Partington (Ed.), *Essential skills for management research.* London: Sage, Ltd.

Whyte, W. F. (1955). *Money and motivation.* New York: Harper & Row.

Wilkens, A. L. (1989). *Developing corporate character: How to successfully change an organization without destroying it.* San Francisco: Jossey-Bass.

Witherspoon, R., & White, R. P. (1998). *Four essential ways that coaching can help executives.* Greensboro, NC: Center for Creative Leadership.

Wortman, M. S. (1982). Strategic management and changing leader-follower roles. *Journal of Applied Behavioral Science, 18,* 371-383.

Young, A. (1976). *The reflexive universe.* Lake Oswego, OR: Robert Briggs.

Yukl, G. A. (1998). *Leadership in organizations* (4th ed.). Englewood Cliffs, NJ: Prentice-Hall.

Zaccaro, S. J. (2001). *The nature of executive leadership: A conceptual and empirical analysis of success.* Washington, DC: American Psychological Association.

Zaleznik, A. (1977). Managers and leaders: Are they different? *Harvard Business Review, 55*(3), 67-78.

Zuboff, S. (1988). *In the age of the smart machine: The future of work and power.* New York: Basic Books.

Index

About the Author

W. Warner Burke is Professor of Psychology and Education and coordinator for the graduate programs in Social-Organizational Psychology, in the Department of Organization and Leadership, at Teachers College, Columbia University, in New York. He is also senior advisor to the organization and change strategy practice of PricewaterhouseCoopers LLP. Dr. Burke earned his BA from Furman University and his MA and PhD from the University of Texas, Austin. Prior to Teachers College, he served as Chair, Department of Management, at Clark University, head of management programs and organization development at the NTL Institute, and as Executive Director of the OD Network. Dr. Burke's consulting experience has been with a variety of organizations in business-industry, education, government, religious, and medical systems. A Diplomate in I/O psychology, the American Board of Professional Psychology, he is also a Fellow of the Academy of Management, the American Psychological Society, and the Society of Industrial and Organizational Psychology, and past editor of both *Organizational Dynamics* and the *Academy of Management Executive*. He has authored more than 130 articles and book chapters in organizational psychology, organization change, and leadership, and authored, coauthored, or edited 14 books. He has received numerous awards, including, in 1989, the Public Service Medal from the National Aeronautics and Space Administration; in 1990, the Distinguished Contribution to Human Resource Development Award; and in 1993, the Organization Development Professional Practice Area Award for Excellence—The Lippitt Memorial Award—from the American Society for Training and Development. His latest book (2000), coauthored with Bill Trahant, is *Business Climate Shifts: Profiles of Change Makers*.